Talking Culture
Ethnography and Conversation Analysis

MICHAEL MOERMAN

With an Appendix by Michael Moerman and Harvey Sacks

upp University of Pennsylvania Press | Philadelphia

University of Pennsylvania Publications in Conduct and Communication

Erving Goffman and Dell Hymes, *Founding Editors*
Dell Hymes, Gillian Sankoff, and Henry Glassie, *General Editors*

A complete listing of the books in this series appears at the back of this volume

Permission is acknowledged to quote material from the following sources.

"Thick Description" from *The Interpretation of Cultures: Selected Essays*, by Clifford Geertz. Copyright © 1973 by Basic Books, Inc., Publishers. Reprinted by permission of the publisher.

Person, Time, and Conduct in Bali, by Clifford Geertz. Cultural Report Series #14, Yale Southeast Asia Studies, 1966. (Reprinted in *The Interpretation of Cultures* by permission of Yale Southeast Asia Studies.)

Library of Congress Cataloguing-in-Publication Data

Moerman, Michael.
  Talking culture.

  (University of Pennsylvania publications in conduct and communication)
  Bibliography: p.
  Includes index.
  1. Conversation.   2. Language and culture.
  2. Ethnology—Methodology.   I. Title.   II. Series.
  P95.45.M64   1987   401'.9   87-14973
  ISBN 0-8122-8072-5
  ISBN 0-8122-1246-0 (pbk.)

Design: ADRIANNE ONDERDONK DUDDEN

3rd printing, 1990

Talking Culture

Ethnography and Conversation Analysis

For
Leo Moerman
Harvey Sacks
Ahmed El-Senoussi
Albert Grodner
my teachers still.

Contents

and memory. Its data consist of audio and video recordings of naturally occurring occasions and of transcripts of those recordings. Conversation analysis studies the organization of everyday talk, of language as actually used in social interaction. Its hallmark is exacting transcripts of naturally occurring talk analyzed for what the talkers orient to in producing its orderliness. By explicating elements of the social organization of speech, conversation analysis provides a component that has been critically missing from the realistic examination of such issues as how language relates to thinking, how "structure" relates to "practice" and institutions to experience, or how actors can be both agents and objects in the social world. But conversation analysis can do this only when it is coupled with ethnography, informed by the context in which speech occurs, and sensitive to the apparent purposes of speakers.

Ethnography is directed toward understanding and explicating how people make sense of their lives. As a fieldworker, I had become convinced that such standard research strategies as asking questions, or even announcing one's professional interests (Moerman 1967:66, ff.), distorted the native relevancies that it was my task to uncover. I devised ways of working that seemed to circumvent them (Moerman 1969a), and, by trying to merely listen in on native talk, became an ethnographer-consumer of conversation analysis (1972, 1973). But the dismayingly accurate predictions that conversation analysis permitted (partially reported in Chapter Three of this book) forced me to interrupt ethnography in order to learn the techniques of conversation analysis. This was a difficult, exacting, and time-consuming task: intellectually rewarding, but less satisfying than fieldwork.

Anything ever said is said by someone, to someone, at a particular moment of some specific socially organized and culturally informed occasion. Casual everyday conversation is the most common, frequent, and pervasive way in which speech is socially organized. It is also the most thoroughly and successfully studied. By attending to the specific here and now, to embodied and actual details as demonstrably oriented to by participants, conversation analysis could be a paragon of ethnographic practice. But ethnographers have so far shown little interest in its findings, and some distaste for its procedures. One reason is that they have not known much about it. This book is directed toward correcting that. But to know conversation analysis is not necessarily to love it. Its high-powered lens sacrifices range, breadth, and *mise-en-scène*. Moreover, the world it has discovered is startling and strange. There are general, powerful, and intricate abstract structures and processes of human conversation that do not correspond to the social order we commonly recognize or to the cultural world that we admire. This can make conversation analysis seem bloodless, impersonal, and unimportant to anthropology's central concerns. Few of our lineage's publications connect the technical organization of conversation to richly experienced human reality. Instead, there is the clacking of "turns" over their "possible completion points" (Sacks, et al. 1974), the neat scattering of "repair initiators" in their three-turn space (Schegloff, et al. 1977; Moerman 1977): dry bones of the talk with which roles, passions, institutions, and private strategies are embodied and lived.

Harvey Sacks understood with deep compassion that we are fated to live in a world of talk. We are successively exalted or bored, enraptured, embarrassed, made anxious largely by talk organized as conversation: talk with which we seduce, threaten, or pour out our hearts to one another. In every moment of talk, people are experiencing and producing their cultures, their roles, their personalities. Not just "the natives," but you and I live lives of talk, experience the social world as motivated talkers and listeners, as tongued creatures of the social order; each with our own bursts of pleasure and pain, each with our own proud differences of personal style. Conversation analysis has some promise of precisely locating and describing how that world of talk works, how the experienced moments of social life are constructed, how the ongoing operation of the social order is organized. Its transcripts are tracings of social events, analogous to the cloud chamber photographs that record physical events. But our events are human events, events of meaning. Their description, explication, and analysis require a synthesis of ethnography—with its concern for context, meaning, history, and intention—with the sometimes arid and always exacting techniques that conversation analysis offers for locating culture *in situ*. That melding is this book's goal.

Some conversational phenomena—overlap, person identification, and repair—will be given more attention than others. This is a matter of convenience and pedagogic utility. My insistence that conversation must be studied in ways sensitive to the languages, cultures, and settings in which it occurs extends to all conversational phenomena, and certainly to those such as announcements, assessments, category-bound activities, discovery markers, downgrades and upgrades, instructions, laughter, noticings, orders, stories, summonses, tokens, understanding, and word searches—that we will have occasion to examine. For my insistence to be more than programmatic, and your reading to be other than pro forma, you must study each transcript (Appendix A) when I comment on it. If you do not, you will not have really read this book.

The first chapter presents the scholarly setting and aspirations of culturally contexted conversation analysis. Chapter Two, by showing that even sherds of marred talk have rich contexts of source and meaning, entices you to examine transcripts. It points to identities of sequential organization between Thai and American conversation, proposes some technical specification of "context," and suggests that the conscious actor cannot be the author of his or her talk. Chapter Three, "Nature and Culture," is more technical. It demonstrates that the sequential organization of American references to persons holds for Thai, an unrelated language spoken in a quite different society. This should please conversation analysts, and surprise other students of speech. It then argues that ignoring the context and purpose of such references distorts their description. This will not surprise anthropologists, but may discomfit conversation analysts. The next two chapters make use of the sequential organization of repair and of references to persons to explore some central questions of social order. Chapter Four, "Motives in Action," uses Thai courtroom talk for investigating the relationship between actions and intentions. It examines Bourdieu's concept of *habitus*, and criticizes Weber's and Schutz' model of the actor. "Society in a Grain of Rice," the fifth chapter, is an exercise in microethnography. Its line-by-line examination of some three minutes of talk in a Thai village is intended to expose and to teach the methods of culturally contexted conversation analysis. The chapter rejects the Saussurian notions of meaning that underlie structuralism and symbolic and "interpretive" anthropology. It also discusses some ways in which the ethnographer affected the talk he participated in and recorded. "Talking About the World," the last chapter, investigates "noticings." Its main argument is that since talk about the world is socially organized on the occasions of its occurrence, consensus—the criterion used by philosophers of science—cannot guarantee the nature of reality. The final chapter and the first transcript-bearing chapter, "Finding Life in Dry Dust," are lighter in tone and less formal than the others. But their purposes are no less serious.

These essays about conversation are conversational in origin. They stem from talk with others in various places over quite a few years. It was my privilege to participate in seminars and classes in conversation analysis at UCLA and UC Irvine, my pleasure and nourishment to have Gail Jefferson, Anita Pomerantz, and Emanuel Schegloff as senior colleagues, and my blessing to have been a friend of Harvey Sacks.

The initial stimulus for this book was the 1978 conference on "The Construction of Realities" sponsored by the EST Foundation, a princely host. Among the participants whose help and challenge I remember most clearly are Gregory Bateson, Alton Becker, Werner Ehrhardt, Heinz von Foerster, Ernst von Glassersfeld, Erving Goffman, Joseph A. Goguen, Charlotte Linde, Humberto Maturana, Gabriel Stolzenberg and Francisco Varela. My ideas developed at the Naropa Institute—a world of discipline, freedom, and fellowship from which it would be inappropriate to single out individuals to thank.

For the environment that encouraged and permitted me to write this book, I am grateful to the Australian academic community, most specifically to the Working Group on Language and Culture of the Department of Anthropology in the Research School of Pacific Studies of the Australian National University where I was a Visiting Fellow in 1981–82 and briefly in 1983. I appreciate UCLA's providing leave for the first visit, airfare for the second, support for a 1979 trip to Asia, and the always efficient services of the Central Word Processing Office.

Since each chapter arises from a somewhat different mix of discussions, each addresses somewhat different audiences: here a linguist, there an anthropologist, sometimes a student of literature. But each of us at various times might be any one of those. And anyone can occasionally benefit from overhearing a remark addressed to another.

My arguments are cumulative and modulated. In order to budge a linguist one way, an ethnographer another, I sometimes tack rather than sail before the wind. In juggling Wittgenstein and Popper, I may occasionally try to derive poise from a blur. I will be concerned to demonstrate the universality of conversational structures, yet point to their manipulability and contextedness. I will cite transcripts as hard data, chiding other scholars for not providing any comparable evidence. Yet I will insist that meaning lies neither in an apparent object nor a privately experienced subject, but in a world composed by the interaction and interpenetration of the seeming two. I approach social interaction with a rough-and-ready applied phenomenology which recognizes that the phenomenon is neither objective nor subjective; not unitary in its significance; essentially "witnessed," yet part of the natural world which it is my obligation to describe rather than "obliterate in the name of science" (Wieder 1980:77). My empiricism is that of the art critic who cites the pigments and brush strokes of the paintings he interprets.

Another way in which this book is like conversation is that no theme ever dies, no issue is ever sure to be finished. Arguments are hinted at in one place to be developed in others; conversations and segments are repeatedly re-cited and re-analyzed. Re-attending to the same talk will show how elaborately organized it, and all the natural world, really is. Re-inspection of these "data," repeated interactions with them, "hanging out with" them, will help to open their worlds to us. It is in those worlds, the worlds of its participants, that all talk has meaning.

1
Conversation Analysis Among the Disciplines[1]

Social Interaction and Social Theory

The existence and survival, and hence the character, of *Homo sapiens* is profoundly social. For other species, "social organization" principally means the ways in which individuals regulate their co-presence. Man deserves no pre-Darwinian exemption, with face-to-face interaction accorded some minor, secluded status. While there are certainly other legitimate concerns for social science, face-to-face interaction is the constitutive substrate of social phenomena. Every thing that matters socially—meanings, class, roles, emotions, guilt, aggression, and so forth and so on—is socially constructed. Theories about how such things are learned and experienced, and about how to study them, which are not built to the specifications that interaction requires are wrong. The theories may be elegant, erudite, morally uplifting, or politically useful. But they are, in the first and critical instance, wrong.

Those to whom this view of the centrality of interaction seems too extreme might agree with, and be reassured by, Cicourel's (1980: 18) observation that "the status of normative rules during social interaction still remains unclear in sociological research," and that this requires "Building a bridge from microphenomena such as discourse or social interaction to macronotions such as occupational careers, social indicators, dominant cultural values, and patterns of inequality in a population." In this book, as I think is universal and unavoidable, that bridge is built out of normal talk and thought and writing. It is tempting to take up Cicourel's (perhaps unconscious) distinction between micro*phenomena,* out there in the world, and macro*notions,* housed solely in our heads. The tedium, frustrations, and career delays occasioned by listening to a tape recorder, sometimes altering the speed of what is said, and straining to write it all down as marks fixed on paper; staring at a frozen image on a video screen, timing it in hundredths of a second, and replaying it in slow motion are all sustained by mythologizing myself a scientist, a humble pure conduit through which the majesty of a real, separate, independent, objective world speaks unimpeded. But if there is a pure score of conversational structures, it is plucked and played and sung by embodied instruments and voices, each with its own resonances. And the pipers are always paid, a supper always being sung for. I and you are of that world, our ears and minds no less totally situated in our time and place, our observation and arguments no less furnished and motivated by our circumstances than any pickpocket's.[2]

■

Anthropology has lately (e.g., Kapferer 1976; Moore 1978) come to realize that such traditional explainers of social action as "class," "ethnicity," "values," etc., are not *things,* but processes—processes manipulated or, more radically, composed during the course of interaction. More conservatively, insofar as different social rules modify each other in particular circumstances, and insofar as such rules somehow "manage to produce practical action as part of a locally defined set of circumstances" (Cicourel 1980:19), we must study the actual scenes and occasions that constitute those circumstances. It is in interaction that people encounter, experience, and learn the principles, institutions, and ideals that characterize their society and culture. It is only in interaction that things social are manipulated. It is on occasions of interaction that they, and language, and persons live. The main reason for an interest in "macronotions" is what they tell us about the actual encountered life experiences and circumstances of the people we study.

Because its procedures and findings provide our best access to the features of face-to-face interaction, conversation analysis is central to understanding the social order. To learn from it, for example, that such categories as role and gender are motile and locally invoked, that social activities require but cannot assure the close-grained cooperation of the interacting parties, or that ongoing accomplishments are contingent and defeasible, is to learn some of what any respectable theory of society must take into account.

■

Conversation analysis focuses on talk. But talk, and other human sound, is only one component of interaction. Like all components, it is neither impermeable nor functionally specific.[3] A word, a wink, an intonation, can each, in context, do the same job. The undoubtedly great weight of setting, costume, or physical orientation cannot be found in this book's transcripts. But the student of talk inherits a rich tradition of writing language and of studying what was written. We must make the best use of it we can.

We pay a price for writing. Just as Ong (1982) claims, writing down sounds as words and marks on paper encourages us to rip life from its context, to mask processes as products and fields as objects. It "arrests" those objects (Volosinov 1973:78), freezes continuous and contingent flows into irreversibility, and "condemns us," in Husserl's phrase, "to see all practice as a spectacle." We must guard against, but can never completely avoid, these dangers. But we do know how to write down words and the grosser features of other sounds, and so can hold the smoke of interaction still for study. The absence of a natural orthography delays the absolutely necessary contributions that the technology of film and video will make to the analysis of interaction.

Conversation is not talk's sole form, but it does seem to be its most general one, composing many social scenes, leaking into others, and probably providing the source from which other forms of speech and writing derive. There is no doubt that some societies are more silent, some more terse, some more formal than others. Some communities—the deaf, for example—do not talk at all. The social occasions which feature conversation in one society might contain only veiled glances in another. The tasks for which we converse, or hold to Robert's Rules of Order, might elsewhere be done with songs or staves. These are all important issues that await empirical investigations based on recordings, transcripts, and analysis of actual occasions of natural interaction. It is all too easy, even irresistibly tempting, to suppose that some persons might have said this or that, to imagine that in some other place or time they do some other thing. But imaginings have no standing unless supported by data.

Conversation Analysis and Ethnographic Practice

Most of the speech-occasions that conversation analysts have examined have been in English and among Americans.[4] My investigation of Thai talk is thus a contribution of a straightforwardly anthropological sort. It asks to what extent are procedures and findings for our culture useful and correct for another, unrelated, one. That issue echoes in most chapters and dominates some. But mentioning it makes it appropriate to at least acknowledge a frequent question: "Well, *is* Thai conversation like American conversation?" The question is basic and important, but its initial answer not very interesting. "The same, but also different, much as the Thais and the Americans are." The extent to which it is the same came as a surprise, even a shock, to me. Like most ethnographers, I am fascinated by the different, the exotic, by the ways in which living with and studying an alien people could stretch my sense of what it means to be human. In some very important ways, Thai conversation *is* different from American conversation. Not only is it in

Thai, but the people doing it are being Thais together, an activity rather different from being an American. Indeed, being a Thai official is different from being a Thai woman, peasant, priest, child, and so forth through all the categories that compose Thai society. Inasmuch as face-to-face interaction is the major analytic and experiential locus of social organization, and conversation a major component of interaction, Thai conversation *must* be radically different from American in what it substantively communicates, expresses, and represents.

Adam Kendon (1972, 1975) rightly insists upon an essential distinction between interaction as a vehicle through which individuals express themselves and through which the society (with its classes, races, dialect groups, etc.) is represented, and interaction as the system by means of which co-presence is organized. Conversation, as the system through which turns at talk are coordinated, is—so far as we now know—essentially the same in Thailand as in America. Subsequent chapters will demonstrate this with respect to such features as the occurrence and negotiation of simultaneous talk, of repair, of references to persons. These correspondences depend upon the organization of turn-taking being the same, such that SELF and OTHER are the basic parties, and the turn-constructional-unit the basic metric. This, in turn, permits the conversation analyst to trace such apparently more cultural matters as assessments, agreement, questions, commands, significant absence, and even laughter. The ethnographer is thereby provided with rather refined instruments for investigating substantive divergences between cultures and complementary differences within them.

∎

Anthropologists have criticized conversation analysis for ignoring cultures other than our own. This book addresses that: both by attending throughout to Thai materials, and by proposing that regularities of sequential organization be used to locate, describe, and provide a metric for cultural variations.[5] The criticism, and this response to it, is based on a rather simple notion of "culture" as the uniformly owned property of a discrete society. A more complex concept emphasizes that culture is a set—perhaps a system—of principles of interpretation, together with the products of that system. In this sense, the materials of all conversation analysis are inextricably cultured. When an American analyst handles American conversation, he or she can fail to notice this. All natives take their native knowledge for granted, take it to be nothing other than the nature of the world (Geertz 1975). But how could the conversation analyst recognize an utterance as a pre-invitation, for example, without trading on covert native knowledge of dating practices and the special significance for them of Saturday night? It is with a native's recognition of an exaggeratedly Yiddish accent, and of what that means for participants of this kind, that the analyst locates an attempted, and possibly offensive, joke. Attending to exotic (Thai) materials exposes the processes and the problematicity of culture.

Ethnographers comment on, translate, and embellish the native world. The transcripts will anchor us in that world. Rather than pretending to read a culturally standardized finished text over the shoulder of an imagined native, we will be living in the line-by-line production of ongoing actual native talk. Techniques for the analysis of the sequential organization of conversation will locate such recurrent patterns and perturbations in that talk as "overlap" or "repair." To show how those conversational events were meaningful parts of the world created and inhabited by their participants, I will have to point to such larger features of the social world as the obligations of friendship, or fealty, or fear;[6] to the power of the Thai state and the practices of its police;[7] to the programs and proclivities of its officials.[8] It will be my task to show that it was from those particular institutions that what was actually said or, by means of specified pauses and hitches of speech, *not* said derived its meaning. Searching my knowledge (And what more can any ethnographer or any native ever do to make sense of something?) for the structures specifically invoked in making actual situated talk meaningful for its talkers reverses the ethnographer's usual practice of selecting bits of the native world as illustrations for pre-existing theories.

■

I do not know whether culturally contexted conversation analysis provides a "discovery" or a "verification" procedure for ethnography. Rather, I think it alters the terms and diminishes the importance of that distinction, making discovery and verification more complements than alternatives. Both become less matters of abstract correctness than of situated salience. I will be gratified when Thai participants show by their actions that things I had found important enough to describe as an ethnographer are used by them for doing significant face-to-face activities. But readers who have not studied Thai culture should be able to use sequential organization for locating important activities (like co-categorizing, ordering, insulting, etc.). Having found them, the reader can inspect some of the ideas, principles, or meanings that the natives then and there invoked and used in order to accomplish those social actions. Or so it might be if transcripts spoke for themselves. They don't. I speak for the Thai data segments in at least two ways.

First, I make them talk English. Those who do not know Thai will be reading my translation. This puts you at my mercy somewhat less than you might suppose. When presenting Thai materials at seminars, I have often been surprised when a student or colleague who knew no Thai challenged, sometimes successfully, a gloss or translation. Line #588 of Segment XXXIII is a convenient instance.

Lazily relying on dictionary Siamese, I had translated it as "And then::,". A student objected that line #588 was not like an English "And then,". Topically, it starts something new; sequentially, it seems to be a summons. These are unlikely jobs for "And then::,".

Culturally contexted conversation analysis simplifies and helps to fulfill the criteria of adequate translation. Nida's stricture (1959:190) that "the relevant unit of meaning for the translator is not the word, but the message," is helpful. But what kind of message? Poet, psychiatrist, historian, and missionary translators would rarely agree, nor should they. Each is concerned with a different notion of meaning. Culturally contexted conversation analysis strives for a translation in which the item in the receptor language does the same job as the item in the source language, a translation whose criteria of equivalence are *sequential and interactional*. This is not always easy to do. But the goal is straightforward. "And then::," for XXXIII:#588 failed to accomplish it.

It is encouraging that the failure is evident to those who study the transcript. In every transcript, because in all talk, each utterance is tied, however loosely, to the conversational and interactional place furnished by other utterances. The net of proximate utterances guides, constrains, and tests the translation. In translating *Mencius on the Mind,* I.A. Richards observed (1932:6, emphasis added) that issues of meaning and intention

are not settled by inspection of the syntax of the passage. They are to be settled, if at all, only by the influence of our interpretation of other passages—many of them almost equally indeterminate *by themselves.*

In natural conversation, unlike Richards' written text, utterances do not occur "by themselves." Nor are the interpretations solely ours: What participants said next guides them. Translation remains an "indirectly controlled guess" (Richards 1932:7), not a mechanically determined process whose products are straightforwardly correct/incorrect. But these differences between written texts and interactively organized talk narrow the possibilities. Strangers to these materials and dialects can continually judge and challenge my translations of them.

Second, having translated the utterances, I tell you about them. No native, and no ethnographer, can hear a conversation or see its transcript with virgin ears and eyes. Nor can readers without a word of Thai preserve their innocence. Whenever I dip you into a segment, you emerge with mind increasingly plated by it. The segment thus becomes each time a new, yet progressively and restrictedly known, text. Culturally contexted conversation analysis cannot silence that knowledge. It aims to explicate it.

Organization and meaning, expression and coordination, skeletal anatomy and physiology, if you will, are not separate and independent systems. It would be a mistake to picture the structure of conversation as a set of wires and hooks from which cultures hang their differently shaped and colored artifacts of meaning, so that we can comfortably understand and admire humanity's mobiles.

■

All meaning is in relation to a context. Explicating the meanings requires stating the context. Every context is multi-layered: conversation-sequential, linguistic, embedded in the present scene, encrusted with past meanings, and more. I do not believe that the ingredients of meaning can be listed, and am certain that they cannot be listed in advance. The interpretations that conversants make are, in fact, *post facto*. Each utterance, and each of its components, calls up the ingredients that participants (and so, imperfectly, us) needed to interpret it. It cannot be said, "with these 6, or 600, or 6^n features, all meanings become clear, every interpretation predictable." Rather, as the present utterance calls attention to its dialect, its rhythm, its enunciation, to the etymology of a featured word, the living, listening, talking interpreter must always be ready to think, "Oh yeah, that one too."

Components of meaning, ingredients for interpretation, are locally occasioned. They are triggered into relevance then and there. The analyst, so long as he claims to be working empirically, finds them after, not in advance of, the uttering. This can make his reasoning sometimes seem (and perhaps sometimes really be) gratuitous and *post hoc*. But the list of ingredients is guided by the participants' finished product: The interpretation of this utterance that the next utterance shows them to have made.[9] Further, culturally contexted conversation analysis tries to limit the ingredients of interpretation, the components of meaning, to ones that are locally significant and locally occasioned. Whenever I point to "class" or "dialect" or "gender," I take on the tasks of reporting as an ethnographer on how those things work in this society, and of showing as a conversation analyst that and how they were invoked and used in that very moment of talk. I will sometimes fail at these tasks. But I count it an accomplishment of culturally contexted conversation analysis to be able to state them, and to state them as a challenge to the adequacy of competing modes of description. Culturally contexted conversation analysis provides means for accomplishing those tasks, and exposes failure.

Talk as Data

Ethnography's central and sacred data are what one native says or does to another, or to the ethnographer. The objects we record, examine, consider, and write about occur in the course of social interaction. Whether observing a meeting, conducting an interview, or just sitting and chatting around the campfire, our primary data are things said as part of socially organized scenes. We collect the droppings of talk.

■

We all know that all talk is thoroughly and multifariously embedded in the historical, cultural, social, biographical, (and so on and so on) context of its occurrence. We make use of this in constructing and interpreting the sense, import, and meaning of every bit of talk we encounter. But—there being no limits to folly—as professional investigators we can deny this, and suppose that some special category of talk—answers to a questionnaire item, the intense whisperings of a favorite informant, the shouts of a drunkard, the "free associations" of a therapy client, or some phrases imagined by a "native speaker"—is somehow immaculately conceived and thus empowered to provide magic earphones to hear and magic lenses to see pure mind, to tap pure culture, language, thought, or whatever other vital essence we search for, collect, distill, package, and sell. The investigator can disparage as trivial or self-cancelling the socially organized specificity of all talk. But he has no grounds whatever for doing so unless he first investigates how talk works.

A question I ask an informant, for example, requires him to orient himself to my relevancies and meanings, and so alters the world I had set out to investigate. In order to use his answer, I must understand how the processes of questioning and the relevant features of the encounter influenced it. Keesing (1981:19) points out that: "we are crucial agents in the micropolitics of elicitation, not simply passive recorders of what people can or will tell us." "Micropolitics" works through the structure of interaction itself. A study of "mystical experiences" in Los Angeles (Anderson n.d.), for example, reported with some surprise that those experiences had a strong "religious" component regardless of the experiencers' attitudes toward particular religions or toward religion in general. Transcripts showed that the researcher asked about religion and then—like any properly trained interviewer—limited his responses to the answers to noncommittal "uh huh"s. But the answers were usually formed as opinions or assessments. In American conversation (as Pomerantz [1975, 1978] has shown) these make agreement relevant. The "uh huh"s were heard by the interviewees as other than agreement, so they produced more talk about religion. The substantive finding, then, was to no little extent produced by the interpenetration of conversational structures with orthodox interview technique. In examining the data of this book, we shall often find that something is said, or repeated, or emphasized, or notably *not* said by virtue of the conversationally organized exigencies of its occasion.

It is simply and neutrally the case that the social organization of occasions of talk affects what is said. Any social investigator, reporter, policeman, medical interviewer, etc., who ignores or derides this is deluding himself. Questioning, discussing, proposing, arguing, the whole gamut of speech activities comprise and nearly exhaust the ethnographer's methods of investigation. Like all methods, they influence, constrain, perhaps even determine what one finds by means of them. It is the investigator's clear duty to take this into account as explicitly, consciously, thoroughly, and generally as possible. It is incumbent upon ethnographers to find out what questioning, telling, arguing, etc., are like; what they do to participants and how they affect what gets said. There is no way in which we can do this without accurate and appropriately detailed records of actual natural occurrences of these activities.

I am not proposing that ethnographic data be restricted to conversational transcripts and ethnography to their analysis. But I am insisting that those who use talk in order to discover what people think must try to find out how the organization of talk influences what people say. The data and techniques of conversation analysis permit this. All talk, even native speech recorded by native agents and concealed machines, is the product of a moment in an organized encounter among categorized actors. Any verbal event of ethnographic notice—a kinship term, dialect shift, price agreement, insult, etc.—exists as the living creature of social interaction. Unless we know how occasions of speech are socially organized, we can neither fully understand nor properly evaluate our data. We collect cultural artifacts that come mounted in a context that gives them their momentarily enlivened meaning. We must preserve their interactional matrix, not pretend to scoop nuggets from a swamp.

∎

In saying that native talk and action are sacred to ethnography, I meant to applaud our reverence for it, our professional ethic of holding it to be the bedrock and warrant for what we report. But it is oddly sacred in another way as well. It is secret.

A distinctive (albeit unrealistic) claim of science is that it uses public, explicit, and consensually regulated means for transforming observed events into description and analysis. This is the force of Bloch's demand (1975:2) "that we must start with what we can observe and make deductions from it according to set rules and criteria." But the best of us are not very good at stating how events were observed, and how their observed features relate, in turn, to our description and analysis of them. Even the most situated ethnography relies on such common-sense transformations as: "a *tight abridgement* of many hours of talking. From it we can *discern*" (Parkin 1976:179, emphasis added) or "a *selected portion* from *notes* of many hours of talk. But it suffices *to give the sense* of *what went on*" (Moore 1977:171, emphasis added).

Ethnography's technical lexicon, its labels for the procedures by which events are transformed by description and analysis, is our lay vocabulary, our native tongue. As ethnographers, we want to explicate how the people we study make sense of their world, to explicate how *they* perform such operations as "abridging," "discerning," locating "what went on." And to do it, we, quite as inexplicitly, use our version of those operations ourselves, thereby building a fire in a wooden stove, trying to dissect the social world with the unexamined muddy instruments of its own talk.

The difficulties are in some ways insuperable. Blount (1975a:5) credits ethnomethodology for realizing that:

social information is obtained by the researcher as a participating member in interaction, doing work to make observable and accessible the meaning of the interaction in ways that are similar to and often coincide with the ways that anyone else in society does the work.

"Selecting," "discerning"—all such ways of "giving the sense of what went on"—whether native or our own, are socially organized ways. They are thus always situated and contexted in their application. Any rule-like, principled description of their operation would therefore distort them. But conversation analytic transcripts provide at least a rendering of what was said.

■

As long ago as 1970, Labov (1972:184) observed that:

It seems natural enough that the basic data for any form of general linguistics would be language as it is used by native speakers communicating with each other in everyday life.

However, even those who study not "general linguistics," but "the components of face-to-face interaction as they bear on, or are affected by . . . speech"[10] or "the use of language in the conduct of social life"[11] rarely let us see those data. In Bauman and Sherzer's classic *Explorations in the Ethnography of Speaking* (1974), for example, only two papers (Darnell's and Sacks') present unedited speech in context. Few of the authors in Bloch's *Political Language and Oratory in Traditional Society* (1975) present the data they describe. Brown and Levinson's important paper (1978) provides the conversational context of hardly any of the few actual speech events it analyzes. The observed world seems always to elude even its most dedicated ethnographers. Was Labov perhaps ironic, rather than hopeful, when he wrote in 1972 (p. 205):

There are now in print a number of empirical studies which demonstrate convincingly that the direct study of language is a practical and fruitful procedure. Th[is] research . . . is relatively recent: the work of ten investigators . . . who use as their primary data accurate records of language in its normal social context.

Can any discipline claim to be a science while giving such tentative attention to natural events in a real world?

Prominent among those who do study "accurate records of language in its normal social context" are Labov himself, John Gumperz (1982), and, perhaps, scholars in "the ethnography of speaking" tradition founded by Dell Hymes. "Perhaps," because ethnographers of speaking do not provide or refer to transcripts or other public records, and have largely concentrated on special sorts of speech events other than everyday conversation. But conversation analysis, if it is to be culturally contexted, has much to learn from this school's consistent recognition that societies differ in their ways of speaking both from one another and internally, and from the prominence it gives to the historical background, ethnographically investigated contexts, and rich cultural meanings of speech events (see Sherzer 1983).

Labov's mastery of linguistics and close attention to phonology could also benefit conversation analysts, however murky and misleading his interactional analyses are (cf. Levinson 1983:294, 352–3). But conversation analysts cannot accept his claims of privileged knowledge of "what is really being talked about" (Labov and Fanshel 1977:52–3, especially the note), his formulaic definitions of types of discourse units (e.g., 1977:104–10), and his assumptions that there is a limited and finite set of social actions, and that these can be mapped one-to-one to utterances (cf. Levinson 1983:288–92).

Every type of "discourse unit" that has been studied in conversation—telling about one's experiences (Jefferson 1978a), giving instructions (Goldberg 1975), making announcements (Terasaki 1976), even "pro forma" greetings (Schegloff 1968) and formal performances (Tedlock 1983:285–301)—is organized interactively and built to meet the exigencies of reception and interception by other participants. None are either pre-planned by a single speaker or made coherent by extrapolations from his sentences (Schegloff 1981). No model of natural speech events that does not take account of the properties of conversational interaction can be correct. Utterances, social actions, and the expressing of cultural themes are simultaneous and mutually constitutive. But their units rarely coincide. Because conversation is a process of social interaction, the content and boundaries of its units are sometimes *essentially* unclear: not because of faulty analysis, but because participants are themselves centrally engaged in negotiating, interpreting, and disputing them.

Conversation analysis can certainly profit from Gumperz' work (e.g., 1982: 172–86) on the conflicts of interpretation that develop when individuals of different conversational traditions and of differential power conduct important business together. One of the most immediate ways in which structure and meaning interpenetrate is that speech is not value free. In talking with friends, strangers, fellow citizens, immigrants, and foreign hosts we react to such features as lexical choices, intonation contours, breathiness, pacing of speech, or placement and frequency of simultaneous talk as to moral matters which tell us something about the kind of person we are talking to and the kind of activity we are engaged in.

Gumperz and his students (Gumperz 1983) investigate this ingeniously, sometimes helping to ameliorate important practical problems. Gumperz is also concerned to set his conversational data and their interpretation in their institutional and motivational setting. But he generally regards conversation as language plus the "prosody" which he finds (1982:100) that "conversationalists use to initiate and sustain verbal encounters." This "prosody" is a list of linguistic items other than lexicon and semantics (loc. cit.). Its coherence as an entity thus derives from the accident of what linguists now study. His prosody is waxed over language, serving merely to color, shade, and modify meanings that are already in the syntax and semantics.[12]

None of these approaches sufficiently appreciates the demonstrated properties of conversation as a process of social interaction. Like earlier work by anthropologists, they regard culture as an arena for talk or as something "embodied in lexical knowledge" (Gumperz 1982:104). Maintaining the dominant paradigm of sociolinguistics, they regard language and society as mutually independent entities, and investigate their correlations.

■

A major contribution of conversation analysis is its insistence upon making, citing, being constrained by, and publishing a close-grained transcript of mechanical recordings of real events. I must emphasize that—and will later specify how—the transcript is not an inert object out there on a page. Indeed, its inconstancy and non-objectivity are among the ways in which it is most instructive. But the transcripts represent, or render, events that occurred in the world; they provide an inexhaustible resource for your own, and future, interests. My descriptions, analyses, arguments, and claims are based on the transcriptional evidence they cite. You can therefore evaluate them. Many of the analyses, arguments, findings, etc., are unabashedly intended to be universal. My hope and claim is to be investigating quite general processes, quite uniform structures. So, for example, descriptions of simultaneous speech, or of the situated motility of social roles—while pointed to some particular segment of some specific transcript—purport to be true of all occurrences of the phenomena in each transcript, in transcripts not yet made of conversations not yet held, and in any language. This is clearly a preposterous claim, one which you are invited to use these very transcripts (or others *of situated real talk*) to qualify or demolish.

That would be one of the ways in which these transcripts furnish an inexhaustible resource. Unedited by the transient professional concerns that filter our rarely published fieldnotes, unpolished by the rhetorical and theoretical motives that produce lapidary quotations from informants, they, like the African conversations Powdermaker (1962) published over twenty years ago, show "a many-dimensioned picture of human realities. . . . New abstractions can still be made from the published . . . conversations" (Powdermaker 1966:283). In writing that the transcripts record events that occurred in the world, I want, initially, to be taken naively. I mean no more than that the words, deformations, emphases, pauses, overlaps, etc., set out on the page[13] result from quite painstaking efforts to write down the sounds made during an actual interaction, an interaction that no researcher consciously elicited or influenced,[14] an interaction that was part of the natural lives of its participants. The specific features the transcripts reveal are features of the natural world in which the talk actually occurred. I wince at, and will later water down, this positivist assurance. But it means at least that we are bothering about something that matters, with things that mattered in the world inhabited by these participants in that place. Since the work of transcribing and analyzing is often dull and frustrating, it helps to know that we are mining real ore. Moreover, adhering to a detailed representation of real events permits discoveries and disconfirmations. Made up or remembered instances can come only from what we already assume, know, or think we know. They cannot surprise us or reveal anything new.

■

I hope to have made the transcripts so valuable to you that we can examine their flaws sympathetically. They are ugly to look at and clumsy to handle and refer to. Their splatterings of "⌐ ⌐" and "(·)" and ":::" would try anyone's patience and aesthetic sensibilities. But the study of conversation progressively reveals it to be built to very fine metric and scale. It need take no more than .2 seconds of silence for any of us to know that a request, however momentous, has been denied; no more than an intra-morpheme aspiration to know that a joke, however offensive, is being assayed. Transcript, description, and analysis must be sensitive to the units from which conversational interaction is constructed, and which participants in conversation regularly use and are used by. Rather than criticize their detail, we might better fear that they are too crude. Tedlock (1983:5) reminds us "that no score can ever be so detailed and precise as to provide for the re-creation of the full sound of the tape," no transcript ever capture "the intricately modulated temporality of the voice" (ibid.:206). Our deprivation is not only aesthetic. Every close investigation of every record of interaction shows it to be densely, complexly, reticulately organized, often in quite unexpected ways. Dimensions of rhythm, tune, intonational mirroring—and many others which our current transcripts do not record—promise to be as regular and forceful a part of the organization of conversational interactions as those to which we now attend. Before Schegloff showed some of the intricate organization of overlap,[15] our transcripts used to record merely "((simultaneous speech))." Until Jefferson's exacting analysis of the sensitive interactive import of laughter forced us to attend to the transcriptionally enervating distinctions between "huh" and "ha," or between overlapped laughter and laughter in the clear, our transcripts could comfortably leave it as "((laughs))." But once a phenomenon is shown to matter in some talk, it must be recorded in all talk, lest our analyses become opportunistic and deaf. One way in which a transcript is not an objective *thing* is that new work and acute re-listening change it.[16] As Tedlock (1983:6) observes for his own, non-conversational and more culturally standardized corpus, "The audible text will remain the primary document . . . providing the basis for any number of future transcriptions . . . of its own content."

■

Ethnographic purposes and Thai materials impose some special disabilities on my transcripts.

For acultural non-contexted conversation analysis, SPEAKER and OTHER(s) are sufficient identifications. The world of such transcripts can be peopled by a neat column of "A"s and "B"s, with an occasional "C" or "D". Culturally contexted conversation analysis emphasizes the fact that every transcript is the script of a scene that really occurred, one acted by real individuals.[17] I represent them with capital letters at the left of the page. Each letter or pair of letters stands for a different individual. Whenever I recognized Khamping's voice, for example, the transcript says "KP;" similarly for the other individuals. Sometimes I could tell only the gender of a speaker. The transcript then says "M" for a man, "W" for an unidentified woman. When I could distinguish one unidentifiable person from another, subscripts are given: M_1 or M_2, and so on.

Tell an actor to play such a scene. He or she would ask: "Who am I? Which of these characters?" No actor will be satisfied if told merely, "You are MK." He— like any reader of a play or any anthropologist interested in the culture and community in which the interaction occurred—will insist on knowing more. "What kind of person is MK? Old? Rich? Educated? Lazy? Who is he to the others? W_2's father perhaps, or lover? How well do these characters know one another?" And so on and on and on through all the features and interests and fashions ("Is MK a cultural innovator?" "A sexist?" "A Capricorn?") that readers and anthropologists and natives from some particular time and place use to categorize actors. Labels for persons are never neutral, never atheoretical. That is why ethnographers are interested in them. Listing characterizations in advance honors and commits us to some theory about what kinds of things are important. The analyst should restrict categories of persons to those the interaction shows to be salient for the inter- actants. That way, we might get at *their* theories, and not just at our own. I cannot characterize these speakers without prejudicing your interpretation of what they say. Yet I cannot withhold characterization if their speech is to be meaningful. For participants talk, and make interpretations of what is said, on the basis of who they find and make themselves to be.

Like most dilemmas, this is eased (albeit never solved) by compromise. I will ply between the general ethnography that recommends some characterizations as culturally appropriate, and pointing to specific utterances to show that and how those characterizations were invoked. That way, you can track my course: evalu- ating the plausibility of the ethnography, the local salience of the category in- voked, the logic of the conversational argument. We will miss something by restricting ourselves to those categorizations which can be shown to have been invoked. Some of the native's world is hidden from the analyst. Might MK be angry at what KP once said about MK's wife? False consciousness can hide things from participants' own awareness. But the restriction will at least avoid "false- positives" and keep us closely attentive to our data and to the moment-to-moment activities and accomplishments of the conversants.

My Thai materials were collected during two field trips. The bulk were re- corded in 1965 in the Thai-Lue village I call Ban Ping, Chiengkham district, Chiengrai (now Phayao) province.[18] Some, largely restricted to Chapter Four, were recorded in courtrooms, prisons, and lawyers' offices in 1968–9.[19]

The citizens and government of Thailand properly insist that they and their lan- guage are Thai, not Siamese. But for ease of expression, and so as to not imply that any of the dialects are more general than another, I will use "Siamese" for the Central Thai dialect, and "Thai" for the family of languages that scholars usually call "Tai". The Thai people are found in southern China, northern Vietnam, the Shan States of Burma, Laos, and, of course, Thailand. The Lue are the Thai whose historical capital was Chiengrung (*ceenghung* in Lue, *Jinghung* in Chinese) in the Sip Song Panna region (Xishuangbanna Dai Autonomous Prefecture) of Yunnan. The late nineteenth and early twentieth centuries were a time of popula- tion shifts and political muscle flexing in northern Southeast Asia. The Lue found- ers of Ban Ping were brought to Chiengkham in the middle of the eighteenth century. Khon Myang (Yuan) settlers soon followed them. At the beginning of this century, the Siamese took direct administration of Chiengkham from the Prince (*caw ciwit*) of Nan. In the early 1960's, many Lao-speaking immigrants arrived from northeast Thailand.[20]

In 1965, ethnicity still closely paralleled social class in Chiengkham. Although some few had become officials—mostly teachers and low-ranking policemen—Lue, Yuan, and Lao speakers were usually peasant villagers; Siamese speakers, officials. There is national and regional diglossia in Thailand. Yuan ("Y" on the transcripts) is the *lingua franca* of the rural north. Siamese ("S" on the transcripts) is the national, official, prestige dialect. The villagers on these transcripts, if they know it at all, learn it in school and hear it on the radio. Local dialects, like Yuan and Lue ("L" on the transcripts), are rural, and so less prestigious, sometimes embarrassing. During my first field trip (1959–61), even officials whose long service in an outlying region would make one expect them to be able to understand local dialects often claimed to be unable to. As a consequence of the more recent "friend of the people" (*mit raatsadɔn*) ideology of government service, they might now claim otherwise. At neither time do claims constitute competence. Conversation analysis can show the extent to which speakers seem to understand one another. Any transcript that contains switches of dialects, languages, or levels also displays the sequential-interactional loci at which switches occur. Analysis can suggest their apparent motives and consequences.

I am not always sure that my dialect labels are correct. In assigning them, I was guided by a native speaker of Lue who is also fluent in Siamese and Yuan. But although I have been reasonably fluent in Lue and Siamese (and indeed once took pride in translating between them for villagers and officials), and came to handle Yuan, my own ear is always foreign, and no longer that good. For native speakers themselves, these dialects shade into one another both in recognizability of production and in degree and source of interintelligibility. Tonal structure (Brown 1962) is the best evidence for genetic relations among Thai dialects. But native speakers readily compensate for it, and are more struck by other phonological discrepancies and by differences in lexicon. The former are generally quite regular, so a little effort surmounts unintelligibility. The latter are largely produced by the borrowings Siamese has made from Sanskrit and Pali, and so reflect language contact, not genetic relations.

Dialect production is continuous rather than discrete. A phrase or utterance can have lexical items from one dialect pronounced with the phonology of another, and with a compromise tonal contour. Forms from one dialect often occur in an utterance largely in another. Participants do not listen like dialect geographers: closely monitoring the tonal, lexical, intonational and other components of dialect shifts. Instead, I suppose them to hear such things as "now he is talking like an ———" or "now he sounds more like I do." Dialect distinctions vary in clarity, degree, and importance. Like labels for persons, they are active and malleable features of the interaction, not its inert precursors.

The phonemic orthography, word-for-word glosses, and capitalized abbreviations for syntactic particles will probably annoy linguists and not mean much to non-linguists. But they are needed if readers of English are to make full use of these transcripts. The glossed words say things. The particles do things for which English usually relies on syntax, lexical choice, or intonation. "Why that now?" is always critical to conversants. Since Thai particles and word order are different from English, a translation rarely shows where in the course of an utterance a conversational event—like an interruption, a pause, an in-breath—occurred. The word-for-word and particle-by-particle glosses do.

The Thai orthography is not as close to the actual sounds as the orthography of the English transcripts. This is because my Thai ear is not as good as my English one. I suspect that it normalizes my hearings, and know that it makes me distrust divergences from standard forms.

Envoi

This book's goal is one set by I. A. Richards (1932:28):

[to] go beyond the mere elucidation of the passage in hand; [to] aim indeed at nothing short of a generalized technique by which all meanings of all kinds on all necessary occasions can be systematically displayed.

In order to expose—let alone teach—a mode of analysis, I will often forego presenting finished work and, instead, invite you into the kitchen so that you can see how the work gets done. This will make for exposition that is sometimes messy. But that is how kitchens are. I dare request your forbearance in I. A. Richards' (loc. cit.) words. We have not progressed much in the half century since he wrote them.

Naturally, such a thing as this must at first seem ungainly, otiose, or pedantic. But we are, as regards our systematic sorting and dividing in the field of meaning, much as primitive man was before the early mathematicians or systematic measurers came to help him divide his grasslands. Doubtless these early measures seemed to him pedants, over fond of indulging in unnecessary complications.

Richards explicated *Mencius on the Mind,* a grand and classic text. Our segments are more humble. The social sciences are unaccustomed to devoting close attention to a few moments of action. I hope to convince you that there is much to be learned from doing just that. For ethnography, there is no richer ore than everyday conversation. Bourdieu (1977) has shown that the anthropologist, because he asks the natives to remark on their practices and then tries to account for them, can never get what he exactly wants: the unremarkable, everyday, and taken-for-granted as they appear to the native in the course of his practices. Culturally contexted conversation analysis asks nothing of the native and concentrates on the commonplace. Its investigations are directed toward what participants orient themselves to in order to produce their everyday talk. That talk is where culturally contexted conversation analysis finds the nexus of society, language, and culture. It is there that the "problem" of interpretation is solved, and the disjunction between society and culture resolved.

2

Finding Life in Dry Dust[1]

This chapter examines some contexted instances of a fleeting, humdrum, imperfect and in some sense purely formal conversational object: overlap—the simultaneous talk of more than one speaker.[2] In presenting these specimens of overlap, I confess to a matchmaker's motives. I want you to admire their interactive liveliness, close choreography, strategic precision, and cultural depth. Not that there is anything special about these homely "mistakes" in turn-taking. Under close examination, any real conversational event reveals some of its intricate beauty. The specks of talk visible through the lens of conversation analysis swarm with life, are packed with meanings, and are artfully constructed in recognizably human ways.

In conversation, normatively and by definition (Sacks, et al. 1974; Leiter 1980:217) one party talks at a time. Yet as conversants and as analysts we notice that sometimes more than one person is talking. To a critic of conversation, as to a participant, overlap may seem a violation, an error, a fault. But apparent breakdowns of conversation's orderliness can be the ordered product of interactive processes. Just as impeded speech, bad grammar, or faulty logic are usually perfect conversation, so are the "mistakes" in turn-taking that we will examine perfect and complexly human interaction.

Sacks, Schegloff, and Jefferson's seminal paper (1974) accounts for the occurrence, violative character, and correcting of overlaps. That so many overlaps occur at speakership transition points provides evidence that conversants orient themselves to and use the turn-constructional and speaker-selection principles that that paper describes. The argument, roughly, goes like this.[3] A speaker's right to be sole talker is a claim to a turn of talk. Turns are built and measured with such units as a possibly complete utterance. An utterance can be built so as to be possibly complete at the possible end of a sentence, a phrase, intonation contour, etc. So there is some pressure upon a person who wants to speak next to come in a little before such a possible end. Moreover, if he doesn't come in *now,* he may not get to come in *next.* Via the ordered set of speaker selection rules, current speaker might otherwise select someone other than him to talk next, or might himself go on, or some other participant might start up first. And since utterances are expected to be relevant to what has been said immediately prior, an aspiring speaker who doesn't get to have his say *next,* might *never* get to have it. So principles of floor-allocation and turn-construction found in American conversation account for there being a profusion of overlaps at turn-initial and turn-terminal positions. Those positions are also the most common loci of overlaps in my corpus of Thai conversations. This implies that the same turn-constructional and speaker-allocation principles operate.

"The Leper"

The first conversational event we will examine is the overlap at lines #43/4 of Data Segment I, entitled, "The Leper." As an ethnographer, I am interested in the meaning, consequentiality, and interpretability of this and other conversational events, not solely in the sequential basis of their production (cf. Leiter 1980:223). This fleeting terminal overlap is a fragment of a text whose integrity must be preserved. No less than for the formal and polished cultural productions Becker (1979:2) points to, understanding a conversational text "require[s] that we know a good deal about who said what to whom about what and why. *The meaning of a text is its relation to its context*" (emphasis added).

   Segment I was recorded in the sheltered porch (*hoox ɔm* [Moerman 1969a:461]) of a Thai-Lue village home in 1965. Some half dozen villagers, the district officer (DO on the transcript), and I (MM on the transcript) had been talking about recordings of Lue folksongs. At line #1, S begins to talk about a recorded performance of which he knows. The artists he mentions at lines #6 and #8 are men the villagers know and recognize.[4] After some thirty seconds of talk (not shown in this data segment) about how the recording was made and whether it can be bought, the district officer asks the question (I:32) translated as, "Where was the singer from?"[5] Sequentially, #32, like #37 begins a repair sequence (Schegloff, et al. 1977; Moerman 1977). By conversation's rules, whether Thai or American, line #32's completion shifts the floor to its recipient for an answer which is, thus, significantly absent[6] at line #33's .7 second silence. Line #34 is, again, a quite regular conversational event, whether Thai or American. The asker of a question, noting the absence of its answer, goes immediately next, and uses his entire turn to propose its answer in question form.

The answer S finally gives (at I:35) is accurate and, like every utterance, formed for its recipient and its occasion. The district officer is not the kind of person whom a villager (like S) would expect to know and recognize the singer by title (*bâ* for an unmarried man) and name, as villagers do. Instead, S's reference is made by means of such things as an official would be expected to know about. But B, a village elder, doesn't get it. Returning to this conversation after a brief exchange with another elder, he initiates repair at line #37. In Thai as in American conversation, successive repair initiators on the same repairable locate it with increasing specificity (Schegloff, et al. 1977, note 15; Moerman 1977:873, f.), as line #39 does relative to line #37 here. S, at line #42, explicitly (with the /nân/) repeats his earlier (line #6) reference form; S's wife (at line #43) adds Nɔ̌·'s eponym.

Many villagers have the same personal name. Eponyms are often added to village names, sometimes to accomplish more specific reference. S, for example, is sometimes referred to as "Sɛ́·ng with the withered arm." Villagers commonly refer to the pipe player as "bâ Nɔ̌· the leper," just as one of them does at line #43. But on this occasion the normally inert eponym is treated as, and so becomes, a sudden source of danger. Precisely upon its appearance, S overlaps it (line #44) and then immediately challenges it as if this mere standard identificatory device had been a considered diagnosis.

Labelling what S does at line #44 "a challenge" relies on the following observations. "He is sort of sick" topicalizes the eponym, reacting to it as to a description rather than as to a mere part of a name. Insofar as "Yeah:ah, he's so::rt of sick" correctly translates this occurrence of /phā*jā*:t nângkǎw lɛ/,[7] the topicalization is substantively a disagreement, challenge, or dismissal. What it argues with is made visible—to participants as to us—by its sequential placement: on top of and obliterating WS's reparative re-reference.

Not every overlap is obliterative.[8] In this segment, the precisely placed obscuring of the eponym and the substantive challenge with which S replaces it, warrant the characterization. When overlaps *are* obliterative, when, as here, one speaker clearly places his talk so as to blot out the talk of another, the intruder's precise placement discloses him to have been attending the talk he overlaps very closely indeed. It is not faulty listening or imperfect participation. The mechanical image is of pinpoint bombing, not careless collision, of turns.

We needed translation in order to recognize and label the event as an obliterative overlap of a person-reference repair. To account for its occurrence and interpret its meaning, we need "ethnographic background" of a particular sort: a statement of the local knowledge that this situated occurrence calls to mind or makes relevant.

S is a client of the missionary under whose protection, and in whose compound, Nɔ̌· lives. S sometimes visits Nɔ̌·, relying upon missionary nurse assurances that Nɔˇ· has a harmless skin ailment and not leprosy. Were the district officer, to whom S knows that townsmen have complained about Nɔˇ·, to regard him as truly a leper, he would have him removed to a leper colony. In the presence of the district officer—the highest official a villager can hope or fear to meet—the otherwise harmless identification sequence tumbled S, and no other villager, into a sensitive matter.

The entire drama took less than ten seconds to perform. Its specifiable moves and units of action—turns, repairs, adjacency pairs, sequences—were conversationally organized. But we never merely exchange turns of talk. In all conversation, people are living their lives, performing their roles, enacting their culture. The motives and meanings of all talk are thick with culture. To understand what the moves mean requires (or recalls) cultural knowledge. The techniques and texture of conversation analysis precisely located the motivated, ongoing, actual operation of major social institutions. In "The Leper," naming practices, the authority of officials, loyalty to patrons, identificatory social memberships were momentarily and momentously invoked and enlivened. This does not mean that the social institutions and cultural patterns produced the talk. But they are implicated in its meaning. The immediacy and complexity of every real social event precludes producing, interpreting, or accounting for it by some single set of rules (like those for repair, turn-taking, loyalty, or kinship). It is also why no segment can be exhaustively explicated, and certainly never in a single pass. "The Leper" is an example of the reciprocal illumination of conversation analysis and ethnography. There will be other, more fully explicated, instances in this and subsequent chapters. No instance or sum of instances proves any claim, except as "proof is in the pudding," bite after bite.

Overlap and Social Categories

Every bit of talk is both special, i.e., a product of all its immediate circumstances, and general, i.e., sequentially organized. By playing one against the other, we can learn about both. Inasmuch as talk is interactionally organized and also meaningful, it is a prominent nexus of society and culture. Each component informs us about the other. Sequential analysis of Data Segments II–IV will let us track the shifting of co- and cross-categorizations, the currents and eddies of cooperation and competition among participants.

The organization of turn-taking makes both the ends and beginnings of turns especially susceptible to overlap, with one turn's start overlapping another's end. Segment I was an instance. Another common form of overlap is for two speakers to start up simultaneously, or close to it. Schegloff (in lectures) has shown that one source of such turn-initial overlaps is for rules of talk to assign a turn or task to a type of party for which more than one participant qualifies.

The American middle-class participants of Data Segment II observe a social occasion they call "having friends over (to the house) for dinner." The occasion bifurcates its participants into two teams: "hosts" and "guests." The teams, the occasion, and much of American middle-class social life is peopled by "couples," pairs of spouses. Indeed, it is a common complaint of those who have lost their spouse—and this is not infrequent among them—that, "Nobody asks me over for dinner anymore." Little of this would make sense to a Lue villager. But he would understand, as it is perhaps universal, that the activity of "being friends" requires showing that one monitors and takes an interest in the world of the other. In American middle-class culture, alterations of household decoration and furniture are quite important. So, in this society, on this occasion, it is proper for guests to notice,[9] and hosts to acknowledge, changes in how the hosts' home is furnished or decorated. A major locus for noticing is early in the interaction; the proper locus for the acknowledgment is immediately after the noticing. Doing "being friends" assigns these tasks to hosts and guests, but does not say which member of their respective teams should do it. Thus, overlap of the sort found at lines #21/2 and #23/4 of Data Segment II are quite common. George and Gwen, guest husband and guest wife respectively, are dinner guests and friends of Helen (host wife) and Hal (host husband). At II:19–20 the guest team does its noticing which the hosts acknowledge, first in overlap with one another (#21/2), then (#23/4) in overlap with them.

Some methodological lessons are perhaps in order. We noticed a conversational perturbation, the overlaps. A conversation analyst takes events to be orderly unless proven otherwise. An ethnographer takes them to be meaningful. Noting the content of the overlaps and recognizing their problematicity got us to explicate cultural patterns no less unusual for being our own. By asking who was party to the overlaps, we located the phenomenon of talking as a team. The same strategy can be used elsewhere. Lines #32–49 of "The Leper" compose a person reference repair sequence. It is a standard, even compelling, feature of conversational repair for the speaker of the utterance targeted for repair to repair it him/herself.[10] WS is S's wife. For her, at I:43, to repair S's talk suggests that Thai spouses sometimes present themselves as teams. If it turned out that one partner regularly corrected the other (as is the case for American parents and their young children), this would be evidence of power differentials between them.

In the overlaps of Data Segments III and IV number of speakers is not equal to number of parties, but the bases of team formation are different. In Segment III, MM's question at line #530 is treated as one that any local person might answer. The answer at line #533 (if it appears at all)[11] is treated as insufficient; MK and

KP, whom the stranger's question invokes, but does not individuate, as locals overlap (#s 534/5; 542/3) in expanding on it.

In Thai society, the categorial distinction between peasants and officials is paramount and almost always relevant. But few categories, if any, are absolutely full-time. "Who are those Lao?" invoked the categories of 'stranger' and 'native' by which DO, otherwise an official, is co-categorized with MK and KP. All three (at III:549–54) answer III:548. The metric of conversational sequencing provides co-ordinates—a sort of background graph paper—for tracking the motile shiftings of roles and relationships that characterize interaction. We can use it to tune into the rustlings and alarms of talk with which we are summoned to and released from our occasioned duty as policemen, daddies, neighbors, and friends.

At lines #162/3 of Data Segment IV MK and KP again start to perform the same action at the same time, but now as mates on a slightly different team. MK and KP, like all individuals, can be correctly categorized in many ways by the rules of their culture. They are Lue, former novices, villagers, middle-aged, men, etc., etc. One of conversation's main and constant jobs is to invoke categories, and thereby enliven norms for current interactive relevance (Moerman 1972).

Thai typifications, their "ethno-ethnography" as it were, take it that all ethnic Thai are either clergy, officials, or peasants (Moerman 1967). Peasants farm rice, officials do not. Rice farming (*tham naa* [S]) is an activity categorially ascribed to villagers, one they are expected to know and to enjoy talking about. By asking "Are the fields done yet?" (IV:149), DO invokes the category of which MK and KP are together members, and from which he himself is contrastively excluded.

Few questions are principally requests for information. The district officer's question—like a 'professor' asking a 'student', "How are classes going?"—is more a move for friendly talk. Fieldworkers administering a cultural inventory, or being themselves asked about the airplane fare from America or Australia, are well acquainted with the aridity of such categorial questions. By asking others only what they are categorially supposed to know and to be interested in (talking to garage mechanics about cars and football, for example, or to farmers only about their fields), we can easily prove to ourselves that they are as ignorant as we thought they were. And we, of course, are proved reciprocally and equally dumb. By asking someone who could be categorized as a 'student', "How are classes going?" I both make him/her into one and make myself—who could otherwise have been friend, companion, or lover—into the categorial 'professor', with all the expectations entailed therein.

The question "Are the fields done yet?" (IV:149) engenders a series of repairs of which one, at line #156, is of the type called "word search" (Schegloff, et al. 1977). By its grammar and delivery (the stretch /::/ and the /,/ intonation), line #156 presents its speaker as missing what he needs for completing his utterance.

KP provides a version of it at line #158, therein actively joining the team that the official's question (#149) invoked, and performing some of its work. But as spouses, siblings, and linesmen for fancy (American gridiron) football quarterbacks know, there are ways in which only team-mates can compete with one another. By switching into Siamese, the more prestigious and official dialect, KP is also showing that he is better able to talk to the district officer than MK is.

MK, in line #160, accepts KP's contribution to his utterance, and continues the expansion that line #156 began. But at #161, the district officer interrupts this expansion with /ɔ̂·/, a "surprise" or "discovery" marker (Jefferson 1973). "Interrupts," like the "obliterate" of "The Leper," is a social, not acoustic, matter. Here, the grammar and the delivery (/:/ and /,/) of MK's #160 project continuing; DO's interruptive onset might easily have occasioned an overlap rather than a latch (/ = /). So note, first, that two persons need not make noise at the same time, need) not overlap, for one of them to be interrupting the other. Second, the notion of "interrupt" rests on there being an owned unit that can be interrupted. This is an interactively negotiated matter (See Chapter Five, p. 82.) Two friends once each separately complained to me about the other "always interrupting" him/her. One, a sexagenarian raconteur, would begin a candidately multi-turn unit (a story, say, or a logical argument) after an /uh huh/ or similar receipt marker from the other, a young woman, only to find her soon competitively overlapping one of its turns. For her, the unit cleared by the receipt marker was not the multi-turn one he intended.

And, thirdly, we must note that interruptions, like overlaps, are not always naughty, breaches, etc. An interruption can be quite legitimate, spurred by the elaborate courtesy which Gail Jefferson (1973) has shown exact placement to embody. DO's IV:161 is a quite proper piece of conversational repair.

Lines IV:149–54 comprise an "adjacency pair" into which a "repair sequence" has been inserted.[12] With overwhelming regularity, whether Thai or English is being talked, inserted repair sequences take the form found here:

1 A: First part of paired action (e.g., question, request, etc.) (#149).
2 B: Initiates repair on #1 (#151).
3 A: Does repair on #1 (#153).
4 B: Does second part of paired action (e.g., answer, grant, etc.) (#154).

This satisfies a set of multiple constraints:

1 The recipient of #1, regardless of how many and who else is present, initiates repair on it;

2 the speaker of #1, whoever else is present, speaks next and uses his entire turn for repairing #1;

3 the speaker of #2, whoever else might be present, then speaks immediately next to perform a second action appropriate to #1.

There are no extra turn-types or speakers.

A general and overriding rule for repair, albeit one balanced by a preference for self-correction, is "do it as soon as possible." This is just what DO does by interrupting at #161. His "discovery" or "surprise-marker" claims that what follows it is a revised, repaired, and hence legitimately interruptive understanding. Its legitimacy is sequential, a matter of repair as soon as possible, and not related to his status. Part of what marks #161 as a repaired understanding is the question particle (/lўy/) which makes it a proposal to be accepted or rejected by recipient next speaker. In this, too, the organization of repair is quite the same in Thai as in English, although Thai uses a syntactic particle for the questioning that American does intonationally. (See Chapter Three, p. 39.)

As mates on the team DO called into being, and by their teamwork in together forming the utterance (#156 + 158) that gave him the new understanding he proposes, *both* MK and KP are recipient, and thereby next speaker, to #161. This produces the turn-initial overlap at #162/3 that first interested us in this segment. The overlap, engendered by teamwork, is handled as teamwork. Each withdraws: first KP at #163, then MK (after #162's /tham:/), to allow the other to finish. Thai and English conversation negotiate overlap with the same devices for competition and withdrawal. Lines IV:162 and 163 will look familiar to readers acquainted with American transcripts, as will the withdrawal of Segment III's line #535, the competitive stretch of III:542, and every other instance of overlap encountered in the transcriptions of this volume.

Overlap in Context

For one speaker to intrude upon the talk of another sometimes means aggression and domination. To quote the (Australian edition of the) *New York Times Weekly Review* (30 Aug. – 5 Sept. 1981, p. 1):

Mr. Meese's domination was underscored by the public silence of Richard V. Allen, the national security adviser. . . . Those who have talked to the two together say Mr. Meese does not hesitate to interrupt or talk over the once highly visible Mr. Allen.

But for overlap, as for every word, every phrase, everything that occurs in conversation, there is no one-to-one mapping of form to function, of item to meaning.

The overlap in lines #258/9 of Data Segment V is not obliterative, contentious or aggressive in any way. Rather, it provides a delicate device for cooperation, for showing that parties are of a single mind, for allowing them to become a single social person by together fabricating an utterance: one of the most minute of social artifacts, and a paragon of individually owned and often defended private property.

Segment V comes from a telephone call made in Southern California in 1968 soon after Robert Kennedy's assassination. Two sisters are discussing politics. In Orange County terms, B is the more liberal of the two. She is less bellicose than A and appreciates the merits of President Kennedy.

Pomerantz's lovely work (1975, 1978) has shown that assessments and expressions of opinion, like A's at lines V:249–53, make agreement a relevant next activity. When a second action can come in opposite forms—agreement or disagreement after an opinion, a grant or a refusal after a request—the form that is preferred is normatively delivered strongly and straight away. Parties can interpret its absence or downgrading as a sign of the dispreferred form, here disagreement. This is the business of the .8 second pause at line #254, a pause that the rules of turn-taking assign to B. With a move quite common to the negotiation of agreement, B, not quite agreeing with A, gives her, in turn, something to agree with at line #255. But now A, in line #256, withholds agreement. Instead, at line #257, she provides a whole barrage of delayers and disagreement markers. The pile-up of delaying "well"s and "uh"s, of mere tokens of agreement (the "yeah"s), and of "Yeah but"s is quite striking. This is what disagreement typically sounds like in American conversation. Will these two sisters never get together? This is just what they begin to do through the beautifully orchestrated overlap that follows at lines #258/9. With a stock phrase about President Kennedy and the homophony of "No" and "know" as cultural resources, they speak chorally and in unison. Speaker A cuts off her turn (/−/ after "in") at line #258, and B completes for A the utterance that A started and withdrew. With delicate choreography, the two have spoken as one: in the content of their opinions, the structure of their joint utterance, and the form of their monophony. A immediately (at #260) provides a token of agreement with B's assessment, and they proceed, after all the jostlings that preceded, to produce a parallel orientation to the events. Agreement is relevant, and often required, for conversational closure, so their ending the topic is further evidence for describing this overlap as not conflictful. It was a way for two to talk as one and therein shift toward the metaphors whose negotiation will bring the topic, and the conversation, to a close.[13]

In neither this instance nor "The Leper" did the overlapped utterance invite invasion, as hitches, upward intonation, pausing, or word-search can. In that sense, both overlaps were interruptive, and neither occupied what has been called, misleadingly (Schegloff 1981), a "back channel." But they were quite different social actions: one conflictful and combative, the other cooperative and conciliatory. Whether as analysts or participants, we could not tell what each meant or did without taking account of both sequential organization and cultural context. That is how the units and counters of interaction—whether utterances, winks, words, or interruptions—always work. That is why we cannot learn much by merely counting them, unless we first analyze each instance to see what it did. Such *analyzed* interruptions and overlaps might then be useful for such projects as diagnosing the dynamics of a relationship or discerning patterns of control and submission among social categories. Here conversation analysis can again be helpful. Social investigators, lay and professional, wantonly assume that the categories they are interested in (gender, for example, or race, ethnicity, class, or party) are the ones that actively mattered in the situations they investigate (Moerman 1972, 1967). Culturally contexted conversation analysis can track which categories and relationships were actively invoked. It will require wider social analysis to trace the mechanisms that relate doctor–patient, for example, to male–female or Anglo–Chicano to boss–worker.

Every interruption, every overlap, every bit of talk is culturally—as well as socially, sequentially, and linguistically—constituted. Between speech communities, regions, and even individuals, the form, placement, and interpretation of overlaps may differ, often invidiously. Tannen (1981) claims that "interruptions" which East Coast Jewish Americans intend to be "supportive" are not heard that way in the West. Kyoto dialect speakers complain that Tokyo speakers steal the floor by coming in on their drawled polite particles. The Scollons (1981) report that White Men pace their speech differently from Athapaskans, whom they therefore interrupt, so making themselves aggressive and the Athapaskans inarticulate. And I have been told of an Australian institute director angrily leaving a meeting after an American, no more pushy than most, had twice finished a sentence for him. The student of interaction, and of language, must take culture, social institutions, and meaning into account—but not by assuming a one-to-one relationship among them.

■

When I eavesdrop on Segment V with my "natural" ears—that is with those of a leftish American intellectual—I hear comically vapid talk that tickles my prejudices. As conversation analysts, we can hear its lovely intricacy. This appreciation comes from close and sympathetic attention to an interaction on its own terms, without pre-judging its importance, its pleasing or displeasing character, and so forth.

Analysis of the sequential organization of conversation permits locating interactive events in the context that gave them their meaning. To the social sciences, "context" usually means something like vague surrounding features that cannot be stated except, perhaps, in retrospect. Sequential analysis provides some foothold on the technical specification of context as significant place. To find the meaning and consequence of a conversational event, we, whether as analysts or partici- pants, orient ourselves to its position within a turn, within a specified and bounded type of sequence (like assessment, noticing, or question-answer), and within the unit of a single conversation with a beginning and ending. As participants, but not yet as analysts, we also place conversations in the history of the interactions that compose a relationship and a biography. Sequential position produces the nodes from which we hang our chimes of talk. But without the scale and resonance of categorial ascriptions and the situationally occasioned normative cultural knowl- edge they invoke, the clacking of talk across turns is mere noise.

The overlaps we have examined are typical, trivial, turn-taking events: the dull- est clods of talk. But life consists of its details. It is experienced, and so lived, moment by ephemeral moment, each successive moment a complexly reticulated intersection of numerous processes. Some of those processes comprise the sequen- tial organization of conversation. By tracking that organization we can perceive what some of our social life consists of, and provide loci and a metric—a place and a scale—for observing the actual ongoing operation of such mystifyingly grand processes as patron-client bonds, cooperation, social networks, or being a peasant.

Much of our social life consists of talk organized as conversation with which we conjure up and deal with our fellows, expose our character, bespeak our cul- ture. Conversation analysis provides a technical description of how that talk is or- ganized. From this we can each see and use what we will: sometimes placing some object of scholarly interest—an insult, say, or terms for a kinsman—in the context which gave it local meaning, sometimes using the structure of conversation as na- tives do: to hook, display, articulate, and fashion things out of the web of culture. Subsequent chapters are concerned with such issues. Here, the overlaps we have examined encourage me to less disciplined reflections. I wonder at the transience with which we experience our self-interest and our social world, or at the instanta- neous and unauthored complexity of each successive moment of anonymous talk. John Cage (1968) observed that:

The relationship of things happening
at the same time is spontaneous
and irrepressible.
It is you yourself
in the form you have
that instant taken.
To stop and figure it out
takes
time.

A speaker who took time to think before he talked could not have produced these complex, artful, and exquisitely choreographed overlaps. Were the overlaps solely creatures of the rules for turn-taking, mere "natural" events like the delicate operation of enzymes, they would be less challenging.[14]

The essential subject of the social and all human sciences is meaningful conduct. Social, purposeful, intensely personal meaning permeates these overlaps. As ethnographers, sympathetic observers, co-members, fellow humans we noticed in the most accidental dust of their talk what these actors were up to: being teammates, for example, as in Segments II–IV. In "The Leper," we could discern a display of what they were aware and afraid of. In Segment V, an instant of simultaneous speech revealed and constituted what two sisters were trying—in an intelligible sense of that very human word—to accomplish.[15] Yet all of these meaningful, consequential, structurally complex, and densely cultural overlaps were certainly undeliberate, unanticipated, unconscious, and unremembered. No individual human actor is their author. We build our experienced, lived in, significant social reality out of a mesh of interactive processes too tiny and too quick for the thinking, planning "I" to handle.[16]

3

Nature and Culture

Introduction

This chapter is the first and most technical of three that focus on a single conversational 'structure'[1] as a means for exploring connections between conversation analysis and ethnography. The structure is the sequential organization of (initial) references to (non-present) persons, as described in a paper written in 1973 by Harvey Sacks and Emanuel Schegloff (Sacks and Schegloff 1979).[2] I will summarize their 1979 description of references to persons in American conversation, briefly discuss the procedures used for comparing such references in Thai, and show that Thai and American conversation have the same sequential organization. I will then point to some implications, applications, and limitations of this surprising correspondence.

Chapters Four and Five emphasize relations between conversational structures and cultural content, using the known structures to locate interactants' motives and meanings. This chapter describes and develops the sense in which those structures are known and universal. This involves an examination of conversation analytic arguments and data that may sometimes seem uncomfortably close and detailed, but providing the tools that subsequent chapters put to ethnographic use requires it.

My focus on person reference is somewhat accidental; its initial basis autobiographical. But I would like my report of correspondence between Thai and American sequential organization, my evaluation of that correspondence and of the procedures that produce it, and my suggestions for using conversational structures as instruments for ethnography and interactional analysis all to be read as standing for—or against—other claimed universals of sequential organization.[3]

The intellectual autobiography is straightforward; its consequences for my career severe. I had become convinced that standard research techniques distorted the native relevancies that it is ethnography's task to uncover (Moerman 1967: 66–8), and had begun to devise ways of working that seemed to circumvent them (1969a). These made me an ethnographer-consumer of conversation analysis (Moerman 1972). The transcript I was working on (Moerman 1973) contained the fragment presented here as Exhibit I. I thought I had accidentally erased the tape (by stereophonically recording Handel's *Messiah* over it). This was distressing, but not destructive to my interest in studying what natives said to one another when I was not asking them questions.

1	MK$_{((Y))}$	phóm	tham	xán		wâj	mōt	lē.	
		PRN	PRV	boundary		PRV	all	PRT	
2		děwnî·	mi·	nǎ·n	phīan	haw	nī	ā	nǎ·n
		then/now	PRV	T	N	PRN	PRT	PRT	T
3		phīan	phan	sɛ·n	nî·				
		N	T	N	D				
4		aw	lōt	xâ·w	thǎj ləj	thǎj	tǐ·	xán	ləj.
		PRV	vehicle	enter	plow	plow	at	boundary	entirely

I made a boundary dike all around my plot. Then our Nan Phian Phan Saen's Nan Phian brought in his tractor and plowed, plowed right at the boundary dike.

E<small>XHIBIT</small> I

Reading a manuscript of Sacks and Schegloff's paper on the interaction of competing conversational preferences in the domain of references to persons suggested that Exhibit I might be a Thai instance of what they had studied in American conversation: an instance of a pattern called "try-marking," central to their analysis. If Thai conversation was sequentially organized as they had discovered American conversation to be, my tape, could it be recovered, should show *phan sɛ·n*, on line #3, to be surrounded by short pauses.

Replaying my tape on a monophonic deck showed that it had not been completely destroyed. Behind the ghostly trace of "Every valley shall be exalted," the Thai voices, and the Thai silences, were clearly audible for re-transcription (as Data Segment VI) with detail finer than our understanding of the organization of conversation required when Exhibit I was made (in 1969). The predicted pauses do, indeed, appear (at VI:219, 221–3). As we will see (pp. 38–9), those pauses help to show that Thai conversation is sequentially organized quite like American conversation. A "mechanical" transcript of naturally occurring talk among individuals I knew well, recorded in a sociocultural setting made familiar to me by intensive fieldwork, revealed a fine-grained structure that conversation analysis could predict in striking detail and apparently account for. A little "hmm," a .5 second and a .8 second pause may seem small matters. But Sacks and Schegloff's 1979 unplanned prediction was unnervingly more exact than anything I had ever encountered in the social sciences. It convinced me to interrupt ethnographic research in order to learn more about a sequential organization of conversation that apparently had great influence on what gets said.

The new transcript was "mechanical" in the sense that it was made to current standards of transcript adequacy without regard to any hypotheses about what its details would reveal. It records turns of talk without respect to any other social science notions. It is "out there" on the page for analyst and reader to encounter, cite, be responsible to, and make sense of according to explicit systematic conversation analytic procedures. Unlike scenes culled for our research interests, the transcript was edited only by turning the recorder on (upon entering the scene of talk) and off (when the batteries ran out). In these ways, the data were objective. But they are not objects: external to our intelligence, sympathy, and understanding. Meaning is integral to structure, not its optional veneer.

Some readers may have seen the Monty Python skit in which two clerks barely notice some vague objects dropping past their window, then observe that they are bodies, and finally recognize them as known corporate officers jumping to their deaths. The black humor reminds us that assigning labels to conspecifics transforms mere physical or biological objects obedient to gravity, momentum, and metabolism into members of the social order whose activity is conduct: meaningful and morally potent. Labelling is cultural. Anthropologists have often studied the definitions, taxonomy, or semantics of some of the words variously used to do it: kinship terms, personal names, ethnic labels, etc. But the social organization of actual occasions of labelling had never been systematically examined. Sacks and Schegloff 1979 investigates one class of such occasions and finds it to be organized by general rules of conversation without respect to culture. Referring to persons lies where "Culture" (in Dilthey's sense of *Geist* as "a field within which diversity and variety are the rule and 'general laws' are not to be looked for") intersects with *Natur* (in Wundt's sense of "human behavior [manifesting] only 'general laws' dependent on universal ahistorical processes and so free of all cultural variability").[4] Chapters Four and Five build toward the situationally specific as against the typological, function or physiology as against structure or anatomy, the symbolic as against the cognitive, the cultural as against the natural. But these are only our divided ways of talking about unified natural events. Neither aspect can be correctly described without the other, so all chapters have their unequal shares of both.

Summary of Sacks and Schegloff 1979

Compared to studies of turn-taking (Sacks, et al. 1974), repair (Schegloff, et al. 1977), or laughter (Jefferson 1979), Sacks and Schegloff 1979 is slight and not well known. But in addition to its substantive interest, the paper offers an explicitly conversation-systemic, and so *naturwissenschafter,* argument that is general, straightforward, and simple enough to summarize here.

Conversation as an orderly phenomenon can be described by means of rules. As with many rule-governed phenomena, there are numerous actual occasions on which different, yet applicable, rules have inconsistent outcomes. One way for a system to provide for the orderly organization of such occasions is by containing superordinate priority rules. That is, by providing that when two (or more) rules are relevant to a given situation, but have inconsistent results, one of them is to be given priority over the other(s). Sacks and Schegloff 1979 reports that in conversation a characteristic organization of priority is for one rule to be relaxed step-by-step in favor of another.

Among the general principles which our research tradition finds helpful for characterizing conversation are two which Sacks and Schegloff 1979 calls "the preference for minimization" and "the preference for recipient design." [5] In the organization of references to persons, minimization is expressed by it being the case that

massively in conversation, references in reference occasions are accomplished by the use of a single reference form (Sacks and Schegloff 1979:17).

One component of recipient design in this conversational domain is a "preference for recognitionals." That is, despite the availability in the language of such non-recognitional forms as /somebody/, /a guy/, etc.,

if recipient may be supposed by speaker to know the one being referred to, and if recipient may suppose speaker to have so supposed [there is a preference for the speaker to use] such reference forms as allow a recipient to find . . . who, that recipient knows, is being referred to (loc. cit.).

Quite commonly the conjoint operation of these rules produces a consonant result: a recognitional label. It is short, and the recipient will use it to recognize its referent person if he can. In American conversation,[6] the typical recognitional label is a personal name. Sacks and Schegloff's study of a large corpus of American transcripts reveals (and mine confirms) that the most common identificatory reference form is the one exemplified by Data Segments VII–IX, quoted from them.

Sacks and Schegloff further report that when the recipient of a recognitional label does not recognize its referent, minimization is relaxed step-by-step. The recipient uses his next turn for no more than /Who?/ (Data Segments X:4; XI:711); referrer uses his next turn for no more than a single proposed recognizable (X:5; XI:712).

The second try in the 'who' engendered sequences is very commonly a repeat of the problematic reference form [XI:712]. Moreover, 'who' engendered sequences very commonly occur as insertions into other sequences [as in XI's "announcement" (Terasaki 1976) sequence]. [W]hen they do, [minimization is further preserved by the recognizer dispensing with] the assertion of recognition . . . and instead, upon recognition, proceeding with his next move [XI:713] in the sequence his 'who?' interrupted (Sacks and Schegloff 1979:20).

Perhaps the most compelling evidence advanced for the step-by-step relaxation of minimization in favor of recognitionals is what happens on occasions in which the minimization-consistent label is not consonant with designing a reference term for a particular recipient. Minimization is maintained by proffering the reference term with what Sacks and Schegloff call a "try-marker." The recognitional label typically is proffered with a rising intonation (usually recorded on our transcripts by a /?/ or /,/) which marks it as a *try* for recognition, without adding to its length. Regularly it is followed by a pause. The recipient is to use this pause for no more than briefly signalling recognition by means of such a "token of recognition" as /uh huh/, /yeah/, or a nod. If the speaker gets this, he proceeds with his ongoing unit. If he does not, this is taken to mean that the recipient does not recognize referent by that recognitional label. The speaker then delivers a short second try, also try-marked. This second try is typically an addition to the name or a "recognitional descriptor," a one-bit[7] piece of information about the referent person that the recipient can use to recognize him by. This is followed by another pause in which the recipient is again to produce a token of recognition. Failure to produce one is taken as failure to recognize, and the speaker produces another one-bit try-marked recognitional descriptor, again followed by a pause for the recipient's recognition token. If, on the other hand, the recipient claims recognition in the pause after a first or subsequent try, the speaker proceeds with his ongoing unit. To quote their exemplary data, the surname in XII:1 is a try-marked recognitional label, as is the added name of XII:2. /The cellist/ (XII:2) is a recognitional descriptor. In Data Segment XIII, A leaves a pause (XIII:3) after the recognitional label /Max Rickler/ and, finding it unfilled by a recognition token from B, offers the recognitional descriptor of XIII:4. Receiving the recognition token (XIII:6's /Yeah/), he proceeds with his unit.

Thai and American Sequential Organization

Finding out how well Sacks and Schegloff's 1979 description fits Thai conversation requires ethnography as well as sequential analysis. Ethnography involves translation; conversation analysis involves making a "collection." Neither operation is straightforward or without troubling assumptions.

In our tradition of conversation analysis, a student begins research by discovering a few instances of some "candidate phenomenon." The investigator then proceeds to make "a collection" of all the instances that he/she encounters in a large corpus of conversations. These are continuously inspected to see how well they seem to cohere as a conversation-sequential phenomenon. A broad collection is encouraged because doubtful instances can help to define and delimit the phenomenon. They may also turn out to be instances of similar and related phenomena which speakers might have used as alternatives.[8] But actual inspection of the phenomenon and the definition and analysis such inspection yields is concentrated on clear and simple cases.

The Thai materials that I examined for my collection consist of transcripts of conversations in a Thai-Lue village recorded in 1965, talk between a lawyer and his clients and witnesses recorded in 1968–9, and courtroom testimony also recorded in 1968–9.[9] I went through these materials and collected all references to persons. My initial report of correspondence of sequential organization (pp. 37–39) is based upon examination of *all* instances of person reference encountered in my Thai transcripts.

To speak of "a Thai collection" begs a number of ethnographic questions. The collection purports to be a set of instances of a recognizable social action, one equivalent, or at least informatively comparable, to an American social action. Making a collection of Thai references to persons assumes that there is some "it," some object or entity to be plucked from any culture, much as earlier ethnologists thought it sensible to compare the kin terminologies of different societies as if they were equivalent objects. Despite its ethnographic crudity, such a collection was necessary. Science replicates procedures. To check your results, I collect materials like yours and use the same procedures on them. Of course, what I find is thereby the product of how I looked and of what I was looking for and at. Making and examining such a collection will answer the question: How are initial references to non-present persons *sequentially* organized in Thai conversation? How are they organized with respect to such units as turns, sequences, pauses, recognitional labels, recognitional descriptors, etc.?

A Thai collection presented for comparisons is a product of translation. Every practitioner of conversation analysis, like every conversant, every ethnographer (e.g., Haviland 1977; Rosaldo 1980:20, f.), every social thinker and investigator, trades on his knowledge of language and (in Cromwell 1982's sense) idiom. The turns and turn constructional units of which conversation consists make use of syntax. Recognizing recipients and social actions requires knowledge of semantics. Some relevant differences between Thai and English must be mentioned here, but solely for their immediately relevant (and least interesting) consequences.

In my corpus of village conversations, the usual recognitional label for an absent person is a title or title plus name, rather than the American personal name. Sometimes a second name, typically that of a spouse but sometimes of a parent, is added. Since coupled names and epithets are sometimes used as initial recognitional labels, but other times added for making reference more specific, the distinction between recognitional labels and recognitional descriptors (which can also sometimes serve as recognitional labels) is less clear than in American conversation.

The dichotomy between present and non-present persons, and distinctions among co-present persons, is less clear in Thai than in English. In the first place, Thai syntax does not require that subjects or objects always be overtly stated (see Grima and Strecker 1976, Campbell 1969, Panupong 1970). In my corpus, an unmentioned subject or object is sometimes a non-present person, sometimes the speaker, and sometimes his recipient or another co-present person.

Furthermore, when Thai talkers *do* mention themselves or other present persons, they rarely use pronouns. They usually use a title, title and name, or (typically only for children) name. This, it will be remembered, is also the dominant way of making recognition-relevant reference to non-present persons.

These features have implications for the Thai notion of person. The only observation that need be made here is that because there is less distinction between recognitional labels and recognitional descriptors, and because the same forms are used for referring to absent as to present persons (including the speaker), the domain of references to non-present persons (and the distinction between self and other) is less clearly separate from other references to persons in Thai conversation than it is in American conversation.

It is nevertheless possible to compare Thai with American collections of initial references to non-present persons. Doing so discloses striking correspondences in how they are sequentially organized.

1 Thai, like English, permits initial reference to non-present persons to be made by means of such "non-recognitional forms" as:

1) pronouns (XIV:1);

2) O-form subject or object nominals (XV:1);

3) categories like the 'kids' of XVI:1, especially when preceded by such words as *phûak* or *mùu,* meaning 'type of,' 'kind of,' 'group of';

4) "descriptors" of the kind instanced by XVII:3, 20–21.

But "recognitional forms" are used commonly and very often.

2 In American, personal names are the usual recognitional labels. The Thai use titles, to which names are sometimes added. The titles, names, and eponyms with which villagers propose absent persons for recognition are all compoundable. Nevertheless, most of the recognitional labels encountered in my corpus are short: consisting of a title or two, a name, a title + name, or a name + epithet.

3 Working toward recognition is the typical task for which minimal recognitional forms are expanded. In XVIII, a pair of names is provided at line #9 in response to line #8's apparent failure to recognize by a single name. In XIX, a second title is provided at line #14 when a single title did not do the job, and epithets later (XIX:31, 33) added to that.

4 Thai use of "Who?" parallels the American pattern described by Sacks and Schegloff 1979. When a recognitional label is used in the course of talk, a recipient claims that he does not recognize its referent person by using the immediately next turn for no more than one single syllable person-referent repair-initiator (S: /khraj/, L: /pháj/). As in American, "this often produces from speaker a repetition of the problematic reference form" in next turn.

5 In person-reference repair, as in all types of repair, successive initiators on the same repairable locate it more precisely, and are often longer.[10] In Data Segment XX, DO's "which Phian?" (lines #268 & 274) after his "who?" (lines #262 & 265) is an instance. And, like the American recipient of the news about Sibbi's sister (Data Segment XI:713), DO claims to have recognized (at line #276) by "proceeding with his next move in the sequence his 'who?' interrupted" (Sacks and Schegloff 1979:20).

6 Try-marked sequences furnish the most elaborate evidence of parallel sequential organization. In the Thai datum (Data Segment VI) with which we began:

(i) MK makes recognition relevant by proferring a recognitional label (/năn phǐan/) at line #218.

(ii) He then repeats it, stretching (/:/) its terminal sound.

(iii) He stops speaking and no one else speaks; the concerted action producing a pause (VI:219).

(iv) MK, and none of the other half-dozen or so persons present,[11] then speaks again,

(v) with a one-bit recognitional descriptor (VI:220) for Nan Phian.

(vi) This is followed by another conjointly produced pause (VI:221).

(vii) DO then produces a recognition token (VI:222), following which

(viii) MK proceeds with his unit.

In this datum and others (e.g., Segments XVIII:7–9; XIX:12–14, 31–34; XXI:446a–447; XXXIII:679–81) the impressively detailed and closely calibrated correspondence to try-marked sequences in American conversation is quite striking:

1) A class of clear recognitional labels exists.

2) These recognitional labels are quite short.

3) When a speaker uses a recognitional label and leaves a pause after it, that pause is to be filled by a recognition token from the recipient.

4) Failure to provide a recognition token is taken as failure to recognize,

5) and speaker then uses an entire next turn for providing just one more item about the referent that recipient could use for recognizing him.

6) He again leaves a pause;

7) again for recipient's recognition token,

8) the absence of which produces still another single item useable for recipient (and no other) to identify referent by,

9) and so on through successive turns until recognition is attained or abandoned.

There is a substantive divergence in that Thai conversation does not much use intonation to mark a try. Thai conversation generally uses particles for many interactional tasks that American conversation accomplishes with intonation.[12] It is tempting to account for this on the grounds that Thai's phonemic tones and the supra-segmental contours they set up restrict the conversational use of intonation contours. But Japanese, in which tones are not phonemic, also appears to use sentential particles when English uses prosodics. Whatever the local reasons, the general implication is clear. To the student of communication it is not helpful to sequester "language," as something that includes syntactic items like sentential particles, apart from "speech" that includes intonation, stress, stretch, and the other items that appear on a conversational transcript.

Ethnographic Implications

The sequential organization of reference occasions is part of the technology of talk. Insofar as talk is used as a tool, as a means to an end, as a device for realizing plans and so disclosing motives, we need to know its mechanics. My vocabulary of tasks and jobs is deliberate. Much of comparative ethnology, and no little ethnography, supposes actors to confront an obdurate world of land, water, or game with purposive techniques for accomplishing their ends. For rice to be grown, soil must be loosened, water made to flow. To analyze farming anywhere in the world, we take such technical, "natural," features into account. The sequential organization of reference occasions might provide a similar purchase on aspects of the social world.

Thai talk that refers to non-present persons is sequentially organized like the American talk that Sacks and Schegloff 1979 describes. First, it is *conversation,* as that phenomenon is recorded in tapes and transcripts made, used, and published by the lineage that Harvey Sacks founded. It is organized by means of the units, principles, and structures more or less well described by our research tradition. It consists of sequentially organized locally allocated turns composed of utterances built of turn-constructional units. It exhibits "preferences" for "agreement" and for "minimization," etc., that interact with an organization of understanding and its repair.

More specifically, Sacks and Schegloff's 1979 description of the structure and distribution of recognitional labels, recognitional descriptors, and recognition tokens; the concerted work to attain recognition; and the constraint of minimizing the number and size of the turns used, characterizes every instance of initial reference to non-present persons encountered in my corpus of Thai conversations. In Thai conversation, as in American, a recognitional label is the main device for making the work of identification relevant. Once identification has been made relevant, the work done by Thai to attain it is governed by the minimization metric and constraint that Sacks and Schegloff discovered in American conversation.

I must emphasize that I am not reporting correspondence of features unexamined by their paper: features like the occasions at and purposes for which recognition is made relevant, or the meaning of the forms by which recognition is proposed and accomplished. Chapters Four and Five will use the sequential organization of references to persons for exploring issues of meaning, intention, and the nature of the social actor. This requires a "clinical," case-by-case, approach rather than the "epidemiological," collection-based, one of Sacks and Schegloff 1979. But I do not think that the two approaches can be fully complementary unless the description and analysis of sequential organization itself takes account of cultural, contextual, and intentional factors eschewed by a narrow version of conversation analysis and precluded by excessive reliance on collections.

■

Thai and English are unrelated languages. Thailand and America are quite different in socio-economic structure. Since Thai references to persons are sequentially organized like American ones, this sequential organization may be universal. The universality is, of course, a deliberately rash proposal awaiting empirical discon-firmation. But the only admissible basis for proving or disproving any proposed universality are recordings, transcripts, and analyses of actual conversations.

Correspondence of organization furnishes ethnography with a background, metric, and structure for precisely locating and specifying the socially important and frequently done task of making identificatory reference to persons. Whether or not universality is confirmed, Sacks and Schegloff's 1979 discoveries and analysis provide a basis and a vocabulary for comparisons.

- Divergences encountered in other cultures and scenes can be noted and de-scribed in ways that might help to account for them.

- Referring to someone in ways that assure (or attempt to assure) his identifica-tion by those who can or should be able to identify him can be recognized on a transcript. Inasmuch as occasions of reference are organized with respect to whether "recipient may be supposed by speaker to know the one being referred to" (Sacks and Schegloff 1979:17), we can learn from transcripts whether a person like the speaker expects a person like his recipient to know a person like the one he refers to. We can see whether this expectation was correct. A ma-jor component of the ethnosociology of knowledge thus becomes directly observable.

- We can learn what categorial memberships are invoked by the natives them-selves in order to do their own job of pinning down, labelling, tracking, con-structing social actors. (See Chapter Four, pp. 60–61 and Chapter Five, pp. 85–6.) We can see whether it is done differently on different types of occasions, or among different types of persons. But in applying Sacks' and Schegloff's dis-coveries, we will come to modify them.

■

Reference occasions are produced by people talking to some purpose. Like all con-versational events, they are thoroughly contexted moments in which roles, values, institutions, passions, and strategies are embodied, experienced, and lived. They are inescapably *occasions,* contexted and embodied. They are the products of so-cial interaction, and therefore negotiated, contingent, and sometimes momentous. We cannot understand the substantive, pragmatic, human and meaningful nature of any such occasion without attending to its situated particularity. Moreover, the specifically conversational organization of "occasions of reference"—whether they occur at all and how they are sequentially organized when they do occur—has a motivated,[13] contextual interactive basis that influences:

1 whether a person is mentioned in such a way as to make individual recognition relevant,

2 the conversational structures used for doing it,

3 the length of the forms used, and

4 the particular labels, descriptors, etc., used.

■

The sequential structure of person reference is conversationally, and hence inter-actively, organized. Sacks and Schegloff 1979 shows this; my report confirms it. But sequence organization is a rather narrow order of social action. A speaker always invokes non-present persons for his/her current speaking purposes, and does it at a particular conversational locus. When a person-reference occurs, it is usually as part of some larger sequence (like giving instructions) or discourse unit (like telling a story). It is typically done to serve some other, more vital, activity like blaming, taking sides, showing off, and so forth. When, as is often salutary, we inspect this conversational phenomenon "top-down" rather than "bottom-up," we can see that the reference and the recognition that always matters is "recognize enough for now," "recognize in the manner and to the degree consistent with current speaking purposes."

Conversationally occasioned identification and recognition vary in kind and degree. Recognition does not always amount to answering the policeman's question, "Do you know this person?" In designing a reference form for co-participants, a speaker often takes into account more of them than a single recipient, and more about them than suppositions of whom they know (Chapter Five, pp. 85–6). The general and universal case is that referrings serve the current speaking purpose of the referrer: locating, invoking, creating the properties of the referent for which he was mentioned. If persons are most often mentioned in such ways as to implicate who specifically and individually is being referred to, this is (to quote an earlier paper on another matter by Schegloff [1968:1080]) "no less a 'special case' for having many occurrences." To say that such references are "preferred" can be a convenient term for capturing the observation that they seem to be preponderant[14] and, more strikingly, that they can be demanded when they have not been offered initially.[15] But just as the reference "occasion" is always the product of interactive work by participants, the "preference" is theirs as well: the product of situated purposes, pertaining to persons, not to conversation. Many socially organized tasks, like gossiping (Haviland 1977) or testifying in court (see Chapter Four) require that the person referred to be uniquely identified. A speaker who proffers or insists upon a term that makes recognition relevant is sometimes therewith proposing one of those tasks. It is of quite general social import for participants to know whether the person they will be talking about is someone with whom they might be co-implicated (cf. Moerman 1972). If speaker's mention is of someone who will be talked about as a fool, or as a wit, or just as someone who was present at a scene when he or she could or should have been elsewhere, everyone had better know whether A's referent is B's wife or neighbor. Sacks and Schegloff's 1979 paper posits two independent and intersecting entities: a set of persons whom A supposes B to know as individuals and a set of occasions of reference. The frequency of and pressure for recognitional references would be better described in terms of, accounted for by means of, and used as an instrument for investigating meaningful social action, rather than ascribed to cognitive suppositions and to the "preference" evinced by regularities of conversational sequencing itself.[16] Heuristically, the best place for starting to show all this is the "reference occasion" with which we began (Segment VI).

Ethnographic Application

In the scene at which it arose, Segment VI is part of the start of a story.[17] As I have pointed out elsewhere (Moerman 1973), this story is, more potently, a plaint or accusation of land theft. MK, a villager, is telling his district officer (DO) that Nan Phian has stolen his land. For his purpose of complaining, accusing, and obtaining redress, it is critical that the district officer know who, *as a specified individual*, took his land. Hence MK's identificatory (by full recognitional label of title and name) and insistently try-marked reference. In Chapter Two's discussion of the "The Leper," I observed that Sɛ·ng's recognitional descriptor for Nɔ̌·, "who lives with Acara Byer," was formed for its recipient townsman official, this same DO. MK's recognitional descriptor, "[the son of Police] Major Saen," fulfills the same specifications. Furthermore, it provides the right personae for his drama of injustice and helplessness. Immediately after a number of versions of MK's story and DO's reactions to them have been repeated, KP, a villager colleague of MK, tells how he, too, had land stolen by an official. In KP's story, which starts with the Data Segment XXI, the referent villain is initially (line #436) referred to solely by title. It is quite unlikely for the district officer, who had only recently taken office, to recognize by title alone which individual KP is referring to. Nor is it the case that KP does not know the more identificatory form of title + name, for he uses it, but only much later in his story (line #493), and after numerous pronominal and zero-form re-references to Accounting Officer Keet. The events of KP's narrative are four years old, and he had resolved them to his satisfaction. To his supportive "second story," not itself an accusation or plaint, it matters only that the culprit was an official. For this, title alone will do. The situated interactive purpose, the motive for talking, is implicated with the form, length, and specificity of recognitional labels.

■

KP's story has characters in addition to the accounting officer. One of them is introduced at line #446a of the Data Segment XXI. This person, a peasant from another village, is certainly not known to the recipient district officer. But KP refers to him individuatingly, by name. This spurs a sequence, quite like our "try-marked" sequences in which there are:

   (i) a pause after the reference (line #446b),
   (ii) followed by a recognitional descriptor from the speaker (line #446c),
   (iii) followed by a recognition token from recipient (line #447),
   (iv) followed by speaker resuming his business (line #448).

But the recognitional descriptor, "my helper there," is not designed to specify "who, that recipient knows" has been referred to. Rather, it characterizes its referent solely as a personage in, and for purposes of KP's story and what that story is told in aid of.

■

In Segment XXI, for the district officer to recognize Ma Na merely as a character in KP's story is for him to hear that story (and the order of recognition its purpose entails) as KP intends it. In Segment XX, on the other hand, the district officer's "Who" (at lines #262 & 265) and "which Phian" (at lines #268 & 274)—although completely consistent with the sequential organizations of repair and of references to persons—are quite another matter. They occur after the "successful" identification sequence with which we, and they, began (Segment VI), and in the course of an immediately subsequent version of MK's plaint. To the first version, which contains Segment VI's apparently successful identification of Nan Phian, the district officer responded merely with a receipt marker, "Yeah" (/khap/). This spurred an amplification of the story, one that showed, by referring to him anaphorically (via the zero-form), that it assumed that recognition of Nan Phian had been accomplished. For that amplified version, MK obtained sympathy (for the loss of his dikes, not his land) and vague advice ("You ought to work it out together.") from the district officer. MK then gives a still more amplified version, during which the "Which Phian?" segment occurs.

  By the person-reference repair-initiators of the "Which Phian?" segment, the district officer shows or claims himself to not have identified Nan Phian as a unique individual. He therein shows or claims or makes himself to not have acknowledged that MK's story was anything other than a "mere story," was anything like the accusation that would require him to have made an individuating identification now, and to take action in the future. DO can sustain this obtuse and inconsequential hearing of MK's story by relying on the availability to conversants of such a standard (the one used appropriately in Segment XXI) as "recognize merely as a character in a story" to account for the recognition token (VI:222) that permitted MK to proceed. MK's sustaining the intelligibility of the plaint he regards himself as making relies upon the availability to *him* of "recognize the referent individual" as Segment VI's standard.

■

In an early paper, Moerman and Sacks (Appendix B) recognized that "understanding" is a socially organized phenomenon. But we restricted our attention to speaking the sequentially appropriate next utterance. The instances examined here show one way in which that formulation is too crude. Displays of understanding are not all-or-none, now-and-forever, stimulus-response signals of some firm entity. Understanding is negotiated, on-going, prospective and retrospective, defeasibly consequential. Understanding is differentially meaningful on different occasions of its occurrence and to different participants at the same occurrence. The district officer's person-reference repair-initiators are part of the same systematic misunderstanding evinced by his "Yeah" and his vague advice about loss of dikes.[18]

Claims of understanding are one of conversation's "multiguities." These multiguities are always locally negotiated, and thereby resources for the exercise or constituting of differential power. Power's appearance here, as everywhere, is active, *interactive,* and so requires the close complementary complicity of co-participants. My own sympathies are all with the peasants who could not shout, "What d'ya mean, 'Which Phian'? We've been tellin' ya about him over and over again!" But like a physician dinner guest told a tale of possibly cancerous symptoms, a district officer is always "on call," always in peril of having to react to any next thing said as a summons to duty. The very extent of his power requires him to cultivate some degree of stupidity and inattention.

It is a pervasive and central feature of Thai society that peasants and officials systematically misunderstand one another, and complain about it. Yet they do converse with one another. Conversation requires its participants to demonstrate their understandings turn by turn, and makes available powerful devices for the repair of misunderstandings. In any society, the recurrent and systematic attainment of misunderstanding between members of social categories who regularly converse with one another must thus be regarded as an artful, complicit, and damning accomplishment, rather than a fault or error. Conversation analysis can show how misunderstanding is accomplished.

One of the items used here, DO's little "hmm" at VI:222, may seem too slight to sustain much weight. But like every item in interaction, it is made meaningful and given its specifiable meaning by sequential position. Here it is a recognition token. Recognition tokens, understanding tokens, confirmatives—all the little sounds and signs we make to allow the other to go on talking—are also traps the other may spring, or we elude. As conversants, we have all used them to go along with someone up to a point, only to discover that point to have been the goal we intended to keep him from, and so found ourselves hung by our own "uh huh"'s.[19]

■

By aspiration, tradition, and constant effort, conversation analysis shows and exactingly delineates the contexted, problematic, moment by accomplished moment character of the social order. It is a practice that enforces constant sympathetic attention to the details of the on-going lived-in social world. But it gains its purchase on that world by freezing it into a transcript for the analyst's distant and impartial inspection. Conversation analysis must therefore always be mindful that

the detemporalizing effect that science produces when it forgets the transformation it imposes on practices inscribed in the current of time . . . is never more pernicious than when exerted on practices defined by the fact that their temporal structure, direction, and rhythm are constitutive of their meaning (Bourdieu 1977:9).

Fixedness on the page and in collections must not make us forget the emergent and prospective character of talk, in which nothing appears until it is said, and each utterance can only invite or try to avoid—but never require or guarantee—some next utterance. Turns, repairs, reference occasions—all the units of conversation analysis—are the locally occasioned products of ongoing interactive work: contingent, negotiated, defeasible, prospective, sometimes retroactive, and always thoroughly, personally, and meaningfully contexted. When conversation analysis loses sight of this, it misleads us about those units and about the processes of interaction.

Sacks and Schegloff's 1979 use of "reference *occasions*" and of "recognitional" and "non-recognitional *forms*" risks reifying the transcripts. The paper shows that "Whether A supposes B to know the person being referred to, and supposes B to suppose that A has so supposed," is basic to how persons are referred to. But this is always a locally motivated concern. "Reference occasions," "recognition," "knowing," and "a person" are produced and problematic. They are problematic in that they are contingent, consequential, defeasible, etc. for the members, speakers, actors themselves; problematic because negotiated by the actual situated agents of society, language, and culture. Formulations of "recognition" or "person" or "knowing" as entities that exist outside of and determine what happens can never account for what happens. Such formulations make it difficult "to conceive of speech and more generally of practice other than as execution within a logic which . . . is that of the rule to be applied" (Bourdieu 1977:24).

Reference occasions and their sequential organization have an interactive, and in that strong sense, social and occasioned structure. Each occasion is accomplished over its course by parties who are oriented to the kinds of regularities that Sacks and Schegloff 1979 describes; who make bids, allowances, interpretations, strategies, and obfuscations informed by those regularities; and who do so in the interests of their lives, not of our collections.

4

Motives in Action[1]

Introduction

This chapter makes use of the sequential organization of conversation in order to investigate how social actions relate to the planning actor and how fleeting moments relate to perduring institutions. The actions it examines will, perforce, be quite small. But they all actually occurred as part of natural social scenes. Unlike the objects studied by "impression management" or "transactional analysis," these actions are neither literary creations nor synthesized scenarios. Unlike the episodes described by "extended case" or "situational" analysis (van Velsen 1967), or alluded to in ethnographic anecdotes, these small actions were not chosen or edited for their intrinsic or theoretical interest. They are mere examples of a phenomenon that the previous chapter equipped us to analyze: initial references to non-present persons, some of them repaired or otherwise "worked over" (p. 52). These data are the recalcitrant stuff of a doggedly real world.

All speech occurs in some particular socio-cultural setting that must be described if we are to understand what is said. The talk of this chapter is restricted to a single setting, with its peculiar connections to institutional arrangements, organizations of motives, and rules for speech. It all comes from tape recordings of direct examination of defendants in Thai criminal trials.[2] I chose this setting because of concern with "intentions" or "motives." In everyday talk these can be quite mixed. A doctor might be trying to impress or seduce a patient as well as to elicit a medical history. A garage mechanic might be trying to brow-beat his customer while presenting a cost estimate. Thai criminal trials are simpler than that. The courtroom, like the market place (Daden 1982), offers unitary normative goals to the student of the strategic use of speech. Lawyers and litigants want to win their case, and are talking to that purpose. But Thai courtroom testimony is not governed by the turn-taking system that defines natural conversation. In order to use such conversational notions as "repair" and "person-reference" for it, I must describe how its turn-taking *is* organized.

The Social Organization of Speech at Thai Criminal Trials

An ethnographer of occasions to which talk is central must describe its organization. To point this out belabors the obvious. But even exemplars of "the ethnography of speaking" shy away from such description. Ben G. Blount's (1975b) "Agreeing to Agree on Genealogy" is one of the finest studies in this tradition. It demonstrates that the vagueness and motility of genealogies, features essential to our understanding of kinship organization and of the difference between the histories of literate and of non-literate peoples, are produced interactively on occasions of speech. Although its

major objective is to identify the structure of the speech event, i.e., the rules that underlie the event and that members may invoke in the course of the event in order to influence its outcome, the sequential organization of conversation . . . is viewed more in terms of background structure and expectancies than in terms of the logical structure of conversational sequencing rules (p. 118).

But one simply cannot "identify the structure of [a] speech event" unless one describes "the rules that underlie the event," the rules that govern the social organization of speech at occasions of the type being investigated. It is these rules that the participants use and are used by "to influence its outcome." It is these rules that the ethnographer assumes and uses in order to describe and understand the event.[3] Sequential organization therefore cannot be regarded as a mere "background structure" or set of "expectancies" (whatever "expectancies" might mean, and whatever sense there is to conceiving of the structure of a thing as its "background").

The alternative to description is mystification. Blount (1975b:133) reports that:

The historical picture [from genealogies] is amorphous to the degree that . . . competition [for a definitive genealogy] is acted out in the absence of strict rules of procedure, where the privileges of rank are minimal in comparison to individual initiative, and where individual initiative is countered by group pressure according to cultural norms.

But to claim that there is an "absence of . . . rules" is to fail to describe. There *are* such rules for the organization of talk. When we are told (Blount 1975b:134) that "The counting of ancestors and, thus, tracing of genealogical relationships within the speech event is subject to the manipulation of information according to social relationships and cultural norms," whatever the product of "manipulation" is "*according to,*" the manipulation itself is done by means of the rules for speech on such occasions. Without being able to directly investigate what the manipulations consist of and how they are done, we are thrown back, perhaps inevitably, on the comforting, traditional, opaque, and unexamined reifications of "social relationships and cultural norms." If, however, we recognize that talk is socially organized and if we use conversation analysis to track its organization, we might be able to show what "the privileges of rank," "individual initiative," and "group pressure" actually consist of on particular occasions.

■

Criminal trials in Thailand consist mainly of public talk.[4] The sequential organization of trial examination is thus a major resource and constraint for litigants and legal practitioners. To understand how references to persons, or anything else said, fit into that talk and do their work there requires some description of the social organization of turn-taking in Thai courtrooms. Despite the ethnographic dangers of relying upon covert idealized contrasts (Moerman 1969a), it is natural to begin with what we already know about conversation and about trial examinations. My account is only a sketch, but will do for current purposes.

The Thai legal system is a successfully hybrid transplant of French and British law, its courtroom procedures exotic only to natives. In Thai criminal testimony, as in the British hearings that Atkinson and Drew (1979) investigated,

turns to speak are allocated between just two speakers . . . to one of whom 'question' turns are allocated and to the other 'answer' turns . . . [pp. 76, f.]. Often very long pauses may occur following the completion of a [question-answer] pair (p. 68).

These features are even more prominent in Thai trials than in Anglo-American courts. Thai lawyers and judges report that oral argument (both opening and summary), objections, and challenges are quite rare. In about 100 days of attending criminal trials, I never heard any. Cases are presented by examining witnesses in question-answer format. Ethnography helps to account for this.

There is no jury to influence. A judge hears and decides the case.[5] Engel's excellent study (1978) ascribes the absence of argument and challenge to the veneration felt toward the court as a representative of Royal power, and to the deference lawyers owe judges. In addition to this normative basis, Thai legal practitioners point out that argument and challenge would expose one's case to the opposition. They hope that the judge is clever enough to discern important points without their being emphasized. In this hope, lawyers also rely on the ease of appeal.[6] If a matter has been entered into the lower court record, it can subsequently be emphasized in the written appeal.

Pauses are more frequent and prolonged in Thai than Anglo-American trials because there is no stenographer. Instead, the judge handwrites the testimony,[7] transforming its question-answer format into a sustained narrative which he reads aloud as soon as a witness has finished testifying. The witness and both lawyers then sign the judge's narrative. The procedure is tedious, stilted, plodding, and dilatory; it is difficult for witnesses and a ground for lawyer's expertise. But the slowed and stiffened pace of talk makes it easier for analysts to track what is going on.

■

The model for testimony is that a lawyer (L) asks a question of a witness (W) who answers it. The judge (J) records the answer, so ending the sequence the lawyer's question began. In that some questions and their answers are not yet the "facts" to be recorded, but are understood as being in pursuit of those facts, the sequential organization of testimony is somewhat more complicated than this. Its basic format is for a lawyer to ask a question of a witness (Data Segments XXII:1; XXIII:1) who answers it in the next turn (XXII:2; XXIII:2). The lawyer or, much less often, the judge, speaks next. As his post-answer turn, the lawyer (or judge) sometimes repeats the answer (XXIII:3; XXIV:3). This is typically followed by a pause (XXIII:4) or by a confirmative (*khap*) from the witness (XXIV:8), after which there is again a pause (XXIV:9). Often the "repetition" is in question form (XXII:7); sometimes it is rephrased (XXII:3).

Litigants and practitioners complain about the unnatural pace of trial talk. Testimony is characterized by long pauses like those of XXIV:4, 17, 22; XXIII:4. Their usual locus is after the witness' confirmative, his answer, or the lawyer's repetition of it. Since the post-witness' turn is the lawyer's, it is he who initiates these pauses. In them the judge is expected to record the answer, ask a question, or indicate that he is waiting for the lawyer's next question.

Repeating the answer is not the only way in which the lawyer uses the turn the answer gave him. He sometimes asks a "new" question, and often "queries," requires "explication/expansion," or initiates repair on the answer (XXV:4; XXX:17).[8]

Repair is of central importance to the organization of conversation. Although the account is not yet full, repair has been the subject of published reports[9] sufficiently numerous to absolve and intimidate me from taking on the task of describing it here. But some orientation, or proselytizing, is perhaps necessary. Conversation is a locally managed system. This requires mechanisms for the mutual adjustment of its separate components and of the interests of parties to it. For the most part, "repair" is that mechanism. Normatively invoked for possible misunderstandings of sense, it is also used to alter possibly unfavorable apprehension of any social action. Its operation is always immediate, compelling, and retrospective. Once repair is invoked, all other conversational business ceases until repair is accomplished or, quite infrequently, dismissed. By "retrospective," I mean that repair always seeks (and almost always finds) something prior to alter, and that it is solely the initiation of repair which makes, or proposes, that the prior item is correctable. "Queries" and "explicative questions" are makeshift notions introduced for the present discussion. I lump them with repair for two reasons.

First, the initiation of repair is neither automatic upon nor restricted to the occurrence of error or unintelligibility (Schegloff, et al. 1977:2.11–2.12; Moerman 1977:2.2–2.23). This is also true of queries and explicative questions.

Second, whenever the lawyer (or the judge) either queries or initiates repair on a witness' turn, it is always the case that:

(i) The witness speaks next.

(ii) He uses his entire turn for repeating, or for modifying, adding to, etc., his prior turn (XXIX:3–6; XXX:18), the one that preceded the query or repair initiation, the one it targeted for repair, explication, etc.

(iii) This witness' turn returns the floor to the lawyer (or judge) who treats it as he does any answer: either querying/initiating repair or repeating/rephrasing it.

An initial version of the lawyer's task is that he elicits answers for the judge to record as testimony and evidence. What the judge records matters critically. His verdict will be examined for how well the recorded testimony supports it. The recorded testimony, together with documents and the written decision, is the sole basis for appeal by either side.

The judge's recording is a sequentially organized matter, an action that terminates a recognizable sequence of socially organized speech. It is thus not something that a single party accomplishes by fiat and alone. The lawyer and his witness speak in ways that influence, and that are intended to influence, when— and thereby what—the judge writes. As one might expect of a matter of such moment, the recording is a conspicuous social act. That the judge is writing, or might be writing, or is considering writing, or is not writing, or has finished writing is available to all parties. The lawyer places his pauses around the judge's writings (XXIII:4, 7; XXX:10, 14). This can be a matter of noticing that the judge seems about to write, and respectfully pausing to accommodate him. More actively, the lawyer has produced a candidate recordable, and pauses to invite or incite the judge to write it down.

In asking a question, a lawyer is working for an answer. In direct examination (i.e., in questioning his own witnesses) the lawyer typically knows, and may have told the witness, what answers he wants. The researcher's transcript reveals whether the answer the lawyer got is acceptable to him, and whether he wants the judge to write it into the record that Thai trial procedure makes so crucial.

One way for a lawyer to accept an answer is by using a "discovery marker" [10] (XXVIII:3, 6, 12) upon receiving it. Another is for him to use the answer as a logical presupposition for a further question (XXV:4; XXVI:6; XXIV:18; XXVIII:3, 10, 12). The lawyer proposes an answer as dictation to the judge by means of pausing:

1) after he receives it,

2) or after he repeats it,

3) or after the witness' confirmative that the lawyer's repetition elicited.

To reject an answer, the lawyer may explicitly repudiate it (XXVI:8) or repair the question that elicited it (XXIX:3+5).[11] But the usual way in which a lawyer rejects an answer is by querying or initiating repair on it. When this happens, the researcher's transcript can reveal the goal of the lawyer's actions.

Queries and repair initiation always obtain a revision or repeat of their target turn, and are understood, justified, accounted for as being directed toward obtaining just that. They are going for the product of an operation that they direct the witness to perform on his prior answer. Furthermore, the specific form of the query or repair-initiation differentially influences the operation done by its recipient, and thus influences the product of that operation. "How" and specificative particles (like *bâang*) direct the witness to give a more detailed version of the answer they target (XXV:4; XXVI:10). The most restrictive reparative question is one in "x or y" form (XXIX:5; XXX:17; XXXI:13). These direct the witness to answer with one of the alternatives specified by the question.

When the lawyer queries or initiates repair on an unrepeated answer, and thereby produces a modified answer which he repeats and then follows with a pause (so proposing it for the judge's record), we can see that the modification was acceptable to the lawyer, while the original answer was not. Inspection of the transcript, along with our knowing the sequential organization of repair and of Thai trial testimony, makes the lawyer's objectives visible to us. They are small-scale objectives, to be sure, but sufficiently actual and unimputed to merit painstaking attention from students of the strategic use of speech and of the relations between intentions and actions. Line-by-line examination of a piece of testimony illustrates this, and confers some ethnographic benefits.

■

Data Segment XXX, line #1, translated as "U::mm::," is one of a number of forms with which this lawyer often marks the beginning of a new line of questioning. That the turn is securely his is embellished by the luxuriance with which he uses it (the pauses of lines #2, #4, & #5; line #3's sniff).

Lawyer's turns are questions. This one ends with line #6. Witness' turns are answers, like line #7. The lawyer repeats the answer (line #8). This elicits a confirmative from the witness (line #9). The lawyer, who goes next, and goes with another question (line #11), holds off asking it, therein making line #10's 3.5 second pause. The pause is to allow, and thereby propose, that the judge record or otherwise note the answer as testimony, as the witness' sworn statement of fact. The fact so proposed is the answer whose repetition elicited the confirmative. Repeating it, and pausing after repeating it—or after the confirmative, should it appear—is how the lawyer proposes it to be a recordable fact.

The same pattern is evinced by the next sequence of:

  (i) the lawyer's question at line #11,
 (ii) the witness' answer at line #12,
(iii) the lawyer's repetition of the answer at line #13,
(iv) and the long pause at line #14.

This, again, is followed by a "new," or "next," question (line #15). Note not only (for the assertion that lawyer's turns are questions) that it is a question, but also that it is a "next" or "new" one. The repairs and queries we will attend to (starting at line #17) show that not all questions are "next" questions. Following his pause with a question that is a "next" question rather than part of "the same" question is a further way in which a lawyer proposes that the answer to the previous question was a recordable fact. He does this in still another way; all of them, as here, often found together. The "next" question uses the answer to the previous question as something established by prior discourse and/or logically presupposed. Discourse ties, presuppositions, and other "linguistic" matters (like syntax used for making and monitoring the sentential units basic to turn-taking) are not given and inert. Like "understanding" (see Appendix B) and everything else that matters in speech, they are interactively organized and interactionally consequential.

At line #1 the lawyer ostentatiously (for the /$\widehat{a}$/ and its equivalents are not always used) began a new line of questioning. Line #5 announces that line to be directions from the murdered man's house. North is the first of them. As a discourse marker, line #15's /lɛ·w/ implies that there has been a prior to which current is tied as a continuation. Indeed, /thaang dâan/ is repeated from line #5, and a new direction, "West," asked about. This implies that the prior direction ("North") is done with, and thus done with by means of the prior answers, which are thereby presupposed as evidentiary facts. In a similar manner, line #11 implies that there is a described "way," and so presupposes the previous answer's description of that way.

The answer of line #16 is accorded quite different treatment. The lawyer, in line #17 (and so still speaking next), initiates repair/query on it, and uses the constraining "x or y" form to do so. This obtains "area, neighborhood, compound," to replace line #16's "house." L initially accepts this (by repeating it in line #19), but further repair/query (line #19/20) obtains "orchard" (line #21). This he accepts by

 (i) his pause (line #22),

 (ii) by his use of /tháangán/'s discourse features to make it a prior,

 (iii) and by the presuppositional logic that "Where do you go from there?" implies that there is an established "there" (namely the one established by line #21's "orchard") as the presupposition for line #23's question.

That question (i.e., line #23) shows itself as a "next" question, thereby further accepting the answer given at line #22. The lawyer repeats (line #25) the answer (line #24) it obtains, eliciting a confirmative (line #26). Line #27's question presupposes the confirmed answer. Its answer in turn is repeated and accepted as a presupposition for a further question (line #29), whose answer is accepted (by line #31's "oh") and allotted its pause (line #32), which the judge (in line #33) shows that he is using for the noting of evidence that such pauses are officially intended for.

Not until the judge reads his record of testimony aloud will the parties know what he has recorded. But by means of initiating repair, mobilizing presuppositions, and positioning his pauses, the lawyer got an orchard, a field, or a forest—with their vastly different potentials for the visibility and escape of the murderer—where a house used to be. His action, like all actions, required the participation of others: the cooperation of the witness and the silence of the judge and the prosecutor.

■

Repair is always directed toward calling attention to and obtaining some modification of the item it targets. Repair in ordinary conversation is vulnerable to accidents of the occasion and to the moves of third (and 4th, 5th, and nth) parties. In casual conversation, repair is a resource for joking or for otherwise altering the business and priorities of speech. But testimony is restricted to its official purposes, limited to just two parties, and deliberate in pace. These features help to make the goals of courtroom repair available to analysis. The lawyer's actions of initiating repair are directed towards obtaining a modified item dictated for the judge's record. Whether as something that will do for now, something discovered along the way to be valuable, or what he wanted from the outset, the modification dictated to the judge was the goal, the purpose, the intention of the lawyer's action of initiating repair. Locked into place by culturally contexted conversation analysis, these sherds of speech show themselves to be purposeful and consequential. They enlarge the scope, by diminishing the scale, of meaningful social action (see pp. 63–6).

Actions and Practice

Through adumbrating the field of the social or cultural as a bridge between private will and brute nature, anthropology's functionalist founding generation and its structuralist successors found rationality and order in the previously bizarre customs of exotic peoples. The locus of sense and meaning was "a culture" or "a society" whose "carriers" or "members" followed "patterns" or "rules." My social science generation's quest is to understand how rules and patterns influence without controlling: How they guide actors, commanding what they attend to, not what they do. Such contemporary concepts as "transaction," "impression management," or "symbolic interaction" acknowledge variation[12] and honor social actors as intelligent beings. But the actors they construct are infantile: omnipotent creatures with ravenous appetites. A constant calculator continuously obsessed by a single motive like gaining power or wealth, good name or image, or simply with not getting mugged, this imagined actor chooses among pre-formed alternatives in a stripped-down world that he or she shares with only one other actor, one quite like himself (or herself). The social dope, carrying his culture like a case of measles, has been replaced by a cardsharp, by a free-wheeling cultural entrepreneur. Those who claim that structural-functionalism's native wears a costume issued by European Colonial Offices may spot "Made in America" on the label of this modern actor's jeans.

Denying that socio-cultural regularities are produced by mere execution of pre-existing rules does not require one to assign the individual actor such crass autonomy. Pierre Bourdieu's rich, subtle, and provocative *Outline of a Theory of Practice*[13] (1977:72) proposes instead the concept of "the *Habitus*":

systems of durable, transposable *dispositions* . . . [that function] as principles of the generation and structuring of practices . . . which are objectively 'regulated' and 'regular' without in any way being the product of obedience to rules, objectively adapted to their goals without presupposing a conscious aiming at ends, [and which are] collectively orchestrated without being the product of the orchestrating action of a conductor.

This notion of *habitus* has tremendous allure: a siren singing the solution to our social science generation's riddle. But even in the hand of its maker, *habitus* remains a name rather than a place, a promise, not a practice, able to fulfill only half of the highwayman's command to "Stand and deliver!"

In opposition to the essential incompleteness of phenomenology and the inescapable distortions of objectification, Bourdieu argues for an analysis of how the durable and material conditions that structuralism strives for impinge on the moment of action that phenomenology and ethnomethodology claim. But his account is never of that moment of action. *How* "the material conditions of existence of a [social] class . . . produce habitus" is left to unexplicated procedures of socialization during unexamined experiences presumed to statistically predominate among the children of a given social class (Bourdieu 1977:81, 85, 87). Bourdieu (1977:76) acknowledges that:

To eliminate the need to resort to "rules," it would be necessary to establish in each case a complete description . . . of the relation between the habitus . . . and the socially structured situation in which the agents' *interests* are defined, and with them the objective functions and subjective motivations of their practices.

But "complete description" is a chimera. This is perhaps why Bourdieu, in his graceful analysis of the Kabyle house (pp. 90, ff.) for example, must himself resort to the practices of "deciphering" its cultural significance and of supposing the Kabyle to be "exercising . . . their mastery of fundamental schemes" of homologous oppositions disclosed by the ethnographer. Having vigorously and compellingly proselytized *la nouvelle cuisine,* Bourdieu serves us a traditional, albeit quite delectable, French ethnographic feast. For "deciphering" and "exercising mastery of fundamental schemes" are the very practices that his book convincingly shows to rely upon the positivist-structuralist assumptions that he rightly rejects.

My own menu is less grand, but also less mysterious. All actions are socially situated and all situations structured. Sequential analysis delineates the structure of social interaction and thus provides the loci of actions. Ethnography can provide the meanings and material conditions of the scenes in which the actions occur. Culturally contexted conversation analysis thus permits a description that, while never complete, is sufficient for showing the nexus between cultural rules and individual intentions. I will limn bones and flesh on spectral habitus by tracking a few repaired or otherwise "worked-over" references to persons in the direct testimony of a defendant prosecuted under Sects. 288 and 289(4) of the Thai

Criminal Code. Whatever their charmless formal character, these repaired person references were all talk that mattered, talk of a man on trial for murder. Our texts are two brief fragments recorded at a trial in the isolated northern Province of Nan in 1969 and set in a context furnished by ethnographic fieldwork. They are presented here as "Father" (XXXI) and "Cell" (XXXII).

"*Father*." In "Father," the defence lawyer's question at line #5 is asked for the judge whose record regularly refers to persons by title (T) + personal name (Np, *chyy* [S]) + surname (Ns, *naam sàkun* [S]). Line #5 begins a person-reference repair-insertion that ends with line #21–24's return to the narrative begun at line #1/2.

Lines #5, 7, and 9 are standard, albeit stilted, items for a collection of repairs on recognitional labels inadequate for identification. But note that the repaired item, "your father" (/phɔ̂· raw/, line #2) is no less referentially adequate than the unrepaired "your mother" (/mɛ̂· raw/) on the same line. Line #5's request for a name as an identificatory label produces (as Chapter Three's account of Thai reference rules should make us expect) a T + N. With T + Np + Ns, the referent has been provided with the standard, and fullest, identificatory label found in court transcripts. The lawyer's line #7, then, is not working just for recognitional sufficiency. The analytic tools developed in our discussion of Segment XXX disclose what XXXI line #7 is going for: to get it said, and thereby noticed by the judge and perhaps entered into the trial record that the defendant's father is (a) *khruu*. The matter must be put this way, with parentheses about the article and the untranslated Thai word. Unlike the American "teacher," *khruu* is a title as well as, or even more than, a job description. Since every reference to a person must contain his/her title, and often consists of no more than that title, getting the defendant's father to be called "teacher" *here* would get him to be called "teacher" every time the trial record refers to him.

Inspection of the transcript shows that it is, indeed, the lawyer's goal to get the defendant's father so labelled in the record. Consider line #21. First, it

   (i) substitutes *khruu* for *naj* as Intaa's title,

   (ii) may emphasize *khruu* by stretching (:) it, and which,

   (iii) by substituting the formal testimentary *bìdaa* for the common and conversational word (*phɔ̂·* in line #2) for "father," shows itself to be intended as dictation to the judge.

Second, line #21 shows itself to be the goal of the insertion sequence begun at line #5. It does this by:

   (i) resuming the narrative where line #1/2 left it;

(ii) treating the initial "your father and mother" of line #2 as a repaired re-pairable (Schegloff, et al. 1977; Moerman 1977) by substituting the new recognitional label, "your father Teacher Np Ns . . . ," for the old one in the same sentence frame.

In this way the new recognitional label is camouflaged as a repair-expansion of the old one.

The title, "Teacher," is not the only item sneaked in by way of person-reference repair, for "who is: (·) who works as headteacher" has been added as well (at line #22). This addition is also via the repair-camouflaged expansion that the lawyer began at line #9. What the lawyer wants in response to his "What [kind of] teacher?" (#9) is "Headmaster." This is shown by his:

(i) using that term in what he dictates for the judge's record at line #22;

(ii) rushing in (/ = /) at line #13 on the defendant's alternative specification (*châw bâan*);

(iii) rushing in with a constraining "x or y" question (*khruu jàj khruu nɔ́j*) that forces the term "Headmaster";

(iv) and by his then (line #15) accepting that term.

Knowing why he might want "Headmaster" requires ethnographic context that subsequent sections (p. 61) will provide.

"*Cell.*" Thai lawyers work without argument. With questions and answers their sole resource, repair is their major, perhaps their only, device for emphasizing. Counsel had learned from discussion with the defendant that Miao (Hmong) tribal insurgents had been crowded into the small holding cell in which the police had kept him. Line #9 of "The Cell" (XXXII) is asked to get this said; line #14, a standard person-reference repair-initiator, asked in order either to get it said that the cellmates were insurgents or, through the repetition or expansion that repair occasions, in order to emphasize "Miao."

The cutoff (/ − /) and hitch (/(.2)/) of line #15—like the stretch (/ : /) and hitch (/(.4)/) of XXXI: 10/11 in *their* syntactic positions—display that their speaker is searching for a word. Here we may presume that the alternatives are emphasizing "Miao" or providing "insurgents." The "insurgents" descriptor having been selected (line #15), the lawyer, again under the guise of repair (#16), works to get it emphasized. This successfully elicits line #17's repetition and se-lective expansion of the political component (/*phuû kɔ̀kaanraʔaj*/) of who these cell-mates were. By his discovery marker (/ɔ̂·:/), summary, and emphasis, the lawyer (at line #18) caps the point.

In #20 he again uses a person-reference repair-initiator. Here it seems, the use of conversational devices for courtroom emphasis encounters some difficulties. By the standards of ordinary conversation, "Miao" has already been said (line #10) and understood. It would take more than line #20's "what kind?" to target "Miao" as its repairable.[14] Line #20 is a repair initiator of a form that targets a repairable in its recipient's (i.e., W's) immediately prior turn (#17). W's line #21 shows that he hears it this way. He provides "Miao" as the repair item only belatedly, after line #22's .2 second delay.

■

I have shown that the lawyer's actions of initiating repair are directed towards obtaining a modified item dictated for the judge's record. Culturally contexted conversation analysis allowed us to locate the accepted, and thus acceptable, end of a "concrete course of action" initiated by the lawyer. For Weber (1947):

A correct *causal* interpretation of a concrete course of action is arrived at when the overt action and the motives have both been correctly apprehended and . . . their relation has become meaningfully comprehensible (p. 99, emphasis added).

[E]xplanatory understanding . . . is rational understanding of motivation, which consists in placing the act in an intelligible and more inclusive context of meaning (p. 95).

Ethnography makes the lawyer's goals intelligible by showing how they are fitted to larger ends.

A main difficulty of the defence case, and a reason for anticipating the need to appeal, was that the defendant had already confessed. A common strategy in such cases, and one that counsel planned to use, is to claim that the defendant had been subjected to torture, threats, promises, subterfuge, or unusual duress. Thai judges know that this can happen. It is to this strategy that the person-reference repairs of "Cell" are fitted.

Ethnic Thai are contemptuous of hill-tribespersons, and find association with them offensive and demeaning. Political insurgents are thought to be dangerous. Having been confined with Miao (Hmong) insurgents until he confessed is a basis for claiming that the defendant's confession was obtained under duress. The lawyer's question at XXXII:9 got the Miao into the cell with his client. Since the repetition occasioned by repair is the courtroom's main device for emphasis, the lawyer's repair-initiator (at line #14) was probably directed toward driving this home. Instead, it got the political component (at line #15) which is thereupon emphasized (#17), again by means of initiating repair (#16). But the working lawyer knows that "Miao" has not yet been repeated. He overlaps (line #23/4) the defendant's strategically correct, but belated, "Miao" (#23) with what in timing, tone, and content sounds like an angry rebuff. But rather than regarding lines #24–27 as "expressing" some inward emotion, we can note how nicely the utterance simultaneously displays and solves a structural "problem" for Thai lawyers: being both an effective patron of his client and a proper servant of the court and the sociocultural hierarchy it represents and enforces.[15]

The resources provided by the sequential organization of repair (and an able lawyer) mean that errors need not be defeats. Defendant not producing "Miao" on time gets "Miao" said (line #28) and added to (#s 30, 32) and re-said (#33).

In Data Segment XXXI, *naj* ("mister"), the title initially (at line #6) proposed for defendant's father, is status neutral. Using it discloses its bearer to have no special status, aside from the maleness assumed of fathers. For the judge to notice, and the record insistently (at every reference to Intaa) repeat that Intaa is a *khruu* or *khruujàj* would be consequential for defence strategy.

The defendant is accused of having killed for hire, a form of murder rather common in northern Thailand at the time of fieldwork. A usual defence in such cases is that the accused is not the kind of person who would do such a thing, that he comes of good family, that he does not need the money. Counsel had told me that he planned to use this defence in this case, and that it was therefore important to get it known and into the record that defendant's father was headmaster of a government school. But he did not want it known that in the isolated district where the defendant and his father live, and where the murder occurred, it was still possible for such a relatively uneducated man as defendant's father to hold such an exalted position and title. He also did not want it known that the father was so estranged from his son as to refuse to visit him in jail, attend case conferences, or pay legal fees. In discussing the case afterwards, counsel said that making a major production of defendant's father's position might have alerted the judge or the prosecutor to inquire into these matters. The reference occasion provided an opportunity for getting the client's father's title and the strategically potent status it entails into the record that the anticipated appeal case would be based on, and of doing it, by way of repair, in a manner that would make judicial and prosecution scrutiny unlikely.

How to specify, recognize, characterize for current speaking purposes is something "The lawyer knows better than you do" ("Cell": 25). His professional competence consists of knowing how to talk. Not all are equally good at it. The defendant, who knows the strategic importance of "Miao," initially failed to yield it up for repair ("Cell": 21, 22). Knowing the defence strategy of invoking his father's position, he searches for an answer to "Father": 9, but finds one (/châw bâan/, line #12) that although accurate and perfectly identificatory is wrong, strategically wrong, for the current speaking purpose of claiming high status for the defendant's father (see Chapter Five, p. 85).

No action can be done alone; no practice, however artful, guarantees success. The judge's record of testimony initially refers to the defendant's father as *Naj* Intaa, then as "my father." About the Miao and other tribals, it says only:

When the police imprisoned me there were no other suspects in the cell at all. Later on . . . the police brought in a Miao murderer, probably a suspected insurgent, and imprisoned him with me.

The verdict, sustained on appeal, specifically rejected the claim that the confession was obtained by bribery, torture, or duress. The defendant was found guilty.

Actions, Actors, and Intentions

Utterance is wholly a product of social interaction, both of the immediate sort as determined by the circumstances of the discourse, and of the more general kind, as determined by the whole aggregate of conditions under which any community of speakers operates (Volosinov 1973:93).

We have seen how L's person references were organized by both the "immediate" regularities of conversation and courtroom discourse, and by those of the Thai social order as (re)presented in its courts. They are instances of the sequential organization of spoken interaction: of question-answer, upon which I have not focused, and of repair, through which regulated and concerted action obtains a modification of the item targeted by a repair-initiator. They are creatures of the organization of Thai courtroom discourse, in which

1) question-answer predominates, largely because there is no jury to be influenced by arguments, summaries, or challenges and in which
2) items proferred as dictation to the judge are made critical by the absence of a stenographer, and by the plan to file an appeal based entirely upon the judge's written record.

In direct testimony, lawyer and client know what they want to appear in that record. In criminal trials, especially, answers to questions are the way to get them there. The tactic of concealing major issues from the opposition makes the initiation of repair an artful means for influencing those recorded answers by altering or emphasizing them. The means are made appropriate by the cultural ideology that a judge's high status should insulate him from arguments and dramatics, while making him sufficiently acute to take in unemphasized points.

In our segments we can see, and in the recordings hear, the enactment of the Thai hierarchy: The absolute reverence that all owe to court and King is the ideological justification for absence of argument; the respect that lawyers owe judges

justifies the extensive pauses; the subordination of peasant defendants to their lawyers is visible in XXXII: 23–27. The case strategies these person-references serve,
although intelligible to a Western reader, involve specifically Thai fears (of tribals), suspicions (about police tactics), and motives ascribable to members of social
classes.

Culturally contexted conversation analysis provides a method for attending to
the actual moment of action, or at least to its trace on a transcript. This brings us
close to the goal of actually showing how durable material conditions impinge on
actual actors in real situations. Like *Terra Australias* before Jansz sailed to the
Gulf of Carpentaria in 1606, Bourdieu's *habitus* is an empty name for a promising
and theoretically necessary place. The confrontation of describable conversational
structures, courtroom discourse, normative goals (of winning the case), Thai cultural principles, and lawyers' expertise makes visible and intelligible *how* "a system
of dispositions can function . . . as principles of the generation and structuring of
practices . . . which are objectively 'regulated' and 'regular' . . . without in any
way being the product of obedience to rules"; *how* "agents [can] cope with unfore-
seen and ever-changing situations"; and how such an accomplishment can come to
be "collectively orchestrated without being the product of the orchestrating action
of a conductor."

The data we have examined embody Thai language, culture, and society in
place. Fitted to institutions, to occasion, and to motives, they can support some
observations about the mutually sustaining, mutually constitutive, triangulative
concepts of actors, actions, and intentions.

■

For Weber and the sociology he founded, mere behavior becomes action when it
reveals meaning. Meaning comes from an analyst, an actor, or a witness surmising
intelligible goals. The goals are intelligible insofar as one can suppose the actor to
be motivated to achieve them. The actions are rational insofar as one judges them
to be well directed toward such goals. This judgement—technical and aesthetic—
is made by analyzing the situation in which the actions occurred, and noting the
extent to which they took account, indeed, took advantage, of that situation for
advancing those motives, while balancing other motives that social analysis im-
putes to this kind of actor in this kind of situation. Action implicates intention;
intentions make actions intelligible; a theory of action is a model of the actor.

I criticized practitioners of "strategic interaction," "impression management,"
"economic anthropology," and so forth for imputing obsessive all-purpose motives
to anonymous actors. The motives we have examined stand on more solid ground.

1. As a matter of institutional structure, lawyers and litigants want to win cases.

2. Thai believe, and sometimes find, that counsel in civil litigation can sell out

clients' interests, and that prosecutors can be bribed or threatened to throw a case. These suspicions are not held of criminal defence lawyers.

3. From working with this lawyer, I know, first, the prominence he gave the strategies I cited;[16] and second, how much he wanted to win this case: the delight with which he imagined how setting confessed murderers free would provide him with clients from all the jails of Thailand, and that he had therefore already spent more time and money on this case than its fees warranted. L's repair initiations were perfectly fitted to the occasions of their occurrence for serving his ends. By virtue of their alignment with motives discovered and ascribed by a theory of litigation, by ethnographic findings, and by L's own talk at times other than the actions' occurrence, they are paradigmatically rational, meaningful and subjectively understandable social actions.

As products of theory, ethnography, recollection, and desire the motives are real enough. But

Purpose or aims . . . belong to the domain of our discourse *about* our actions, that is, they belong to the domain of descriptions . . . [and] have no explanatory value in the phenomenological domain which they pretend to illuminate, because they do not refer to processes . . . operating in the generation of any of its phenomena (Maturana and Varela 1980:85–6, emphasis altered).

Thought really happens. So do public and social actions. Thinking sometimes affects what one does. And what one person does influences what happens next. But the world is too complex for any one thing to be the cause of another. Thought, individual activity, and social action—although certainly systematically connected, and tied to biology, history and all the other constructions—each has its own determinants and organization. To suppose motives to have animated the speakers, inhabited the interactive occasion, and thereby accounted for the repairs, demands excessive faith in the potency of thought and desire.

When Weber claimed "subjectively understandable action" for the subject matter of sociology (1947:90, f.), he noted that we best "understand what a person is doing when he tries to achieve certain ends by choosing among appropriate means on the basis of the facts of the situation." We have seen how L's repairs were such "appropriate means." But it would be misleading to regard him as having selected his actions off a rack of pre-formed alternatives.

Talk is built of the units, like person-reference repair, that conversation analysis progressively delineates. Interactants produce their actions and their public selves by artfully constructing those units on the spot. Their creativity extends not only to the content (e.g., "headteacher" as a recognitional label) and form (e.g., person-reference repair-insertion) of the locally occasioned unit, but also to making it locally occasioned. In "The Cell," L did not merely chance upon conversation's requirement for repairing a reference occasion. He produced one, and its repair, and did both in a way consistent with and constitutive of his social position and case strategy.[17]

Alfred Schutz (1962:67) uses

the term "action" [to] designate human conduct as an ongoing process which is devised by the actor in advance, that is, which is based upon a preconceived project. The term "act" shall designate the outcome of this ongoing process, that is, the accomplished action.

Theories of action impute properties to "persons" (Blum and McHugh 1971:106–8). Schutz' two "that is" rely on an omnipotent actor and on the magical powers of thought.

For Schutz, deliberation must precede action. Actors plan by imagining a future time in which an action will have already been accomplished "and reconstruct[ing] the future steps which will have brought forth this future act" (1962:69). Schutz applauds (1962:68) John Dewey's idea of deliberation as "a dramatic rehearsal in imagination of various competing possible lines of action."[18]

This does capture some subjective experience. I confess (and doubt that I am unique) that I often imagine desirable (and undesirable) future states of affairs, and envision steps which seem to make those states more likely. Sometimes I even imagine alternative steps and compare their fantasied consequences for what I fear and desire. So it is tempting for me to suppose there to be a forceful, even causal and determinative, connection between my plans, thoughts, and dreams—on the one hand (the left, of course)—and interactive events on the other. But the moment of action is too full and too busy for the activities of plotting, dreaming, and thinking. Having done them may make the actor more alert to the opportunities of the moment. But they do not explain his actions.

Schutz (1962:67) writes that

for an action to be manifested into the outer world, the voluntative fiat which transfers the project into a purpose, the inner command 'Let us start!' [*Fiat Lux!*] must have preceded.

This is true only if we *assume* that the world is formed by potent individual wills, that public action emanates from private thoughts; only if we posit the continuous existence of a God-like actor. But neither in my own mind nor in the meaningful social actions we have examined can I find Schutz' actor, a sort of corporate officer for whom

in . . . daily life . . . projected ends are means within a pre-conceived particular plan—for the hour or the year, for work or for leisure—and all these particular plans are subject to [a] plan for life as the most universal one which determines the subordinate ones (1962:93).

Indeed, writing in the 1980's it is embarrassing to look for him.

Conversation analysis constructs a different actor: a "virtuoso" (Bourdieu 1977:79) for whom "The schemes of thought and expression he has acquired are the basis for the intentionless invention of regulated improvisation"; an actor who thinks, if that is the word for it, on his feet. Those feet, in turn, are planted on some craft in a wind buffeted sea.

L's artful actions were certainly too sudden and too slight for his thoughts to have fixed or his plans envisioned. The circumstances which made them appropriate to his situated purposes were irremediably too unpredictable for plotting in advance. As with all actions when closely observed, the participation of others was too requisite and too fine-grained for one person to be credited with their accomplishment. In a real trial, in real time, in real life, as in Conrad's *Victory:*

The trick of the thing, the readiness of mind and the turn of hand . . . comes without reflection and leads the man to excellence. . . . Thinking is the great enemy of perfection (Author's Note).

Reflective, planning consciousness is an often small, always self-interested, and not infrequently delusive component of creativity in action. This seems mysterious only if we suppose social action to stem from the thoughts of individuals. But there is no need to impute thinkings behind actings.

Culturally contexted conversation analysis provides a description of the interactive system in which meaningful actions occur. As Gregory Bateson (1972:338) insisted:

It is important to see the particular utterance or action as *part* of the ecological subsystem called context and not as the product or effect of what remains of the context after the piece which we want to explain has been cut out from it.

The repairs we have examined are an integral part of the situation in which they occurred: a situation that embodies and consists of systems of speech, social order, cultural meanings, and sociotypic intentions. Contemporary biologists, information scientists, and other students of the properties of systems would certainly agree with Bateson's observation (1972:315) that "no part of an internally interactive system can have unilateral control over the remainder or over any other part." Our need to assign such control and responsibility, and the thinking willful person to whom we assign them, arise from our own history and culture.

Writing some 30 years after the Macy Conferences, Bateson ascribed social science's failure to recognize and use discoveries about the organization of systems to the rules by which an individual 'construes' his experience . . . [and] especially [to] that group of premises upon which Occidental concepts of the 'self' are built (1972:314, f.).

To the extent that social science's marriage to the potent private self results from inadequate tools for describing the system of face-to-face interaction, culturally contexted conversation analysis can be of use. It makes social interaction into a technical object whose components can be delineated, their convergent consequences tracked. Applying it to our data showed that and, to some extent, how, L's

"self" as ordinarily understood is only a small part of a much larger . . . system. . . . The "self" is a false reification of an improperly delimited part of this much larger field of interlocking processes (Bateson 1972:331, f.).

The thinking, planning, willful, "self" that Bateson curtails is Schutz' and Weber's actor, the *person* whose thoughts, desires and emotions find their realization and expression in actions which the person is therefore said to cause, his internal states therefore said to underlie. But this "self," like any, is a cultural construction.[19] Systems theory and conversation analysis undermine the Romantic and Bourgeois actor who has "that within which passes show" and Schutz' God-like executive.

If social analysis must construct a person, it is more apt to imagine him as a surfer whose practiced body moves unthinking with wave, wind, and board, or as a martial artist whom empty mind (*mu-shin*)—by virtue of its very freedom from thoughts and decisions that precede action—makes expert. Such an actor, with "No thinker behind the thoughts; no doer behind the deeds," better captures the agent of actual interactive events. It is also the image endorsed by the Thai Buddhist culture in which the actions that this chapter examined were produced.

5

Society in a Grain of Rice: An Exercise in Micro-Ethnography

Goals

This chapter is a teaching exercise in culturally contexted conversation analysis. I will show you my methods, and what they discover along the way. Then I will compare them to symbolic and "interpretive" anthropology. Our data are some three minutes of talk recorded in the Thai-Lue village of Ban Ping. For studying conversation *per se*, dull materials are best. It is hard to concentrate on such technical objects as "re-cycled turn beginnings" or "transition-space repairs" when distracted by interesting talk. But to meld conversation analysis with ethnography, vapidity is not necessary. The segment (XXXIII) we will examine is substantively interesting. As talk between villagers and an official, it contains instances *in vivo* of ways of interacting that typify and constitute dominant, and dominating, features of Thai life. As talk with and about the fieldworker, it permits us to track the effects of the participant observer: once anthropology's secret shame, now the fashionable focus of its self-absorption.

These few moments of talk thus attract our close attention and tempt some speculation. Giving them what they deserve implies no recommendation that the study of history and institutions be replaced by culturally contexted conversation analysis. Physicians know there is much more to diagnosis than cytology. But those who neglect cytology may fail to understand living processes, and so might be guilty of malpractice.

Means

An utterance is likely to be many things at once, some pulling in different directions.[1] This chapter's device for aligning issues with utterances is to organize the sections thematically, but key them to the utterances at which the themes first appear. I will use capital letters to introduce terms that sequential analysis has made technical.

Units get their sense and their meaning through placement in a larger order that ethnography, culturally contexted conversation analysis, and attention to the entire episode of interaction can help us to grasp. Built upward out of utterances and their components, conversational interaction is also built from top down. As Richards (1932: iv) found:

There will be occasion to insist upon the necessity of taking the whole tenor of the work as a guide in interpreting each portion, however small; and upon the folly of fixing meanings for scraps in isolation from the rest. But before we can conjecture as to the tenor of the whole we must provisionally survey the possibilities of the meanings of the parts. Thus interpretation . . . must be cyclical.

This chapter will return more than once to utterances already examined.

Every utterance is nailed into its very place. Participants found its sequential intelligibility there; and there the analyst must discuss it. But showing how a type of utterance or sequence works requires reference to other instances of the same type. In this, I cannot assume that the reader (nor must the reader assume that I) know(s) all there is to know about a particular type of conversational unit. But to try to describe, let alone prove, every conversational finding that this chapter uses would require me to write six books inside it.

Some presentations of conversational "findings" will be qualified, or vague. One reason for this has been given in previous chapters (Chapter Three, particularly). I do not fully endorse all of the findings, nor the methods and assumptions used to capture them. Another reason is more personal: a matter of friendships, biography, and scholarly ethics. My understanding of the conversational phenomena we will make use of—such things as sequence types, adjacency, laughter—is an interpretation of the work of others, much of it unpublished, some of it done in the course of discussions and seminars in which I participated. When I discuss laughter, for example, I can never be sure of how or whether to cite Gail Jefferson. Most of what I know about its sequential organization is based on interpretations that she might reject of discoveries she has made but only partially published. So with her—as with Anita Pomerantz on preference organization, and Emanuel

Schegloff on adjacency and repair, and Harvey Sacks for all of it—I fear always committing either slander or theft. Please blame, and forgive, me so we can get on with it. Even when wrong, sketchy, or vague, there will always be detailed statements of method, and citations of public data. So every weakness gives direction to investigations that others might pursue.

Background and Setting

Whatever methodological purity might demand, there are some characterizations of these participants and of this scene which it would be mystifying and churlish to withhold. DO is a Thai government official: the chief administrator (District Officer, *naj amphə·*) of the district in which the conversation occurred. He has only once, if ever, been to Ban Ping before. MM is me. The others are all villagers of Ban Ping. The setting is the porch of a village home: TM's. The time is the first moments of my return, after four years' absence, to Ban Ping, where my wife and I had lived for 14 months.

The other letters in the left column of the transcript indicate dialects. Interpreting their interactional import requires micro-, or even individual, sociolinguistics: The analyst must know the speakers' competencies. This guides inferences about the significance of dialect choices and shifts. Suppose, for example, that it is normal to proffer a second pair-part in the same dialect as the first pair-part to which it responds. If someone who speaks only Lue answers a Siamese question in Lue, it does not mean what it would were someone able to speak Siamese to answer in Lue. So I must disclose my observations of the language competencies of these speakers. This is not just outsider's knowledge. Participants make use of dialect in order to choose and exclude who might respond to, or be normatively expected to understand, what they say and hear.[2]

MK can speak Lue, Yuan, and very imperfect Siamese.
KP can speak Lue, Yuan, and imperfect Siamese.
DO can speak Siamese and very imperfect Yuan.
MM can speak imperfect Lue and Siamese.
TM can speak Lue and Yuan.
The older women can speak Lue and imperfect Yuan.
The younger women can speak Lue and imperfect Siamese and Yuan.

Contexted conversation analysis is directed toward discovering which of the many culturally available distinctions are active and relevant to the situation, how those distinctions are brought to bear, and what they consist of. To label individuals by the dialect they speak assumes or implies that dialect is interactively salient. I report as an ethnographer that Lue is a village dialect and that villager *vs.* official is a dichotomy basic to Thai society. But so are male and female, young and old, rich and poor. Dialect use, like any of these, might be merely a demographic feature extrinsic to the talk: convenient for casual description, but accidental to the participants' non-language activities and conduct. In this segment, however, it is clear to me that the Thai who talk in Lue are talking like villagers, as only villagers could and would, using knowledge that only villagers have. It is clear to me that DO is not just speaking the national dialect, but that he is talking as only officials can and do. If I am right, attending to this talk can disclose some ways in which Thai bring off a major feature of their society.

I use the strange phrase, "the Thai who talk in Lue," because one of the Lue-speakers is not a Thai. MM, however romantic and nostalgic, is an American anthropologist. It is clear, and embarrassing, to me that his presence is consequential. The occasion of interaction began when the district officer and MM arrived together in DO's jeep. There is no neutral way of saying whether DO "brought" (*maa sòng* in Siamese) or "came with" (*maa tɔj* in Lue) MM. The verb, like the dialect, is entailed by whose perspective—villagers' or officials'—one takes. In their talk from its outset, the villagers are making MM out to be the "homecomer" (Schutz 1964: 106) he so sorely wants to be.

The homecomer . . . expects to return to an environment of which . . . he thinks [he] still has intimate knowledge which he has just to take for granted in order to find his bearings.

Whoever MM is to them, he is certainly not the distinguished foreign consultant on economic development and research training whom the provincial governor had instructed the district officer to receive, escort, and be responsible for.

Personally, I find it ironic, amusing, even rather sweet that an anthropologist so concerned to leave native life unruffled by interviews makes such waves. Professionally, it is reassuring to point out that culturally contexted conversation analysis permits us to locate the perturbations made by the researcher's presence. Ethnographically, I must insist that the contest is only accidentally over MM. The struggle is between villagers and officials, between the autonomy of the local community and the authority of the state, between cultural symbols of village and nation. The weapons that happen to be used are talk about the ethnographer's loyalties and about food. Since the contest occurs as talk, the resources and constraints are the structures of conversation: here, laughter, orders, stories, and our old familiar: references to persons.

The Segment

The total context in which speech echoes is beyond our ken: earlier talk by these parties, memories of what great-grandparents were said to have said, recollected fragments of scripture. But intelligibility and social action also must have units—consensually bounded ones. If "a conversation" were not such a unit, we could not notice and resent the absence of a greeting at its beginning, or remark on the odd-ness of placing one in its middle. If "a story" were not such a unit, where would participants work to suspend and then resume the "current speaker has the floor for a single utterance" rule of the conversational exchanges that surround the story?

We begin formally, and with silence at line #574. This is philosophically and aesthetically appropriate, but my reasons are technical. The units that talk and its analysis require are made by the talkers and found by the analyst. To impose boundaries for reasons of extrinsic theory or convenience is to study wildflowers with a lawn-mower. The analyst wants to start before the beginning of a unit in order to find the unit's boundaries, how it differentiates itself from prior units. Al-though undoubtedly enlivened and influenced by memories of what has been said before, and by hopes and fears for what might be said later, the participants have given one another, and us, fourteen seconds of silence to mark what follows it a new beginning, a somewhat fresh start.

The placement and great size of this silence make it a LAPSE, an object quite different from a PAUSE within a turn or sequence. Not that all lapses are equiva-lent. Some peoples allow, even insist on, them more than others do.[3] Nor are the meaning and suitability of a lapse (or any other interactional event) given by "a culture" stripped of local types of occasions and parties. A lapse far longer than one that would smother a first encounter sits comfortably in a six-hour drive to a campsite. The lapses that embarrass a therapy session can be the same size as those that document a friendship.

It is not silly to ask why a lapse occurred at line #574, but I do not know how to try to answer. No participant's recollection of a conversational event is to be much relied on. The lapse was comfortable enough, I think, except to MM who was worried about consuming tape, batteries, and research time. It certainly did not obliterate participants' memories of what had been said before. For us, the lapse provides a vantage point for line #575/6 as a place to start.

Ethnographers need patterns; transcripts provide them. They are an essential artifice that permit the phenomenologically illegitimate activities of glancing back at what participants might have forgotten and jumping ahead to what they have not yet produced or heard. They also permit us to search other conversations for the same or similar patterns. This introduces a further theoretical difficulty. In that meaning is in context, it must be closely demonstrated for each of the other recorded situations that the pattern was the same. In that the categorization of actors is local, whose pattern would it be? The analyst must demonstrate that the individuals who spoke on those other occasions were actively occupying the same roles or categories as the individuals who spoke at this one.

At #575/6 MK begins new business. With a smile in his voice, he speaks in Lue, about, and perhaps to, MM. Only Lue speakers (MM at #577, KP at #579) respond to #575/6. MK (at #580) joins and UPGRADES their response. At line #581, KP explicates #575/6 and translates it into DO's dialect. This assumes, composes, creates DO as a person who needs such explication and translation, and makes KP into the person who performs those services. DO does not join in. What DO does (at line #588) is to begin business of his own.

With utterance #630, again after a lapse (#629), MK again speaks in Lue to propose a new topic: again speaking about and to MM, again beginning the activity of LAUGHING together (see below). And again, only Lue speakers join in (MM at #631, KP at #634, women at #s 637, 642, 644, and 646). KP then again (at #648) explicates and translates into Siamese for and to DO who again does not participate (except, perhaps, at #652).

A pattern, surely. But what of? And whose? Does this segment show how participants align themselves and act as two sides, and that these sides are villagers *vs.* official? In every conversation, who the talkers are talking *as* is implicated with what they do with their talk. But we must separate the strands if we are to describe at all.

With #575/6, MK proposes a topic, an orientation to it (amusement), and *an activity:* LAUGHING TOGETHER—conversation's great device for conviviality and co-alignment. Jefferson (1979) has discovered interactionally relevant grades of laughter in American conversation. I have so far found the same organization and the same gradations in Thai conversation.[4] Laughter grades upward from the "smile-voice" made when the lips are tensed into a smile and poised for laughing, through puffs of intra-morphemic laughter that blow through but do not destroy words,[5] through the closed vowel forms of /heh/ and /hə/, to the open vowel of /ha/. The more continuous dimensions are roughly:

delayed < prompt;
few particles < many particles;
soft < loud;
slow < rapid.

In America, at least, when a joke's teller laughs with higher grade than his recipients do, the joke has not succeeded. If my loudly laughed possible insult is met by your begrudging "°heh heh," laughter did not ameliorate the offense. If the butt of a joke laughs .2 of a second after the others, he shows himself to be a bad sport.

At utterance #575/6 MK's smile voiced makes laughter relevant and appropriate.[6] KP, another Lue speaker and villager, laughs (#579). MK, by upgrading (#580), bids for continued laughter. KP then translates for DO (#581) and upgrades the laughing. But DO refrains.[7] Anyone can recognize laughter and tentatively propose that he is human by joining in. Every fieldworker stumbling his way with a new language soon learns this. By not laughing, DO rejects, and does not merely fail to understand, what is going on.

Instead of joining the prior talk, DO lets it die. He then utters #588. Sequentially, it is a SUMMONS: a first pair-part that starts something new, demands an ANSWER, and implies new business to which those summoned should attend (Schegloff 1968). #588 is thus produced to be disjunctive with the villager talk and laughter that preceded it.

Actor and action are co-implicative, mutually constitutive. Sacks (1972b) has shown the importance to members and to theory of CATEGORY-BOUND ACTIVITIES: actions (and other predicates) with which types of persons are normatively associated.

A summons expectably precedes and announces new business. At #592 DO begins same. Sequentially, #592 is an ORDER or INSTRUCTION| (Goldberg 1975). This notion is familiar to the Thai. They characterize the usual way in which officials talk to villagers as *kham-sàng kham-sɔ̌·n,* "ordering and instructing." For DO to order and instruct here is for him to enact his official's status that might otherwise be only potential.

Orders, of course, are about something. Their topic is crucial to what participants and analysts make of them. These orders are specifically *ex officio;* the treatment they get are notably *villager* responses. Although it is experientially and ethnographically wrong to separate form from substance, my pedagogic purpose recommends it. First, form.

For talkers, as for analysts, a sequence begun should end. But it is not always clear where. The Thai lexeme *khap* (#595) is a TOKEN, sometimes of receipt, sometimes of agreement, sometimes of understanding, sometimes just a "chirp" with which a male speaker[8] signals, respectfully, that he knows that someone is talking to him. Officials and other superiors often complain that villagers and other subordinates *khap wáj kɔ̌n,* "say yes first," and thus mask whether they have understood, agreed, or committed themselves. My fieldnotes record instances showing that it is not only foreigners whose expectations of commitment are sometimes raised and frustrated by their recipients' *khaps.*

DO expands his order (at #596) after the first *khap* it gets, but seems satisfied by the double *khaps* of #s 597 and 598, for he does not use the floor that they return to him. Spoken jointly, the *khap*s co-align MK and KP (see Chapter Two, pp. 23–24). Insofar as #592/4 + 596 is an order, the *khap*s are tokens of obedience, spoken by subordinates, and thus as villagers.

In substance, the segment starts with villager talk about MM that incorporates him as a familiar person: invoking him by his village name (see p. 85), enacting (by laughter) and explaining (/kháw chɔ̃·p/, #581) an attitude toward him and toward his return. The official reaches into this co-alignment by instructing the villagers about how they are to act toward MM: Tell him the kinds of intelligence information (#596's /thùk súk dyătlɔ́·n/) that officials are supposed to collect.

In #600–602 KP acknowledges DO's topic, but with renewed smile-voice and laughter jogs it back to a villager understanding of the anthropologist's enterprise: harmless, familiar to them, and done independently of official interests. By adverting to "the old stories" that his father told MM (#600/2), KP invokes what Schutz (1964:111) calls "life at home" which

means, for the most part, life in actual or potential primary groups . . . it means, finally, that each . . . has the chance to re-establish the we-relation, if interrupted, and to continue as if no intermittance had occured.

The contest over who MM is, what he does, and as whose agent, has begun.[9]

The Yuan dialect of #600 shows it to be intended for comprehension by an outsider. But an utterance can be designed for someone's comprehension without being built to elicit speech from him. #600, however, is constructed syntactically so as to elicit a response token from its recipient: It starts with its object ("the old stories"), and ends with the /ɛ̌·/ that roughly corresponds to comma intonation in American conversation.

In four distinct formal ways DO does not join, and positively rejects, KP's business.

1 DO repeatedly refuses KP's invitation to laugh together.

    (i) By the smile-voice of #600, KP gingerly invites his recipient (whom we have just seen was DO) to laughter. DO's #601 does not accept.

    (ii) At the start of #602 KP renews and strengthens the invitation by upgrading it from smile-voice to low-grade laughter (hɛ). Still no uptake.

    (iii) KP again upgrades (ha). DO's #603 and #604 contain no marks of laughter, and are withheld until after all of KP's laughter is over.

2 The low volume of DO's tokens in #603 and #604a may be a rejection of the sequence and topic that KP's #600 and #602 proposed. Goldberg (1978) has shown that in American conversation, speakers lowering their volume from the one they last used in the current sequence can be a bid to end that sequence. By raising their volume from the one they last used in the current sequence, speakers bid to start a new sequence. I have so far found the same organization to hold in Thai conversation. With the low volume /°mm/ of #604a, DO receives and ends KP's activity. He uses the same utterance to markedly (by its volume, squeaky-voice, stretch, and "substance" ["And so:::,"]) start something new.

3 #604, much like #588, works as a summons—demanding attention and implying new business.

4 And the new business is his old business: sequentially (giving them orders) and topically (about how to treat MM).

By his serious tone and resumed activity, the official talks as if the villager never had.

#604–628: Having multiply rejected villagers' business, DO renews his own, *ex officio,* activity of giving them orders and instructions. The order gets what orders get, the now familiar *khap:* the token of agreement, understanding, compliance that is often any subordinate's only possibility and best defence. Since authority demands the *khap*s, "yassuh"s, and *si, señor*s that authorities regularly receive, authorities can never be sure how much (if any) agreement, understanding, commitment, compliance the tokens indicate. This /khap/ (#605) is very soft (∞) and sounds pro forma, or so DO seems to take (or make) it.

In #605–625, a speaker who finds his recipient's response insufficient adds to what he has just said. Better, by adding to what he has just said, a speaker indicates that he takes recipient's response to have been insufficient. This vague formula covers such more technical terms as "explicative repetition," "third-turn repair," and "upgrading" or "downgrading" used in prior chapters.

DO's line #606/7 is clearly an explicative expansion of his command (#604b), and thus repairs it: Line #604c's "food" expands to "whatever is needed from the market;" #607's "come look for me" tells the villagers how they can /jàa hâj man khàat/ (#604c). Repairs are often also changes of grade.[10]

The concepts of UPGRADE and DOWNGRADE are extremely useful for the analysis of collections and of interactive patterns. But they are rather abstract. On particular occasions, they take particular forms: an insisting or diminishing of an order, a reason for complying, a reason against resisting, a "sweetening" (as negotiators say), a threat. Attending to their particularity can help us to understand the occasion. It can also help to expose the cultural ideas that made the occasion intelligible to its participants.

There is a mutual trade between cultural knowledge and conversational sequentiality. With the same glance that recognizes line #3 as an upgrade of an invitation, an American who encounters:

1   A: Come on over and we'll talk
2   (.5)
3   and maybe have a few drinks

sees or learns the special value of "drinks" to these parties. Sequences can disclose the presuppositions of their speakers.

Even in the unlikely event that DO took KP's /°°khap/ to indicate a lack of understanding, and so explicated #604c in the interest of intelligibility, the expansion modifies his order so as to "sweeten" it, to make it more acceptable, to downgrade the action it might have seemed to demand, to counter a difficulty that he thus shows himself to have thought that KP might have found in it. "Come find me" (#607) as a sweetener is predicated on DO suspecting that KP took his order to have required the villagers to provide the food themselves. Most of his subsequent utterances are further downgrades[11] that let us trace his ideas of what the villagers might have thought to be difficult.

In #610 DO explicity states that he recognizes and can eliminate what KP might have been worried about.

Line #615 (and #624) makes DO's order an inconsequential difficulty. In almost every turn, the official makes further "clarification" of his order, proposing further ways in which it would be easy to fulfill. Each progressive concession gets but a soft *khap* or (less polite) *hm* (#608, 611, 616, 625).

I find a familiar irony in these order sequences. The villagers' very subservience makes their compliance and agreement uncertain. It is perhaps too strong to say that by his progressive downgrades the official is humbling himself before the villagers. But examining the transcript showed me a relation between villager and official that I had not anticipated. That result alone should make us demand that statements about villagers and officials[12] be supported by reports of whether villagers really do what officials tell them to, and by attention to what actually occurs when villagers and officials speak together.

Familiar and ironic in form, the orders are almost poignant in substance. When this interaction occurred (in 1965), the Thai Government had just begun to direct its officials to behave as *mit raatsadɔn*, "friends of the people." This district officer is doing that, and quite well. But friendship is not consistent with hierarchy, and cannot be *ex officio*. When DO (at #604c) tells the villagers to make sure that MM is properly fed, he *may* be impugning their hospitality. He is certainly imposing his relevancies on them. They are taking/making MM into a "homecomer," into one of them. DO orders the villagers to feed MM at the official's behest, on his behalf. This denies MM the status they are according him—and therein denies them the capacity to accord it—much as it would were a teacher or welfare worker to order you to feed your child properly. The district officer's very kindness to the villagers imposes upon them his official authority and orientation, urban values, and team alignments. The concessions show how kind and considerate he is to them. But they all also assert his—and so challenge their—responsibility for MM.

■

I noted that "almost every turn" contains concessions. This was in order to reserve discussion of another matter that some turns are concerned with in whole (#613) or in part (#607). The food that MM must not lack (line #604c) is explicated (in #607) to be the sort that comes from town, that has to be bought (#613), that both sides agree (#618/619) is unavailable in villages. For KP (in #620) to counter-propose (/tɛ̌·/) chicken as part of a *class* (/ñang/) of foodstuffs provides further evidence that a general dichotomy has been made operative.

Anthropologists (e.g., Leach 1960; Levi-Strauss 1970) are familiar with food dichotomies and their intense moral significance: tame vs. wild, field vs. forest, raw vs. cooked, *kosher* vs. *traif*.[13] I do not suggest adding chicken (#620) vs. pork, meat (#621), canned goods, and bottled drinks (#627) to this list. Binary opposition is a possibly universal, and relatively uninteresting, property of thought. Whenever, as in this interaction, there are sides, there are likely to be dichotomies.[14] In this interaction, at this moment, for these actors, town food vs. village food is the culturally available dichotomy that is used here and now, consequentially, purposefully, meaningfully. Whatever meaning food has, it has in and by virtue of specific interactive performances, not abstract unsituated bifurcations.

Symbolic anthropologists who hold that "a theory of a culture necessarily involves an attempt to explain how some *set of things* . . . can *have* meaning for the members of the society" (Basso and Selby 1976:4, emphasis added) misphrase the problem by suggesting that meaning inheres in the culture and adheres to *things*. They sacrifice

the message for the sake of the code, the event for the sake of the system, the intention for the sake of the structure, and the arbitrariness of the act for the systematicity of combinations within synchronic systems (Ricoeur 1976:6).

I insist, instead, that "meanings . . . need to be studied in small-scale exemplars" (Douglas 1984:8).[15] This is not merely the ethnographer's preference for the petty. It relates to

the Saussure–Peirce contrast . . . between a dyadic sign-relation, in which sound images (the signifiers) acquire their "meanings" . . . (the signified) from a conventionalized linguistic code (*langue*), and a triadic sign-relation, in which the sign denotes an object, signifies a property or relation of that object, and interprets another sign in an endless inter-

change between utterers and interpreters of the signs. The Piercian sign-relation includes
. . . a community of interpreters . . . (Singer 1984:5).

But even this is too non-processual. Rather than divining the consensus achieved
by the "endless interchange," the student of meaning must investigate particular
interchanges. In whatever general way it might be "culturally available," the typological dichotomy between town and village food, the specific items it includes,
and its import and meaning are actively provided through this immediate actual
interactive performance.

The orders, and the responses to them, presuppose a dichotomy of foods and of
eaters. That dichotomy is also the basis for the REASONS that DO uses to follow,
support, and justify his command (#618–628). The official has invoked the dichotomy in disfavor of rural food, and so as to compose MM as the kind of person
who must have town food, and thus as someone not like a villager.

DO's orders and the reasons that justify them get their final *khap* at line #628.
This is followed by silence that participants could, and do, allow to become a lapse
(#629) that thus provides them a place they might use for an activity which would
thereby (i.e., by virtue of its placement) be hearable as new. The place is used by
MK's #630 for resuming specifically villager business.

MK's #630 is like his #575/6 in that it follows a silence, is said in Lue, to and
about MM, and proposes laughter. Like the villager business of KP's #600/2
(which also proposed laughter), MK's #630 is said after the joint completion of an
order-acknowledgement sequence, and nudges the substance of that sequence
from the official's to the villagers' way of describing and accounting for MM's behavior. The laughter is joined by other Lue speakers (#s 631, 634). So is the
nudge.

MK acknowledges the dietary peculiarities (#633) that DO raised, but assimi-
lates them to MM's status as a homecomer (/lùk kaáj haj . . . maa/, #630), and
treats them as personal characteristics that do not have to do with urban-rural typifications. Like KP in #600, MK shifts from official to villager definitions of MM.
Village women join in (#s 637, 642, 644, 646, 647, 649) the village explanation that confirms MM as a familiar being: He eats the delicacies that his wife
(mē·caán), now absent, provided. The women shift the food dichotomy from village vs. town to glutinous rice vs. boiled rice and goodies (# 637, 646, 649,
654/5).

■

In principle and in general, Douglas (1984:28) is probably correct in noting that
"isolated food items in themselves do not make an ethnic diet; the ethnically distinctive aspect is the patterning of a whole cycle of combinations." It is true, be-

haviorally, for the peoples of Northern Thailand. Their curries lack the coconut cream of the center and the south. They rarely use fresh coriander (*phàk chii*). Some items of nutritive value, like fermented bean curd (*thóo-ôo*, "stinking beans") are occasionally noted as local oddities, as are a few dishes (like *nàam phìk nàam-pŭu*, an odoriferous black paste made of field crabs) that lend themselves to being eaten with glutinous rice. But for these people themselves, ethnic and regional dietary distinctiveness focuses on, is expressed by, is talked, boasted, and joked about by means of a single food item: glutinous rice (Moerman 1968:11).

The distinction between eaters of glutinous rice and eaters of ordinary rice, like the distinction between eaters of food produced in villages and those who eat food purchased in town, is category-bound (p. 74). Both make the same sorting of the population. The individuals who eat ordinary rice are those who eat town food. But the categories are members of different "devices" (Sacks 1972a). The distinction between rices is ethnic; the distinction between eating town purchased and locally produced food is one of socio-economic class. The difference is rather like the one Sacks (Lectures, Fall 1965) reported of an American therapy session at which the patients, all teenagers, told a newcomer that they had been discussing drag racing. They therein invoked a teenager-adult distinction that makes the same sorting of participants as would the more embarrassing distinction between patients and psychiatrist.

On the basis of prior fieldwork, I had argued (1967:64) that "the Lue of Chiengkham avoid opprobrious class identification through asserting the higher priority of a non-stratifiable ethnic identification," but reckoned my argument "weakly grounded" (p. 65) insofar as it relied on occasions in which natives presented themselves to me, an anthropologist they knew was interested in them as Lue (pp. 65–7ff). Conversational data lets us see how categories become salient *in situ*. KP's story (p. 82) and the district officer's response to it continue, develop, and sharpen the rice dichotomy that the women introduced.

■

I have shown, sufficiently I hope, that these participants do not merely happen to be villagers, officials, and anthropologist who happen to be talking to one another. They know themselves to be, and are engaged in interactive work to accomplish, both the categorization and the activity. Why else would they explicate and translate (p. 73)? By using the artifact of a transcript to see how their work is going, we can notice that it falls into blocks of participation.

1 #575–587:

  1) MK, a villager, initiates talk.

  2) In substance and in dialect, it is villager talk.

3) It is laughing talk.

4) Another villager (KP) and MM participate in the talk and laughter.

5) DO stays out of it.

2 #588–628:

1) DO initiates talk.

2) In substance (ordering), tone (serious), and dialect it is official talk.

3) It does not become general. Two villagers *khap* to it; the others, including MM, stay out.

In the course of this second block, KP tries something other than a *khap*. By dialect (Yuan) and lexical choice (see p. 85), KP directs #600–602 toward the official, inviting laughter. KP asserts a village claim to MM by adverting to a history the villagers, but not DO, share with MM, reporting what villagers and MM did together without any official orders, and phrasing the activity in terms of kinship and personal relationships. In its immediate conversational setting, this is a challenge to the official's claim. But #600/2 was smothered (pp. 75–6); treated, if treated at all, as a passing part of the official's ongoing series of orders (pp. 76–7).

3 #630–647:

1) initiated by MK,

2) villager talk in dialect and substance,

3) and invite laughter.

4) The talk and laughter are joined by MM, MK, KP, and village women, but not by DO.

This chunky pattern of participation recommends viewing KP's #600/2 as a device for drawing DO into talk initiated by villagers, talk that asserts villager relevancies and claims.

4 KP's #648 is a stronger version of such a device. In *form:*

1) #s 648, 650, 653, and 656 are in Siamese rather than Yuan. This makes them more sharply directed to DO, the only speaker of that dialect.

2) #648 follows villager talk. It does not border on, and so is unlikely to be assimilated to, a sequence of orders.

3) #648 is clearly built as the start of a story (see p. 82), and thus as a bid for extended speakership.

Like #600, it *substantively* adverts to MM's prior visit and the co-history from which DO is excluded. KP's story does more than modulate toward a villager version of MM and how he was with us. It uses the dichotomy of rices to say that MM is just like us.

■

An earlier publication (Moerman 1968:11) reported that:

All Thai eat rice, but the sticky rice . . . of the north is often contemned by Asians who eat ordinary rice. . . . Our own initial rapport was aided by our eating glutinous rice. Villagers had no preconceptions about what kind of rice was eaten in America, but our obvious high status made them assume that we would eat in central Thai style . . . "They eat as we do," provided entree for us as equals.

I am gratified that KP's story seems to verify the observation. More importantly, I hope that contexted conversation analysis permits readers to discover for themselves the active situated use of these cultural ideas. The intelligibility they give the story need not rely on prior extrinsic ethnography. Such analysis also shows that the official misunderstood the villager's story.

■

STORIES are conjoint accomplishments.[16] It takes joint work to start and to end them. Starting a story is "locally occasioned."

That is, techniques are used to display a relationship between the story and prior talk and thus account for, and propose the appropriateness of, the story's telling (Jefferson 1978a:220).

Like all interactional work, this can encounter difficulties. Its specific vulnerability is that other participants can take, or make, the intended story-start into no more than a continuation of the business that preceded it. This is the fate met by KP's #600/2. It is the other, sharper, edge to the irony of hierarchy. Inasmuch as most of what officials say to villagers is intended as—or can be heard as—orders and instructions, most of what villagers say to officials can be heard as but a response to orders and instructions.

Stories take more than one turn to complete. This requires their audience to relinquish the rights to the floor that normal utterance-by-utterance speaker transition might otherwise give them. KP's #648, "When he came the first time," is a clear bid to start a story. By producing it before WI has quite finished her #647, KP might have been trying to rush or force his story into the conversation. But every conversational unit is an interactive accomplishment. Although KP entered at a possible completion point of #647, WI does not allow him to end her turn. Rushing him (note the slight terminal overlap) much as he did her, she (at #649a) finishes the utterance unit that #647 began. More accurately, and more interactively, #649a retroactively turns #647—which could stand quite well on its own—into a prepositional phrase for #649, which need never have been said. She therein makes KP's utterance into one that interrupted hers.[17]

It takes joint work to end stories. The recipient's job is to provide a reaction (like laughter), a capping interpretive phrase, or a parallel story of his own. Each shows not only that he took the story to be over, but also how he understood it. KP's story invited laughter; DO provides none. KP has emphasized (#648 and #656's /thîlè·k/) that he is describing MM at the very beginning of his first stay in the village. DO (at #660) speaks of MM at the end of that stay. But to say that DO *fails* to understand, makes "understanding" too cognitive, too unitary, and too passive. Rather, he *refuses* to understand, refuses to acknowledge and go along with the locally relevant point of KP's story. For he shows that he understands the same dichotomy of rice and its eaters by using it to dispute its implication for group loyalties and membership, and for MM's place in them.

By substance, sequential placement, and syntax,[18] #662 leads to #673 which claims that eating glutinous rice is something one has to get used to. Line #662 invokes and contrasts two groups such that not only the foreign MM, but *these villagers*, are not "we Thai people."

The taxonomy of ethnic labels in which "Lue" is at one level contrasted with, and at another incorporated by, "Thai" (Moerman 1965) is not merely a lexicographer's convenience. Encouraged, even commanded, to think of themselves as "we Thai people," these eaters of glutinous rice are here again made aware of who they often really are. The reminder is made sharper, even offensive, when the official (at line #675/7) tells them that only those who cannot eat and are unfamiliar with the rice that these villagers eat and identify with are "the real Thai, the true Thai." Surely, reformers who encourage officials to talk to villagers should give some attention to what they say when they do.

By speaking in Siamese (beginning at #648), KP shows himself to be working to get and keep DO as his story's recipient, to involve him in villager talk. He failed. Utterance #662 and the insults it leads to elicit only decreasing tokens (from *khaps* to *hmm*). With #677's low volume, the official grinds to a momentary (#678b) halt. He resumes a type of sequence that preceding chapters have made familiar to us.

■

Lines #679–691 comprise a sequentially standard, interlocking, package. With a raised voice that sounds like the start of something new, DO proffers #679, an utterance that would be harvested for a "collection" (Chapter Three, pp. 36–7) of references to non-present persons, and look quite like the other items in that collection (p. 38).

   (i) Recognition is made relevant by the use of the standard recognitional label of title + name.

(ii) There is then a pause (#680), presumably for a recognition token.

(iii) No one fills the pause.

(iv) Speaker then (#681) re-proposes the now problematic recognitional label, and

(v) adds a one-bit recognitional descriptor ("who wore eye-glasses last
night").

(vi) This is marked as a try,[19]

(vii) and followed by a further pause (#682). This may have been filled with a
nonaudible recognition token,

(viii) for speaker proceeds with his unit (#683).

That unit, in turn, would fit into and conform with a collection of PRE-ANNOUNCE-
MENTS (Terasaki 1976). The pre-announcement is

(i) followed by recipient's token of surprise or interest (#685),

(ii) followed by announcer's confirmation (#686's /ə̂·: ./) and expansion.

The sequentially standard person-reference is part of the standard announcement.
But every conversational occurrence is interactionally unique.

■

Previous chapters alerted us to inquire into the purposes served by the subject and
the form of occasions of person-reference and of their repair. On this occasion,
DO makes the immediate purpose of his referent quite explicit. He affiliates the
reference to "Teacher Ya" to his prior talk, citing him and then "the Education
Officer" (#691) as examples of persons who cannot eat glutinous rice.

These men are known to be Northerners. By citing them, the official violates
the ethnic distinction of rice eaters that the villagers had invoked (p. 79) to re-
assert his own, class based, distinction. To again quote from an earlier publication
(Moerman 1968:11):

In Chiengkham, and throughout northern and northeastern Thailand, one can express his
social position by the rice he eats. Officials are forced by their position to try to live as
central Thais: Class becomes culture. The Chiengkham district officer [in 1959–61, not
DO] was born and raised in the northern city of Lampang. But he, and many other high
officials who are northern by birth, eat the ordinary rice and coconut-curries of central
Thailand. People seldom speak of rice as a sign of status, but all recognize it as such.

Here, it *is* being spoken of, and insistently. The significance of this for the ethnographer is that the conversational locus of these person-references demonstrates

the interactive and ideological salience of cultural symbols without informants having to specify it.

At #694, MM, DO's professionally culture-minded co-conversant, shows surprise at this announcement of Teacher Ya's diet.[20] Those who regard taxonomies and cognitive categories as abstract and unsituated will be misled by the official's response. DO certainly knows that the city of Phayao is in the north and, indeed, is the commercial entrepôt for this district. The term is pressed into service by interactive exigencies, as an initial way of distinguishing Teacher Ya without having to use a deprecating term.

MM invoked the repair. DO seems to interpret his silence (at #696) as showing that it did not satisfy him, for he provides another. WORD SEARCHES often produce a delicate or euphemistic term. DO's, at #698, does so here. *Châw bâan* as a term for villagers is less deprecating than the more usual *khon bâan nɔ̀·k*,[21] but no less pointed in emphasizing class, rather than ethnic and regional, membership.

Anthropological concern with terms for persons has concentrated on unsituated correctness (e.g., what is this type of kinperson called: "father," "uncle," etc.?) and on selection among referential alternatives (e.g., "father" or "daddy"? "Ronnie" or "Mr. President"?). Ethnographers know, or should, that which term is used implies or connotes or creates a relationship among speaker, audience, and referent. This is true regardless of whether the person referred to is present or not.

The first non-pronominal label for persons in this segment occurred at line #584 when MK referred to MM as *pɔ̌·cáan*, the title and name by which villagers know, call, and refer to him. It is not a term known or used by DO.[22] *Mɛ́·cáan*, the reference term for MM's wife that MK (at line #641) and the women (#s 642 & 647) use, is also a village label unknown to the official.[23] For villagers to use this community's terms for MM and his wife is not only to talk to members of this community, it is to conjure up the MM who is also a member.

In line #600, KP refers to TM as "my father," /pɔ̌· phǒm/. This too has implications for relationships among those present. The term is Siamese, the kinship relation known (but not normally stated) by villagers. They usually call TM, the oldest man in the village and a renowned ritual specialist, *thâw mǒn*, "great grandparent." Here he is instead named not only in the national dialect, but in such a way as to make sense to just such a stranger as DO.

Talk is designed for its recipients. Chapter Three discussed one design component of references to non-present persons: Will recipient be able to identify the referent? DO's recognitional descriptor for Teacher Ya (#681), "who wore eyeglasses last night," is built for anyone who was with its speaker and Teacher Ya then. Its intended recipient is thereby MM who, along with Teacher Ya and other officials, had been DO's dinner guest. Categorially, villagers do not share such social occasions with officials.

Chapter Four's examination of trial testimony showed us that the occurrence, repair, and form of a reference to a non-present person are all informed, and sometimes determined, by interactional considerations that have little to do with referential sufficiency. The analyst cannot assume that a speaker's providing a recognitional descriptor proves that a recognitional label would have been referentially inadequate without one. By saying /khruu ŷa/ (at #679), then leaving a pause, and then providing a recognitional descriptor, DO retroactively makes line #680 into a conversational place from which a recognition token is missing, and thereby makes (or takes or claims) line #681 into a reference that needed a descriptor.

Throughout this segment, MM has talked only with villagers, DO spoken only to give villagers orders. A recognitional descriptor designed for MM uses the interactionally compelling organization of try-marked reference occasions to draw MM into a state of talk with DO. The reference repair at #681 functions to co-categorize MM with, and to involve him in talk with, its speaker. This, together with the invidious argument to which it is affiliated, might have been enough to motivate the repair.

The next repair of a reference to non-present persons is no less interactively, rather than cognitively, motivated. There is no other teacher Ya in these parts than the one who has been mentioned. But at #700 repair is again conspicuously—in that it is out of the normal three-turn space—invoked, now by a villager, MK. The sequential organization of repair forces DO—who spoke last and who introduced and repaired the initial reference—into talk with him. MK uses the floor and the recipient he gained for reporting that he teaches. The invidious distinction that the official has just been making gives this report its relevance and significance. By teaching, MK claims to be more than a mere *châaw bâan*.

Culturally Contexed Conversation Analysis and Interpretive Anthropology

Chapters Three and Four showed that the intentions of situated actors interact with local systems of turn-taking and with the structure of sequences. They also showed that the occurrence of an "occasion of reference" and its sequential shape sometimes have little to do with cognitive identification of a referent. We have seen in this chapter that the appropriateness, intelligibility, significance, import—in short, *the meaning*—of references to persons involves:

1 the locally invoked categorizations of all those present;
2 the societal issues (like villager vs. official) that have been enlivened;

3 the culturally defined setting;

4 the locally triggered significance of cultural symbols (like rice and other food).

This is by no means a complete list of what participants and analysts must attend to in order to apprehend the meaning of a "person-reference." Most of the items on any such list involve ethnography. Discovering them and how they work requires sequential analysis of a transcript of actual talk. Science and art, *Natur* and *Geist,* nature and culture, conversation analysis and ethnography must be combined. We need not, and must not, make the choice implied by the dictum that:

It is not against a body of uninterpreted data, radically thinned descriptions, that we must measure the cogency of our explications, but against the power of the scientific imagination to bring us into touch with the lives of strangers (Geertz 1973:16).

Ethnography must be provided with explicit methods for testing conclusions against uninterrupted and public data. Conversation analysis must aspire to bring us into touch with the lives of strangers and with our own lives; to resonate with culture's meanings; to acknowledge that talk is placed in a society, one sometimes cruel and inequitable.

The work of Clifford Geertz would seem to offer the most promising and imposing site for building a bridge between ethnography and sequential analysis. The method he calls for (1966:364) is one culturally contexted conversation analysis provides:

What is needed is some systematic, rather than merely literary or impressionistic, way to discover what is given. . . . What we want and do not yet have is a developed method of describing and analyzing the meaningful structure of experience . . . as it is apprehended by . . . members of a particular society at a particular point in time—in a word, a scientific phenomenology of culture.

The program he announces sounds like culturally contexted conversation analysis:

[T]here are three characteristics of ethnographic description: it is interpretive; what it is interpretive of is the flow of social discourse; and the interpreting involved consists in trying to rescue the "said" of such discourse from its perishing occasions and fix it in perusable terms. . . . [T]here is, in addition, a fourth characteristic of such description . . . : It is microscopic (1973:20, ff.).

But close inspection shows Geertz' practice to be inconsistent with his program. Since "interpretive anthropology" is so right-hearted and so influential, even inspirational, it is worth taking some trouble to compare it to culturally contexted conversation analysis. The comparison is facilitated by Geertz having devoted two major studies of "the person" in Bali (1966, 1974) to how persons are referred to.

All "structuralists," and any anthropologist who equates "the analysis of meaning" with "cultural *symbols* and . . . what they *signify*" (Basso and Selby 1976:1, emphasis added), share the assumptions of those studies. The assumptions support methods that are inconsistent with Geertz' stated purposes and program. They are the products of an unhappy marriage of two theories: each, itself, deficient. The first is Saussurian structuralism which posits the existence of mental entities that stand in a one-to-one relationship to verbal forms that refer to and/or express them. The other is an idealist version of American cultural anthropology. It holds that a culture is a system of ideas, one with its own internal coherence. Combining these theories precludes honoring social action, denies language any function other than reference, gives no place to the social organization of the situations in which language is used, discounts the activities of purposive actors, and dismisses the observed world as an obstacle.

■

Geertz (1973) writes that:

the concept of culture I espouse, and whose utility the[se] essays . . . attempt to demonstrate is essentially a semiotic one[24] [p. 5]. . . . The whole point of a semiotic approach to culture is . . . to aid us in gaining access to the conceptual world in which our subjects live . . . [p. 24].

In *Person, Time, and Conduct in Bali*, the conceptual territory explored is how "the people of Bali define, perceive, and react to—that is, think about—individual persons" (1966:360). Geertz reports on how Balinese "conceive, . . . look upon, . . . see, . . . perceive, . . . experience, . . . individuals." All these terms are usually taken to refer to private, mental, internal events. Geertz forcefully maintains that he intends them otherwise.

Human thought is consummately social. . . . [T]hinking is a public activity—its natural habitat is the houseyard, the marketplace, and the town square (1966:360). . . . Thought does not consist of mysterious processes located in what Gilbert Ryle has called a secret grotto in the head but of a traffic in significant symbols . . . (1966:362).

But intentions are not accomplishments; proclamations are not practices. Geertz' studies of the Balinese notion of the person do not attend to the "public," to "activity," or to any "natural habitat." His method is to "construe the [natives'] modes of expression, what I would call their symbol systems" (1974:336). Symbolic, structuralist, and interpretive anthropologists who lack a method for recording and analyzing the patterns of "traffic" are left with only the "significant symbols." Geertz' symbols are words: "an elaborate repertoire of designations and titles" through which the Balinese notion of the person "is realized" (1974:236). They are mystically coupled to mental entities: "symbols embody" meaning; "they [are] the material vehicles of thought" (1966:362); "conceptual structures are embodied in . . . symbolic forms" (1966:364).

Saussure analyzed the sign into its two components: a sound or acoustic component which he called the *signifier* (*signifiant* in French), and a mental or conceptual component which he called the *signified* (*signifié*). . . . The signified is not a thing but the notion of a thing, what comes into the mind of the speaker or hearer when the appropriate signifier is uttered (Sturrock 1979:6).

For Geertz, as for Saussure, concepts are consubstantial with verbal forms; language embodies ideas. In *Person, Time, and Conduct in Bali,* the program is to "refer to the [labels] as 'symbolic orders of person-definition' and consider them first serially, [and then] as a more or less coherent cluster" (p. 368). But the sets or "orders" of labels are ethnographically extrinsic. "Person-definition" is connected to the "symbolic order" solely by stipulation. The serial descriptions inherit these faults. The arguments by which Geertz links Balinese notions of the person to the "symbolic orders" of labels are based upon the connotations of the labels' semantic fields or by reference to the formal social institutions that confer them. Their omnipotent shaping of Balinese consciousness is merely assumed. Their role in social action is unexamined.

Although Geertz forcefully and correctly insists that social action requires categorized individuals, his statement (1966:363) of this is mentalistic and misleading.

Peoples everywhere have developed symbolic structures in terms of which persons are perceived not . . . as mere unadorned members of the human race, but as representatives of certain distinct categories of persons, specific sorts of individuals. . . . The everyday world in which the members of any community move, their taken-for-granted field of social action is populated not by anybodies, faceless men without qualities, but by somebodies, concrete classes of determinate persons positively characterized and appropriately labeled.

"Perceived" has two unfortunate consequences. First, like "thought"—another common term in these papers on Bali—"perception" adverts to an internal, imputed, psychic event. A science *can* focus on and search for secret, hidden, objects like the atom of old physics or the genetic code. But strenuous search should be based on broad theories, close reasoning, and controlled observations that connect the palpable experienced world to its invisible presumed source. "Thought" and "perception" do not have that status. Their relationships to social action are problematic and other than we usually suppose (see Chapters Two, Four, and Six); their connections to the phenomenal world are largely the unexamined artifacts of contemporary Western culture.

Secondly, "perceive" is rather passive, static, or at least a-social. For Geertz, there is a one-to-one mapping of individual to category, a mapping fixed by referential labelling. A given individual simply *is,* and is "perceived" as, the full-time occupant of a single labelled category. It is a sort of aura around him. By attending to actual interactions we have seen that the categorizing of an individual is a social action: situated, motile, shaded, purposive, consequential, negotiated. The category is not simply *there,* pre-formed, to be perceived. It is *occasioned,* and the individual is maneuvered or forced into it.

The relationships between individuals and categories, and between categories and labels, are situated and variable. To call the "somebodies" that interaction requires "concrete classes of determinate persons positively characterized and appropriately labeled," confounds words with people, products with processes. Labels name categories. In the segment that this chapter examined, natives did interactive negotiated work to categorize some participants as "villagers." Individuals do not come fixed into categories. They are squeezed in and out of them on occasions of interaction. Nor need labels be mentioned for categorization to occur. Americans can remain racist without ever again talking of "Nigger Jim."

The relationships between categories and "positive characteriz[ations]" are also situated, negotiated, variable. When participants activate a category, its stereotypic ("category-bound," in our technical terminology) characteristics are made relevant and possibly operative. But this, too, is the product of interactive negotiation. And the characterizations are separable (e.g., honest, but not stupid; a teacher not a farmer) and must be made relevant to the situation.

Geertz confuses individuals, labels, categories, and characterizations. The culturally contexted analysis of conversation investigates the interactional processes through which motivated and situated actors create, manipulate, and align these quite different entities.

Whether as ethnographers or as natives, we perceive many different scenes and occasions; we hear many different uses of a word or phrase; we notice that no one always acts in the same way. This is inescapable natural variety—actual, situated, and vital. It is what most of us go to the field for, and what all of us talk about when we come back. Depending on our theoretical orientation, it is our gold or our garbage.

Saussure distinguished language (*la langue*), a fixed, pure, perfect and self-sufficient system, from speech (*parole*). Language generates speech. But the limitations of memory and the physical fumblings of the tongue make speech a rather clumsy and defective child. For Saussure, as for Chomsky with his parallel notions of "competence" and "performance," the real world is something of a speech impediment. To Geertz, a culture is an "acted document," an "interworked system of construable signs" (1973:14), in short, a text. But, as Kapferer (1983:7) notes, "to analyze a 'text' . . . independently of its performance structure is to risk a serious violation of cultural form."

To suppose there to be a text that is the culture posits the existence of an invisible, inaudible, impalpable, single, homogenized, idealized script-like entity that somehow underlies and accounts for the variety actually experienced. "Interpretive anthropology" wants to read that hypothesized document. The vagaries of the world as actually encountered are, at best, mere variations on that text. At worst—and usually—they are dross that obscures it. To Geertz (1973:10),

doing ethnography [is] like trying to read (in the sense of "construct a reading of") a manuscript—foreign, faded, full of ellipses, incoherencies, suspicious emendations, and tendentious commentaries.

So he is forced to shove the experienced world out of the way, forced to correct it, "forced to schematize Balinese practices severely and to represent them as being much more homogenous and rather more consistent than they really are" (1966: note 7). The trouble is not only that surprises and inconsistencies might be suppressed, although that, too, is a trouble. The trouble is that what is ironed out, neatened up, and straightened away is exactly what is needed: the structures of practice and performance, the processes of interpretation and communication that give symbols and give life their meaning.

Actual encountered variety is the material for, and the product of, the natives' work of constructing and interpreting their meaningfully inhabited world. It is the very resource that the ethnographer must treasure and utilize for delineating and understanding that world. That world is *this* world, the world of events and appearances, the world of "the houseyard, the marketplace, and the town square" to which Geertz (1966:360) directs us but himself ignores.

For Geertz (1966:363), "It is through culture patterns, ordered clusters of significant symbols, that man makes sense of the events through which he lives." "Significant symbols" are "meaningful forms" (1973:10). He (1966:404) recognizes the danger that:

When one deals with meaningful forms, the temptation to see the relationship among them as immanent, as consisting of some sort of intrinsic affinity (or disaffinity) they bear for one another, is virtually overwhelming.

It is to this very temptation that his own studies of the Balinese person succumb. Not because their subject is "meaningful forms," but because he supposes meaning to inhere in a form and does not recognize that forms and meanings are aligned, juggled, sorted, and interpreted by purposive actors in socially organized situations. By default, there are no sources of meaning other than the referential semantics and etymology of words, no principles of organization other than "intrinsic affinities," and no locus for action other than the mind. To a semiologic approach, meaning is located by means of internal relations of signs within the hypothesized cultural "text." These relations are of two sorts: paradigmatic relationships between elements that can be substituted for each other; and syntagmatic relationships between elements that can combine together.

For Geertz, "culture" is quite separate from "society." Like an otherwise formless mass of cotton-candy supported by a paper cone, culture is given structure and a handle by the internal relations among the words that encode it. Chapter One demanded that "society" be located in interaction. This chapter insists that "culture" be located there: where the production, interpretation, and organization of meaning are socially structured and publicly negotiated and enforced. In Geertz' studies of the Balinese person, the culture is in its words.

■

The introduction to the "ethnography proper" of *Person, Time, and Conduct in Bali* (1966:368) begins:

In Bali, there are six sorts of labels which one person can apply to another in order to identify him as a unique individual.

Transcripts of conversations preserve and present "recognition occasions," actual specific occurrences when it was the natives' conscious, deliberate, concentrated business-at-hand to "identify [someone] as a unique individual." This is essential for "describing and analyzing the meaningful structure of experience . . . as it is apprehended by . . . members of a . . . society . . . [: For] a scientific phenomenology of culture" (Geertz 1966:364). But Geertz provides no records of interaction. We therefore cannot determine whether the Balinese are *ever* concerned to "identify [someone] as a unique individual," or, if and when they are, how they do it. Attention to actual instances demonstrated that for "one person . . . to identify [another] as a unique individual" is a social activity, done, like all social activities, concertedly: by means of an interactively organized sequence of actions. This confers some benefits on our researches.

A methodological benefit is that records of interaction furnish "a systematic, rather than merely literary or impressionistic, way to discover what is given" (Geertz 1966:364). Auerbach (1953) and Richards (1932) are exemplary interpreters because they present both texts (their data) and detailed exposition of their methods. This enables a reader to agree, or not, and to argue for or against a particular method or interpretation. We can improve or reject the findings and procedures. Most importantly, we can learn how to do something. Geertz' studies of Bali lack public data and explicit methods. We can only sympathize, or fail to: Either is the product of his rhetoric or our philosophical dispositions. We are either in his camp or not: possibly converted, but never convinced.

A substantive benefit from records of interaction is that the natives show us— because they must show one another—what they are up to, and what they made of it, utterance by utterance. We need not rely on "our own constructions of other people's constructions of what they and their compatriots are up to" as "our *data* (Geertz 1973:9, emphasis added). We need not "*begin* with our own interpretations of what our informants are up to, or think they are up to, and then systematize those" (1973:15, emphasis altered). Transcripts—and a method for their analysis—disclose participants' understandings and interpretations line by line.

Without a single instance of one native talking to another, there is, instead, the anthropologist talking only to himself.

Hopping back and forth between the whole conceived through the parts that actualize it and the parts conceived through the whole that motivates them, we seek to turn them, by a sort of intellectual perpetual motion, into explications of one another.

[W]hen a meanings-and-symbols ethnographer like myself attempts to find out what some pack of natives conceive a person to be, he moves back and forth between asking himself, "What is the general form of their life?," and "What exactly are the vehicles in which that form is embodied?" (Geertz 1974:235, ff.)

Geertz does quote "informants" (1973:7), but their talk—rather than being a social action formed for its occasion, situation, and listener—is a dutiful conduit of culture and history to the anthropologist's immaculate ears. Speech among natives is rarely even alluded to. When it is, as in (1966:373),

Kinship terms appear in public discourse only in response to some question, or in describing some event . . . with respect to which the existence of the kin tie is felt to be a relevant piece of information,

it is presented as the undocumented representative of an unspecified sample. Nor is it respected as speech. From the occurrence of an item (the kinship term) somewhere in the course of some conversations, Geertz infers the presence of a "feeling" that is then used to explain the occurrence of the item.

Person, Time, and Conduct in Bali continues:

Of the six sorts of labels which one person can apply to another in order to identify him as a unique individual, . . . each sort consists not of a mere collection of useful tags but of a distinct and bounded terminological system (1966:368).

Labels are words. Inasmuch as they "embody" ideas, they are the same as Saussure's signs. Noting that there are "sorts" and "systems," however, could leave room for attending to the structure of practice. In the segment examined in this chapter, for example, participants formulated and negotiated locally occasioned types of recognitional labels (e.g., in Lue and in Siamese; those used only by villagers, ones more generally known, and ones directed to outsiders). Geertz' "sorts," "bounded systems," and so forth are extrinsically motivated and come out of anthropology's argot. They are:

> personal names;
> birth order names;
> kinship terms;
> teknonyms;
> status titles;
> public titles.

These classes are our professional ones: *a priori* and without demonstrated connection to social action. The categories exist outside of time: limitless receptacles for whatever time and the natives might produce.

Ethnographers have long striven for descriptive categories that are informed by natives' terms of choice (Goodenough 1956). These do not always correspond to our convenient professional classifications. Geertz (1966:363) assumes that they do, and then derives their meaning from this assumption.

> Kinship terminologies, are ego-centered. . . . [P]ersonal names and sobriquets are informalizing and particularizing. . . . Others are centered on one or another aspect or subsystem of society.

We have seen that when participants formulate, sort, and choose among categories for persons, their terms of choice are based on distinctions created in and potent for the interaction in which the choices occurred. In the segment examined in this chapter, for example, dialect choice was a source of label types; choosing between *majkə·n mɔ mɛ·n* and *pɔ́·cáan* as MM's label had nothing to do with some general property inherent in names ("informalizing and particularizing"), it was based on the locally enlivened opposition: villager vs. official.

"The symbolic order defined by personal names" (1963:368) is the first that Geertz considers. Names are "arbitrarily coined nonsense syllables" without social implications of class, sex, etc. Not widely used or known, they do not individuate. Geertz concludes from this that the Balinese are uninterested in "what we call . . . 'personality'" (p. 370).

Birth-order names come next. They "highlight" an interest in progeny. Their re-cycling "suggests . . . an endless four-stage replication of imperishable forms"

(p. 371). We are not told how or to whom the highlights and suggestions appear.

The Balinese have a "generation-type" kin terminological system. This gives access to their mental images: "For any given actor, the general picture is a layer-cake arrangement of relatives" (p. 372). The picture seems not to matter much: "The system of kinship terminology play[s] a rather secondary role in shaping the moment-to-moment flow of social intercourse" (p. 373). Since we are denied any reports of "the moment-to-moment flow of social intercourse," this must be taken on faith. It is not difficult to do so. Why should one expect a system of terminology, qua system of terminology, to shape the moment-to-moment flow of social intercourse? Terms, persons, and actions are distinct entities, although systematically related. No one of them shapes another.

"For the great mass of the peasantry, . . . most Balinese address and refer to one another" (p. 375) by means of teknonyms: as "Mother/Father of _____," or "Grandmother/Grandfather of _____." The blank is the personal name of their first born child or grandchild. So individuating *is* done, and done via a personal name, albeit not the name of the person individuated. Gender is marked by the titles (as "mother" vs. "father"). [25]

Geertz reports that Bali has an "exceptionally well developed and . . . influential system of teknonymy," and asks (p. 376): "What impact does it have upon the individual Balinese's perceptions of himself and his acquaintances?" From an interactional perspective, the question is certainly odd. Why and in what way should one expect a terminological system to impact on perceptions? But Geertz can answer. Teknonymy's "first effect is to identify the husband and wife pair" once they procreate (p. 376). We are not told how or to whom the effect appears.

In Bali

the father-mother pair has very great economic, political, and spiritual importance. . . . In virtually all local activities, from the religious to the agricultural, the parental couple participates as a unit.

These institutional arrangements are quite widespread in Southeast Asia. In Bali, Geertz tells us (p. 376), "teknonymy underscores both the importance of the marital pair in local society and the enormous value which is placed upon procreation." So "the impact" of the custom is at first merely to "underscore" (a nicely textual word) in Bali institutional arrangements also found elsewhere. But "underscore" is soon empowered. Geertz claims that the pattern of labelling determines what people see and think. Under the

teknonymous regime [*sic!*] . . . an individual is not *perceived* in the context of who his ancestors were . . . , but rather in the context of who he is ancestral to. One is not *defined* . . . in terms of who produced one, . . . but in terms of whom one has produced (p. 379, emphasis added).

"The status title system is a pure prestige system" (p. 380). Via its folk ety-mology (The Balinese say the titles come from the gods.) and intersection with the *varna* system, "it [*sic!*] interprets the implications of that [Hindu] world view [and] . . . make[s] it possible to view social life under the aspect of a general set of cosmological notions" (p. 384). All untouched, it would seem, by human, or at least Balinese, hands, tongues, and ears.

The connections that Geertz traces between Balinese labels and Balinese con-cepts are unconvincing, slight, even (if the word may be permitted for so august an author) silly. This is largely because in the papers on Bali, as in the anthropologi-cal work Geertz later came to criticize (1973:17),[26]

Culture is treated . . . purely as a symbolic system by isolating its elements, specifying the internal relationships among those elements, and then characterizing the whole system in some general way—according to the core symbols around which it is organized, the under-lying structures of which it is a surface expression, or the ideological principles upon which it is based. . . . [T]his hermetical approach to things seems to me to run the danger (and increasingly to have been overtaken by it) of locking cultural analysis away from its proper object, the informal logic of actual life.

Geertz' studies of the Balinese person[27] are not based on what he later (1973) came to call "thick description": on "setting down the meaning particular social actions have for the actors whose actions they are"; on "interpretation that goes all the way down to the most immediate observational level" (pp. 27, f.). They do not fulfill thick description's demand (p. 17) that: "Behavior . . . be attended to, and with some exactness, because it is in the flow of behavior . . . that cultural forms find articulation." Geertz' etiology (1973:18) is accurate for his own studies of the Balinese person.

To divorce [anthropological interpretation] from what happens—from what, in this time or that place, specific people say, what they do, what is done to them, from the whole vast business of the world—is to divorce it from its applications and render it vacant.

Geertz reports (1966:368) that "these various labels are not, in most cases, employed simultaneously, but alternatively, depending upon the situation and sometimes the individual." Labels are words. The polyphonic powers of even the Balinese, those paragons of artistry, could not attain to employing them simultane-ously. The labels are used by actors to refer to persons. That different ones are used "depending upon the . . . individual," hardly advances our understanding. The crucial matter for the use and meaning of these, and any, words is, "the situa-tion." Geertz presents none. Were he to, the symbols might yield their meaning.

Geertz complains (1966:362) that, "The meanings that symbols . . . embody [*sic*] are often elusive, vague, fluctuating, and convoluted." This characterizes symbols negatively, by what they lack: clarity and fixity. To require that the world be other than it is guarantees disappointment. If symbols are to get used as they *are* used, they must have a flexible, multiple, defeasible relationship to meaning. It is on actual occasions of its situated use, if ever, that the meaning of a symbol is fixed and clarified. By paying attention to real talk, we learned that meaning is situated, not abstract; enacted, not embodied; negotiated, not decoded; consequential, not prior, to use; and not exclusively referential. Situated and located meaning makes use of—but is never completely determined by—the dictionaries, etymologies, semantic appropriateness, institutional origins, and other sources and resonances that linguists and symbolic anthropologists rely upon. Meaning, in the course of talk at least, is always in context, situated, negotiated—that is, interactive. Meaning is thus inescapably, *and investigatably,* contingent, proposed, defeasible and otherwise messy in the abstract, but clear enough in the lived reality.

When we do attend to what happens when persons actively engage in "identify-[ing someone] as a unique individual," we learn that it is a social action composed:

1) of a *sequence* of utterances
2) by more than 1 speaker;
3) of spaces between their speech;
4) of sounds (like "er," "um," LAUGHTER) that are not words;
5) of at least as many kinds of perturbations, contours, etc. as our transcript conventions record (e.g., =, °, |, |, :::, -, (.n)); and, of words, certainly.

The words that matter most immediately are those used for non-recognitional labels, recognitional labels, recognitional descriptors, and recognition tokens. All are equally essential parts of a mutually constitutive systematic process.

Geertz considers only the "six sorts of labels": some Balinese words whose referents are persons. He confines his data to the labels and his method to their exegesis. This confuses a systemic social process with one of its occasioned components. If the Balinese use their language as other humans (save perhaps mathematicians while writing proofs) use theirs, those words are often put to purposes other than "identify[ing someone] as a unique individual." If the Balinese perform the task of identification as the Thai and the Americans do (see Chapter Three), they will use words (and silences and perturbations) other than those labels. The presumably finite set of labels and "sorts of labels" does not exhaust the words and phrases used to attempt and accomplish the task of "identify[ing someone] as a unique individual." A large, perhaps limitless, set of recognitional descriptors is used as well.

My criticisms of Geertz' papers do not implicate their eloquent, learned and influential thesis that the concepts of person, of time, and of conduct are interrelated, that they vary, that they generate moral orders, and that those different moral orders—including our own—are therefore the products of culture and history. Nor can I challenge his substantive report of the Balinese concepts of "person, time, and conduct." Indeed, that is my criticism. The data he cites are unrelated to his ethnographic description. Lexical items that refer to persons are the wrong data. Semiologic text analysis is the wrong method.[28]

■

Study of actual occasions has demonstrated that all terms for persons are said and understood by real people with real interests. Those people actively orient to their immediate situation and type of occasion, to the setting, to when during the occasion the reference occurs, to the kinds of actors present, to social actions both ongoing and hinted at. All those factors—and more—influence the terms they use and how they understand them. Whatever the form—label or descriptor or neither —its use and its meaning are often not predominantly referential. There simply is no simple correspondence between a form and an idea. A label is not a statement, and, *a fortiori,* not a culture's statement about what it means to be a person.

When we take account of the conversational structures and social situations in which, and the persons by which, labels are used, labels—along with recognitional descriptors, pauses, try-markings, and the full panoply of devices actually used for person-identification—can help to illuminate the important problem that Geertz set himself, and all ethnographers. Some preliminary observations can illustrate this.

First, Thai speakers often do not mention—whether by name, pronoun, title, or any other form—persons, whether themselves, their listeners, or those they talk about. When mention *is* made, its most common form is a title. The form that the speaker uses for him/herself is the same as the form that others use for him or her. So, for example, if I am older than you, you call me and I call myself *phîi.* Despite the lack of a method, or even a compelling argument, for connecting them, it is hard not to believe there to be powerful relationships between these practices that occur whenever people talk together or think about talking, and the Thai Buddhist ideology of *Selfless Persons* (Collins 1982) or the way in which Thai officials and historical personages disappear behind their titles (Sharp and Hanks 1978:114; Wales 1934:38).

Second, when person-identification has been made relevant, and especially when conversants work to accomplish identification, the ethnographer can see the sorts of labels and recognitional descriptors that natives use in order to formulate social persons. But his reasoning about these forms must honor the structured circumstances of their occurrence. So, for example, we may note as ethnographic data about Lue villagers that they, and those who would talk with them successfully, typically label and describe persons for recognition by means of a limited number of kinship relations (usually mate, parent, or child),[29] a limited number of titles (e.g., current or former religious [Moerman 1966:155, f.][30] or government title [Moerman 1969b],[31] or title of senior age[32]); village, province, or region of origin (especially if the referent is not from here);[33] or ethnicity (if not a Lue). The list goes on, but not on and on and on. It is a list of what Lue villagers take and make to be important for knowing who and what a person is. But the items on the list live and have meaning only in the circumstance of being uttered by and to specific persons on particular occasions. So, for example, when KP belatedly invokes repair (XIX:30) in order to make sure that MM knows for sure whose garden has been talked about, he is also sustaining MM as just the ethnographer sort of person MM wants to be: someone who knows and should know—but has to be told— what villagers know.

■

Published sequential analyses of conversation study the social construction of meaning without sufficient concern for the sense and resonances of words. Geertz' studies of the person in Bali explicate words without recourse to the social organization that gives them meaning. By attending to the interactive organization of conversation in its cultural context we can have both.

To Geertz, "conversation" is an image, not an actual human activity. Only metaphorically does he "trac[e] the curve of social discourse; fixing it into an inspectable form" (1973:24). Only in a very extended sense indeed does he "aid us in gaining access to the conceptual world in which our subjects live so that we can, in some extended sense of the term, converse with them" (idem). Correct in his observation that all ethnographers speak or write for others, Geertz fails to draw the implication when he quotes (1973:13):

"If speaking *for* someone else seems to be a mysterious process," Stanley Cavell has remarked, "that may be because speaking *to* someone does not seem mysterious enough."

Culturally contexted conversation analysis is more simple minded. It takes "social discourse," "inspectable form," "converse," and "speaking to someone" quite literally, and honors mystery by paying it close attention. Those who would obey Geertz' dictum (1966:405) that:

[m]eaning is not intrinsic in the objects, acts, processes, and so on, which bear it, but . . . imposed upon them; and the explanation of its properties must therefore be sought in that which does the imposing—men living in society

would do well to consider not just the semantics of labels, but to confront the actual demands of living in society. Prominent among these are the constant and in-

6

Talking About the World[1]

Language, Talk, and Reality

This chapter examines some actual talk about the "real world." The reader already knows what I mean by "actual talk": transcripts of recorded naturally occurring interactions. To those data, this chapter adds some introspection and recollection. But it is necessary to specify what I mean by the "real world," the world "out there," and why I use quotation marks.

Not all talk is referential in the sense that it is about something. And not all referential talk is about a world external to itself, for there can be talk about talk. Nor need the world outside of talk be one "out there." Both Thais and Americans, for example, consider "It's raining," *fŏn tòk,* and "I'm fine, thanks," *sabāaj khap,* to be equally sensible, but obviously to refer to ontologically different entities or processes, and to spur different kinds of interests in their correctness.

Since not all talk refers to the world "out there," how can one locate the talk that does? Certainly not by asserting prior knowledge of what the world really consists of, by deciding which subjects and concepts are substantive realities, and then tracking talk about them. Views of reality are too biased, science too incomplete. An ethnographer sometimes deals and lives with people who seem to have assumptions, perceptions, judgements, experiences of a world different from his. We may suspect the fieldworker of occasionally exaggerating the differences between the natives' world and his own: taking metaphors to be factual reports, contrasting actual native activities to ones we ascribe to our scientists, and generally inflating the romance and challenge of his calling. But the possibility that others live in other worlds is real and undeniable.

Fortunately, we do not have to know what the world *is* in order to locate talk about it. We need merely to recognize and honor what talk about the world is like. The data of this chapter are instances of people talking in some ways that convey that they are talking about a world "out there." This is what an ethnographer must always work with. According to Heidegger (1967), that radical ethnographer of our own practices, it is also what Western philosophy from Aristotle through Kant has worked with. "Thinghood" (*Sachheit*) is a matter of how we assert, address, and propose (pp. 37, 63–4); philosophical "reality," a way of making propositions about subjects, not a certification of the existence of objects outside of our consciousness (pp. 212–13, 237). For ethnographers and conversation analysts "the world out there" is a verb, not a noun; a social activity, not a pre-formed thing.

We will examine instances of reality being constructed through the activity of talking about it. This does not require an initial philosophical stance about either the ultimate nature of reality or about our ability to know and understand it. We can at least set out in company with such an empiricist as Konrad Lorenz (1978: 233) who supposes that there must be a recalcitrant external reality to which our (and all surviving species') sensory and cognitive apparatus evolves an adaptation, and note with him that the filtering of that reality comes not only from the properties of our sensory organs, but also from the

mysterious and somewhat uncanny way [in which] a culture swallows up all the efforts of the individuals within it and turns them into a form of 'general knowledge,' a sort of public opinion on what is true and real.

But our project does require an *investigative* stance: one that faces toward interactively organized talk, not toward language.

■

So long, and so fruitfully, has it been suggested that there is a peculiar, intimate, mutually constitutive relationship between a people's language and their view of the world that I trust I can be forgiven for concentrating on the expressions of that theme that are closest to my time and profession. For anthropologists the theme is enshrined as the "Sapir–Whorf hypothesis" that those who share a native language—in the linguists' and philosophers' sense of "language" (the lexicon + the syntax)—have a common view of the world, one that comes from, or consists of, or creates that language. The idea has been challenged (e.g., Berlin and Kay 1969; Cole and Scribner 1974:39–60), delicately modulated (e.g., Witherspoon 1977), and made less global and deterministic in many ways. "Language" has been expanded to include "prosody" (Gumperz 1982) and "discourse units" (e.g., Scollon and Scollon 1981). But the way in which Lawrence K. Frank (1966:12) approvingly introduced a quotation from Whorf to a general audience is still rather typical.

Language is probably the most widely and most frequently used symbol. Through its daily use each member of a cultural group continually reasserts and reaffirms its symbolic world and communicates with others.

But notice how "daily use" permits Frank to glide from "language" to assertions, affirmations, and communication. In this he joins Sapir and Whorf themselves, for Sapir (1929:162) refers to "the *use* of language" and Whorf (1940:221) to "fashions of *speaking*" (emphases added). And so they must: For language itself is mute. Anyone interested in how a view of the world is shared, recognized, maintained, or socialized within a community must attend to language made public and socially compelling, must attend to talk.

[B]efore one goes to the length of invoking an unconscious logos . . . one should perhaps first clarify the lived meanings that are experienced by the men speaking the language. In any case, one should join to any logic of the language a phenomenology of the spoken word (Dufrenne 1963:39).

Harry Hoijer, a leading interpreter of Whorf, recognized this in proposing (1954:97–8) that "we need to know, not only that a particular linguistic pattern exists, but also how frequently it occurs in everyday speech." Hoijer, with the descriptive linguists of his generation, envisioned language to be a set of pre-minted patterns of phrases and sentences thrown into the world like countable coins. "Language" now means a system that generates and creates. We learn little by counting those of its outputs we happen to stumble upon. We learn nothing if we fail to take account of the situation in which speech is encountered.

In noting that "a linguistic sign system *per se* exerts . . . influence or constraint . . . only as a result of its *use* in social situations," Kellner (1973:331) sharpens a theme in his earlier work and the work of his colleagues. Although Berger and Kellner (1964:3) state that

The seemingly objective and taken-for-granted character of the social definitions of reality can be seen most clearly in the case of language itself,

they go on to observe (p. 4) that

In everyday life, however, the principal method employed is speech. In this sense, it is proper to view the individual's relationship with his significant others as an ongoing conversation.

But their use of "conversation" is metaphoric. Their interest is restricted to what it takes "silently for granted" and leaves unsaid.

A more influential expression can be found in Berger and Luckmann's *The Social Construction of Reality*. Despite their concentration on vocabulary as the objectifier of social reality (pp. 21, f.), they insist that:

> The reality of everyday life is shared with others. . . . The most important experience of others takes place in the face-to-face situation, which is the prototypical case of social interaction. All other cases are derivatives of it (p. 28).

This position was applauded and developed by Michael Halliday (1976:574–5).

> An individual's subjective reality is created and maintained through interaction with others . . . and such interaction is, critically, verbal—it takes the form of conversation.

Halliday points out that

> Berger and Luckmann do not ask the question, what must language be like for casual conversation to have this magical power. They are not concerned with the nature of the linguistic system. For linguistics, however, this is a central problem, . . . it might be said to be *the* central problem: how can we interpret the linguistic system in such a way as to explain the magical powers of conversation?

Halliday does not ask "What must conversation be like?" As a linguist, he is not predominantly concerned with the nature of the interactive and conversational system. But without this question, we are merely examining the magician's props. The features of language per se are like the rigidity of the magician's rod, the false lid of his top hat. The tricks' sucess needs them, to be sure. But the trick itself, the processes of the magical act, is conversation. Culturally contexted sequential analysis permits us to describe, and perhaps unmask, that trick.

A Plea for Noticings

Philosophers are concerned with "the problem of reference," with how statements can relate to a world external to them; scientists with how descriptions map to reality; anthropologists with the world as natives talk about it. All usual standards of truth, and every possibility for lying, suppose there to be a world about which it is talk's sometime duty to report. Without talk about the world we could not warn our fellows about a cave bear, tell (or lie) about where the fishing is good, or request someone's hand in marriage.

The ways of talking that claim a real world as subject, that call attention to features of that world, and that enforce consensus about it are a principal means by which reality is oriented to, verified, created. Such talk can be a feature of a wide range of situations: courtroom testimony, dinner parties, scientific experiments. Some of the ways of talking that show that we are taking (and therein making) what we talk about to be the real world have been described sequentially. Among them are giving instructions (Goldberg 1975), announcements of news (Terasaki 1976), narratives of personal experience, and—the type on which this chapter concentrates—"noticings."

Noticings call another person's attention to some specific occurrence or feature in the world out there. Berger and Luckmann (1967:20) point out that "Consciousness . . . always . . . is directed toward objects." Noticings direct attention and thereby specify consciousness. Compellingly and with immediacy, they point to "the reality experience[d] in wide-awake consciousness," the arena in which Berger and Luckmann (1967:38) find the origins and primary function of language. An interest in them continues the research program of Evans-Pritchard, one of anthropology's genitors, who "started by seeking the selective principles governing attention, and . . . by expecting the principles to lie in social interaction" (Douglas 1980:38).

Some thinkers ascribe the evolutionary origin and function of human language to its role as a medium for making reports about the world. The "food dance" of the honey bee (von Frisch 1967) intrigues us because one bee uses it to inform others about the location in the world of something terribly important to bees. The discovery (Seyfarth and Cheney 1980) that young vervet monkeys learn to distinguish and then to produce different alarm calls in response to different classes of predators is exciting in its implication that arbitrary referential semantics, socially learned and used stereotyped signs about events in the world, occurs in species other than humans.

Noticings are delivered as if they were the automatic product of their speaker having just made some immediately prior observation of something in the outside world to which he is calling his fellows' attention. In these respects, noticings seem similar to the bee's dance or the monkey's alarm call. But we must not minimize the differences between bees and people, between humans who, in Bronowski's (1978:32) interesting distinction, "convey information," and animals, who "convey instructions." As von Foerster (1966:54) notes:

Communication among social insects is carried out through unalterable signs which are linked to the genetic make-up of the species. While the signs refer to objects and percepts, and serve to modify actions and manipulations, symbols refer to concepts and ideas and serve to initiate and facilitate computation.

Noticings call attention to something hitherto unnoticed. This, too, is not without theoretical interest. They are "shifts of attention *within* everyday life" (Berger and Luckmann 1967:25).

When this happens, the reality of everyday life seeks to integrate the problematic sector into what is already unproblematic (Berger and Luckmann 1967:24).

Noticings are interactionally potent. They always start some interactive business, can properly interrupt other business, and can initiate a state of talk—sometimes with persons to whom one could not otherwise have access. Who of us, riding in a confined vehicle, has not found himself plunged into dreary conversation by some fellow passenger's, "Wow! Did you see that?"

Noticings are sequentially implicative. Their recipients must talk to them, and so talk about the features of the world they mention. This permits us to locate and analyze talk in which participants agree (or conspicuously fail to agree) about the sensibly noticed and consensually discussed properties of their world.

When to Notice

"HEY! Your pants are on fire!" furnishes an apocryphal instance of how noticings are an immediate response to events in the world. "HEY! Your pants were on fire last week!" would hardly do. This "just now" quality is an interactional, not a perceptual, matter. Consider two instances of noticings recorded on videotape. Such taped records permit us to see and hear the managed quality of what we usually take as natural.

On one tape, a hostess is pouring drinks for her guests. She walks around the table at which they have been sitting. One of the guests, Luke, is away from the table, at the sink. We see the hostess look down at Luke's nearly full glass and hold the wine bottle over it. She then says, "LUKE? Some wine?" Luke does not reply. The hostess then says, "OH. You still got some." The video record discloses that the perceptual observation, her looking at the glass, is separated from the social, spoken, noticing. The placement of the noticing politely provides on Luke's behalf a reason for the refusal his silence was interpreted as.

The other videotape records a wedding receiving line. We see the bride's father, to his left the groom's mother, then the bride, then the groom. The guests, their backs toward us, file past them. The mutual coordination this requires is rather fun to watch. If I am the bride, for example, in order to know when to go about ending my current interaction, I have to monitor the engagements of both my mother-in-law, whose interactant I will receive when she is finished with him, and my new husband, to whom I must pass the person I am talking to so that I can start talking to the one whom my mother-in-law sends me. At one point we see the bride turn her head and eyes toward a guest who is engaged with her father, two positions up the line from her. Some time later, as that guest leaves the groom's mother, the bride throws her head back, turns her face toward him with a big smile, and says, as if she had just now noticed him, "CHARLIE!" As in the earlier tape, we can see that the moment of perception is not the moment of public noticing. The noticing is timed by interactive, not perceptual, processes.

For a noticing to come off as having been nothing other than the automatic and truthful report of something just observed in the outside world is the consequence of a successfully managed claim. Such *interactive* success provides no direct access to a world outside the interaction, whether "out there" or in the speaker's head. Temporal separation between stimulus and response, perception and activity, is important to distinctions between "signs" and "symbols," "instructions" and "information," "manipulation" and "computation." This temporal separation is socially occasioned, interactively organized, and culturally informed and informative.

Language, Truth, and Talk

In a recent and influential book, Barwise and Perry (1983:3) propose that

a test for a theory of meaning and a key to its development is the fact that meaningful expressions can be used to convey information (and misinformation), both about the external world and our states of mind.

If expressions were not systematically linked with kinds of events, on the one hand, and states of mind, on the other, their utterance would convey no information; they would be just noises or scribbles, without any meaning at all.

Like many philosophers and linguists, Barwise and Perry place that systematic linkage within language itself. Like most, they insist that the linkage is comprised of truthful description. It is not that Barwise and Perry fail to recognize that people sometimes do not tell the truth. Indeed, they note (p. 18) that

If people said only what they knew to be the case, then we would never notice truth as a property of some utterances and not others. It is because people sometimes [1] violate the conventions of language [1] . . . that we come to recognize truth as a uniformity across certain utterance situations. Obviously, [2] if truthful assertions were not an important part of our life, and if we did not possess a fairly good ability to recognize them, utterances would not carry information for us, and so language would not be meaningful. This is why semantics focuses on truth conditions, as a way of understanding linguistic meaning [2] (numbers added).

Notice that what I have bracketed as [1] makes talking truthfully a property of *language*. And notice, further, that the argument marked [2] is compelling only if "important" is taken to mean constant and universal, and if "information" is taken to mean assertions about the external world. The first equivalence is clearly just a puff of rhetoric. The second is no less incorrect, and more important. Barwise and Perry are not naive logical positivists. They do not claim that truth-conditions are involved in the meaningfulness of all utterances, but concede (pp. 18–19) that:

> Truth is only one constraint placed on speakers by linguistic meaning, a constraint on the legitimate use of simple declarative statements. . . . Austin and later writers on speech acts have forced us to realize that, important as truth is to understanding language, there is more to a theory of linguistic meaning than an account of the truth conditions of utterances. But it is on that first step that we shall concentrate.

This is the wrong way about. The constraint of truth is not a property of *language*, but one placed by the organization of speaking and by speakers. And it is not omnirelevant. "Truth," "accuracy," and other mappings between what is said and what is referred to are locally occasioned. Even if we restrict our attention to talk about the world out there, truth and accuracy are not always the relevant or appropriate standards. Being amusing, touching, or polite sometimes counts too. Furthermore, truth is made relevant, let alone criterial, not by particular types of sentences (e.g., "declarative" ones), but by the occasion on which language is used. It is the circumstances of saying something that determine whether truth is a relevant criterion for its meaning, interpretation, and correctness. It is not that the kind of utterance called a "speech act," or any other *kind of utterance,* is specially exempted from truth considerations. Inspection of actual talk indicates that the constraint and standard of truth-conditions, like every other abstract standard of an utterance's adequacy, must be made relevant to the occasion of its occurrence. Truthful description is in this sense no less exceptional, special, or marked than any other criterion.

   When truth *has* been made relevant, we can, indeed, make use of talk to learn about the speakers' views of the world. But knowing whether and how truth is relevant requires ethnographic information about the situation of the talkers. As with all ethnography, what we learn requires and interacts with what we already know. As with all interaction, when some standard—like truth—is relevant, it is present as a resource to be negotiated over, not solely as a constraint. These observations can be illustrated by some talk from a setting in which ethnography finds truthful description to be relevant and critical.

During a trial in the Criminal Court of Chiengmai, Thailand, the sole eye-witness to a murder testified that by the dim light of an oil-wick lamp he saw one of the defendants fire the fatal shot. Questioned further by the defence attorney, he insisted that the gunman wore rubber sandals with green thongs, his companion leather shoes with black laces. The judge, thinking such acute observation improbable, discounted the eye-witness testimony and acquitted the defendants who would otherwise have gone to jail for fifteen years. In constructing their cases, lawyer, judge, and police made use of normative notions about what humans can notice in the world, and about their society.

"Corruption" is a slippery concept. Thai judges expect police to sometimes produce witnesses who haven't really seen what they testify to. So they ask about minor details that false witnesses would not know. Thai police know this. So they drill all witnesses with such details. Thus truthful witnesses know details they could not have observed; and by preparing truthful witnesses with incredible details, the police and prosecutor might manage to throw cases blamelessly.[2] The truths we conjure are at least two edged.

In another case, Insuan and Somcit were accused of murder. Their defence was that they got drunk and fell asleep in another village at the time of the crime. Taa, a witness for the prosecution, lives in the village where they claim to have been sleeping. He was visiting his neighbor, Tuj, shortly after the murder was committed. He told the police and the court that while he was on Tuj's verandah, a young man came to the foot of the stairs and asked his way. At a police line-up, Taa identified the young man as Somcit. Had Somcit been asleep, he would be innocent. Had he requested directions at Tuj's house while Taa was visiting, he could be one of the murderers.

In the north of Thailand, it is a prominent and widespread custom for young men to visit (ɛ̂w) marriageable girls (sǎaw) in the evening to converse with them on the verandah of their homes. Under cross-examination, Taa testified that Tuj has a marriageable daughter. Pressed by defence counsel, he admitted that he assumed that the young man at the foot of the stairs had come to ɛ̂w sǎaw, to court, Tuj's daughter. He thus did not especially notice or closely observe (sàngkèet) him. The witness then revealed that he had therefore been uncertain of his identification at the police line-up, and could not affirm (jynjan) it now.

The folk epistemology that counsel used to impugn Taa's identification of Somcit is one we share with the Thai. It holds, first, that a person is unlikely to notice the details of something only casually examined. Second, that one examines only casually—if at all—what he immediately apprehends as expectable and unexceptional. Third, that when one sees people who—by sex, age, time, dress, etc.— could be doing the culturally expectable activity, he assumes that they are indeed engaged in that activity (cf. Sacks 1977).

Even when talk is about the world, and—as in the courtroom or the astro-physical observatory (Garfinkel, et al. 1981)—truth is the relevant and dominant standard, we learn about the talkers, their culture, and their negotiation of a situation. Indeed, we can scarcely learn about anything else. What we find out from truthful talk about the world is always the participants' "truth": statements that are accurate and correct for a culturally recognized type of situation as they negotiate it at this very time. The sense of "about" is the local version of adequate description for an instituted situation on an irremediably actual occasion: Here in court when counsel presses. And the sense of "the world" is as the one that participants, on each separate occasion wielders and servants of their culture as of their biology, take it to be. Here, a world in which normal observers notice what is normally noticeable.

What to Notice

Half a century ago, Evans-Pritchard wrote[3]:

Any sound or sight may reach the brain of a person without entering his consciousness. We may say that he 'hears' or 'sees' it but does not 'notice' it. In a stream of sense impressions only a few become conscious impressions and these are selected on account of their greater affectivity. A man's interests are the selective agents and these are to a great extent socially determined, for it is generally the value attached to an object by all members of a social group that directs the attention of an individual toward it.

The observation is by now familiar to anthropologists and their readers. It helps to make sense of the profusion of cattle terms among the Nuer, words for snow among the Eskimo, or words for drugs among those who use them (Agar 1973). Anthropology now has somewhat more complex ideas of "socially determined," of groups values, and of how they are interrelated than it did in 1934. Interests, values, and emotions are taken to vary—systematically it is hoped—among the members of a culture. Commonality and normativity are taken to direct, manipu-late, influence, inform speech and behavior, not to produce, predict, or completely control them. And "social," in this book at least, means not "general to a commu-nity," but active, actual, occasioned social interaction. While it is still infor-mative, and certainly easier, to form an impression about what a people seems generally interested in, and conclude from that some things about their "culture," much about people that is more detailed, more specific, more processual, and more compelling can be learned by examining actual occasions of their noticing and talking about the world.

■

Speakers embody and en-tongue social categories as made relevant and enlivened by the occasion of speech. Consider in this regard some noticings written down while they occurred.

During the five-minute bus ride between Los Angeles Airport's parking lot and passenger terminal, a passenger called out: "He got a cab!" This noticing drew attention to a scene that an accident report would record as Figure 1.

The driver turned his head toward that noticed world and said, "They always do that, run into buses. They don't have any respect for buses." Observe the economy with which he transformed the world's moral order:

(i) it now contains not an isolated incident, but a practice (something "they always do");
(ii) the practice is accounted for by disrespect;
(iii) his repair—the explicative expansion of the pro-verb "do"—turns that world into one in which a bus, like his, is once again the innocent dishonored victim.

Later during this very short trip, the driver used his public address system to make the noticing: "There's a cab run right onto the curb to get by a bus. They crazy, cabdrivers." To my eyes, the cab with its two wheels momentarily off the roadway as it squeezed by a bus was not especially noticeable. The driver, his professional interest enlivened, perhaps by the prior incident, was scanning the world for further reportable cabbie depravities.

What was noticed by driver and passenger is not especially important for a de-

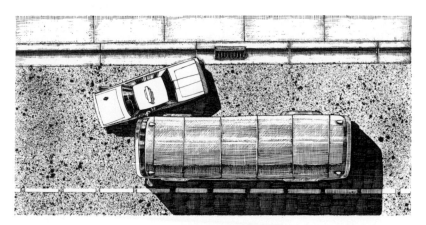

FIGURE 1

scription of the culture of the Americans. But it does show us the local occasioning of the pervasive division between two social categories who contest for passengers, road space, salary levels, and respectability, and how that division and competition affects selective attention to and talk about the world.

■

The world noticed and talked about is often not especially striking or interesting. Much talk is perfectly and valuably humdrum and pro forma, done across neutral and anonymous social categories. We can't, after all, have "deep" and "meaningful" talk without being in interaction. Worn smooth by being passed from hand to hand, the pebbles of "small talk" are warm from human contact and can test the waters for more intimate communication. However commonplace the topic, how we talk to it makes our commonality.

In Data Segment XXXIV, two sisters are doing this in a typical and mundane way. Much of this conversation[4] consists of each sister elaborately informing the other of events in her life and then inquiring into what befell the other. The listening sister rarely shows much interest in, and the telling sister rarely much enthusiasm for, the events related. But there are also lively moments, as when talk about the weather right after a narrative, produced flatly, is allowed to wind down with a whimper (lines #1–12).

Ada takes Bea's enthusiastic, "WHAT A MISERABLE WEEKEND," (line #13) to be about the weather, Bea's weather, and immediately (#14–15) shows that she knows on her own what Bea's weather was like, that she honors a moral obligation to compare it with hers, and that she appreciates what Bea's feelings about Bea's weather must have been. They rapidly match worlds by trading invidiously contrasted reports of each's weather (lines #14–22) and find another world to have experienced together when Bea presents evidence ("I had to turn the furnace up") that she, in her world up in town, experienced cold just as Ada did in her world down at the beach. At line #26, Ada displays that she is doing work to find rain in her world to match to Bea's. Their relationship is actualized and maintained by their mutually orienting to trivial events in the world. A world experienced together—perceived, oriented to, felt, and meaningful in the same way—is much like what anthropologists call "a culture." In talk about the world, speakers show whether or not they share one.

■

In his *Paris Lectures,* Edmund Husserl (as quoted in Douglas 1973:60) noted that:

Everything in the world, all spatio-temporal being, exists for me because I experience it, because I perceive it, remember it, think of it in any way, judge it, value it, desire it, etc.

But how does Husserl, or you or I, come to "perceive, remember, think of" something "in the world"? Childhood traumas, arcane arts, and secret perversions are not inconsequential, to be sure. But more commonplace interactive grounds are far more forceful.

Many social moments demand noticings. Try withholding one from a host who has renovated his home, a spouse with a new haircut, a man whose pants are on fire. As a friendly guest inspecting your home for the changes I must compliment you on (Data Segment II), I invoke and sustain, and require you to orient to, the permanence of objects, the durability of the place in which those changes have been made, and your continuity of personality.

Much talk quite requires reference to the world. To report about the world, one has to attend to it for just those particulars that the talk requires. The social forces that make us say "It's raining" or "There was a lot of traffic" when it becomes interactionally appropriate to do so, motivate and require us to perceive and experience the world in just the normal standard ways that sustain such hackneyed talk. From the ceaseless news reported by our nervous system we piece together the tried and true familiar stories. We search the luxuriant flux of the world for local variants of the pebbles we have learned to pass on to our fellows. We scan for and note all and (to our great loss) only the sorts of items needed to sustain the normal talk about the world that interaction will require of us: In America, the race and gender of conspecifics; the functions, prices and brand names of objects. The furniture of even our most private worlds comes from our culture's warehouse.

If you sneak up on your thoughts, you will observe that they are often formed not as language, but as speech: earmarked by such objects as, "we::ll," with just such transcribable stretches and intonations and, like every utterance, formed for some recipient. Much thought is conversation rehearsed and remembered in the head.

One Spring I was walking in the Rockies. The steady stunning beauty of that world, and a recent period of meditation, had quieted my mind. As I caught sight of a crystalline lake bordered in brilliant greens, yellows, and purples, the thought came: "The lupins're in flower." I observed that my tone of inner voice and the hinted smile of my facial muscles had formed that utterance for the woman I had left behind in Los Angeles. We loved hiking in the country together, and spring flowers. One component of our relationship was my reporting on experiences while away, my talking about them in the ways our particular relationship made appropriate. For us, this was a reportable experience. Part of my loyalty to her was inspecting the world in ways that would make visible the kinds of events she should be told about. I was seeing the world on behalf of another, my eyes working for her ears. An intimate intrusion of the social world, indeed. But what can any of us ever be except the local feeling and thinking embodiment of our biology, our culture, and our age?

■

Talk about the world is essentially talk, servicing and furnishing, as all talk does, the interactively organized occasion of its occurrence. In all talk about the world out there,

1) whether a reference to the world will be made now,

2) what aspects of the world will be mentioned,

3) what kind of reference will be made, and

4) what recipients will do with it

are the products of the current state of an interaction and always influence the next state of that interaction.

On the occasion at which Data Segment XXXV was tape-recorded, guest wife, GW, and her husband, GH, were visiting the home of their friends, HW, the host wife, and her husband, HH. The guests have a vacation home in the country which they had once invited the hosts to use. But when an old friend visited, they withdrew the invitation in her favor. At lines #11–14, GW raises this topic.

The transcript is only a skeletal score of this delightfully animated tape, but it does serve to indicate that the talk that ensues is "difficult" or "awkward." At lines #25–27 GW displays herself as not knowing what to say. The protestings at lines #31 and #32, and the high falsetto voice (line #32) show the moment to be a "touchy" one for both couples. Humor (traded at lines #39–43), a common device for resolving difficulties, reveals its essential vulnerability to being taken seriously. The awkwardness is ended by the noticing with which GW interrupts her own talk at line #51.

HW weaves. One component of GW's job of "being a friend" is to monitor, comment on, and appreciate the world of the other. The beginnings of interactions provide a standard locus for this (see the discussion of Data Segment II), but such noticings also occur at other moments: when the conversation palls, for example. Noticings are not immune to interaction's omnirelevant question: Why this now? Sequential analysis has found that[5]:

1) Noticings are legitimately interruptive.

2) Noticings about someone who is present make assessments relevant.

3) After assessments, agreement work is in order.

GW's suddenly calling attention to HW's weaving, with its sequential trajectory of assessments and agreements, sparks a new burst of talk that leaves the argument it interrupted unreachably behind. It returns the participants to laughing together, as friends should, and just as they were (at lines #1–5) before the topic of the vacation home was raised.

Berger and Luckmann (1967:18) propose that "The central question for sociological theory can . . . be put as follows: How is it possible that subjective meanings become objective facticities?" Is not the question perhaps sometimes answered by being reversed? By using a noticing to compellingly call attention to the objective fact of the cloth HW wove, GW gave it meaning.

By running after the hare of Campbell tartan, these two couples leap over an obstacle to their friendship. Where to place consciousness of this ploy is the analyst's decision. Piaget's recommendation (1954:xii) that "in order to reconstruct the subject's point of view it is enough to reverse in some way the picture obtained by observation of his behavior" is not an adequate basis for ethnography. But inspection of transcripts shows that conversants orient to, use, and in those senses "know," the sequential consequentiality of noticings. "Purpose is a mental construct imported by the observer" (Beers 1980:67).

■

In a passage cited earlier, Berger and Luckmann (1967:38) write that:

Language . . . refers above all to the reality I experience in wide-awake consciousness, which is dominated by the pragmatic motive (that is, the cluster of meanings directly pertaining to present or future actions) which I share with others in a taken-for-granted manner.

For language in use, this chapter has shown that "the pragmatic motive[s]" are critically those that pertain to the immediate circumstances of the interactive occasion. The "shar[ing] with others," although it may sometimes be taken for granted, is often, as in Data Segment XXXV, a locally sparked accomplishment.

Daily experience confirms their view (Berger and Luckmann 1967:21 f.) that "The reality of everyday life appears already objectified, that is, constituted by an order of objects that have been designated *as* objects before my appearance on the scene." Our examination of noticings shows that this appearance is to no little extent an interactive accomplishment. Attention and thus consciousness, and thereby quotidian and normal everyday reality, are subject to social manipulation and radical discontinuity. When someone, talking with others, suddenly evinces a startled reaction to the outside world, we know that, like Luke's full glass, he might not have seen it just now. We know that, like the deep green of Campbell tartan on Helen's blanket, it was summoned to our senses by the interactive purposes of its noticer.

The ethnographer's path that Evans-Pritchard (op. cit.) blazed by insisting that a person's "interests are the selective agents [of attention], and these are to a great extent socially determined" leads to fruitful terrain. When we replace the pioneer's rough assumption that "it is generally the value attached to an object by all members of a social group that directs the attention of an individual toward it" by the examination of actual talk that calls attention to the world, we learn that attention, while its range might be limited by a general biological and cultural program, is directed and focused by the compelling vagaries of face-to-face interaction. Such examination permits us to track the workings of social categories and relationships, to see how they are maintained, enforced, and manipulated by means of ongoing social interactions, and to appreciate how the commonplace cultural world invades and forms our private consciousness.

The World Talked About

Whether as prisoners or bold knights encased in armor, we live within our nervous system. Solely there do we experience objects and consciousness.

[A]ll that is accessible to the nervous system at any point are states of relative activity holding between nerve cells, and all that to which any state of relative activity can give origin are further states of relative activity in other nerve cells . . . (Maturana and Varela 1980:13).

Objects are *Eigen,* tokens, for functions performed by the nervous system and not *gegen-staende,* 'against-standers' out in the world.[6] Objectivity is conferred by discourse. When you and I reciprocally stipulate each other's independent existence and use some word, like "cat," or "table," or "salami" as a token for what we have experienced within, we take our use of the same word as proof that some object—the same object—exists in the communal space outside.

Reality is that which can be witnessed; hence, rests on knowledge that can be shared, that is, "together-knowledge," or *con-scientia* (von Foerster 1966:47).

Whether as Azande diagnosticians, Western astrophysicists, or bored passengers on a airport bus, we prove that the outside world exists, and agree upon its properties, by talking about it together in the same way. Such talk, like all talk, and such agreement, like all agreement, is socially organized on the occasions of its occurrence. It is governed by rules for talking, for behaving normally, for proper comportment. It can therefore never guarantee dispassionate accurate observation and reportage, never transform us encultured and engaged creatures into bodiless satellites cruising cool space with our sensors. Structured by interactive processes and guided by situated purposes, consensual statements about the world cannot be a touchstone of what the world, outside of talk about it, is like.

■

Peter Berger and his associates (Berger and Luckmann 1967; Berger and Kellner 1964) take it that individuals learn and internalize a view of reality that is stable, normal, and shared by the members of their society. The main process they locate is socialization through interaction with other individuals—like parents, spouses, religious leaders—whom social institutions make *significant* others. My view differs from theirs in a number of ways. By pointing to the compelling sequential organization of talk, culturally contexted conversation analysis straightforwardly describes the mysterious "inherent quality of reciprocity" which they (p. 37) ascribe to "the face-to-face situation." More fundamentally, noting locally occasioned discontinuities of consciousness suggests that one need not suppose that a person's view of reality is constant. It is subject to being re-called, re-affirmed, or re-constituted in the course of his interactions. This implies a quite different view of the individual, as well as of the culture. For Berger and Luckmann (1967:137):

Primary socialization ends when the concept of the generalized other (and all that goes with it) has been established in the consciousness of the individual. . . . This presents us with two further problems: First how the reality internalized in primary socialization is maintained in consciousness, and second, how further internalizations—or secondary socialization—in the later biography of the individual take place.

These are false problems. First, for their "maintained in," we can substitute "re-called into," and point to some of the conversational mechanisms through which this happens. Second, we need not suppose there to be a perduring individual whose thoughts and reality-assumptions are durably present in a continuous consciousness which must first have been fixed and filled by "socialization" and "internalization." Our actor need only know how to converse. More specifically, he or she must know how to talk about the world by means of such sequential structures as noticings, announcements, assessments, stories, etc. This approach makes it unnecessary to distinguish either "secondary" later life socialization as especially problematic or some institutionally selected "others" as especially "significant." Rather, as Halliday (1976:574) put it, "subjective reality is created and maintained through interaction with others, who are 'significant others' precisely because they fill this role."

Noticings, like all talk about the world, invoke a world and summon us to inhabit it together, to observe, sense, experience the same things in it. By such talk, we 'put our minds together,' and so form one shared mind. This is one of conversation's principal functions and principal rewards. Sometimes, by throwing out a world that's hard to catch, we press others into being especially significant by joining us in a special world. Not infrequently, a speaker actively probes and guides his recipients into a common cognitive domain rather than "tacitly assum[ing] the listener to be identical with him and hence as having the same cognitive domain which he has" (Maturana and Verela 1980:33). An ethnographer, literary critic, or other practitioner of the "documentary method" (Garfinkel 1967:76–103) who uses native talk to form a picture of the ordinary native's ordinary world therefore must take the specific circumstances of specific talk into account.

Consider the co-habited fantasy of Data Segment XXXVI. At line #22/3, B makes a somewhat opaque announcement: "opaque" in that A's take-up (finally delivered at line #28) is significantly absent from the pauses that B starts, and A joins, at lines #24 and 26. Absent or insufficient take-up produces more talk to aid and point (#s 25 and 27) the take-up that the speaker therein shows himself to be working for. (See Chapter Five, p. 76.) Indeed, A's successive utterances show a lovely gradation of minds increasingly together:

   (i) The "Oh really?" of line #28 is pro forma, showing only that its speaker knows that an announcement has been made.
  (ii) Line #30 both upgrades this, and gives it the more specific emotional tone,
 (iii) that line #35 (via the "profanity") further upgrades.[7]
  (iv) In line #37/8, A demonstrates substantive cognitive understanding of what the announced 'event' means to B, and claims ("I'm glad it didn't happen . . .") to co-orient to B's circumstances and feelings.
   (v) The sharing of B's place in the event is most fully shown by the language[8] A uses and the full event-in-your/my-life's history analysis she gives at line #40/1. She places herself in B's world of events, orientations, and attitudes.

This talk's blending of national tragedy with imagined petty inconvenience may offend civic-minded citizens. Members use public culture to furnish personal worlds. For all of us, when we converse, floods are excuses for being late to a dinner party, earthquakes in Guatemala a justification for postponing fieldwork, forest fires reasons for curtailing a conversation in order to call one's son in California.[9] Conversants are like birds building a nest together with whatever they need for the job at hand. The ornithologist must not be offended by them scurrying about for the locally requisite materials: a piece of string, a bottle cap, a precious gem, a bit of mouse dung.

Notice that the event that B announced and that A finally joins her in imagining never occurred outside of B's head. She, as behooves every American, has been watching television coverage of Robert Kennedy's assassination. She recognized the place where Robert Kennedy's body was now as a place where she once was. And she imagined her *then* to be his *now*, and absorbed the fantasy's implications into her private world. A, a decent friend, finally finds some sense to it. But the world in which time, place, and person coincided is entirely a fantasy, entirely the construction of one friend inhabiting another's imagination.

Yet they are not mad; the talk is not abnormal. Change the parties and the subject and it could be your talk or mine. It seems bizarre only from our privileged perspective as readers of a transcript. From the normal perspective of being the talkers and inhabiting a scene, we, like them, like any A and B, would just be talking about the world. The world talked about can be a *folie à deux,* or *trois,* or of as many as are gathered talking together. The world we unite our minds by talking about might not exist outside of the interaction that attends to and therein constructs it. And no amount and no kind of talk can ever make certain that it does.

Anthropologists have long been aware of this, but only as it pertains to the strange beliefs of exotic peoples. Since anthropologists, thank God, are human, our viewpoint comes as part of our culture. From *its* perspective, some realities are special, problematic. So we examine the psychological conditioning and social arrangements whereby "natives," rational folk like us after all, manage to believe in gods, ghosts, and demons, in cures and dreams. *Those* realities could not be self-existing; *they* must need some propping up by social forces extrinsic to them. But, as Frake (1980:336) noted:

Granted it can tax the anthropologists' ingenuity to make sense of head-hunting, the couvade, asymmetrical circulating connubia, and other strange customs. . . . But it is equally hard to understand how we do what we do all the time; conduct our daily lives. Anthropologists are beginning to discover that it is as hard to study one's "own" culture (if one can find it) as any other. The outcome of ethnography, then, is not to make strange ideas less strange, but to make the familiar unfamiliar—something to be wondered at and puzzled over.

We cannot help but find our own culture, or any other, by closely examining its talk. Doing so jars us into adopting a distancing attitude toward our own assumedly unpropped, free-standing, self-existent world. Our culture's reality, no less than Azande witchcraft, Dinka colors (Lienhardt 1961), or Igorot headhunting (Rosaldo 1980), is constructed by conventions of belief, and subject to interactive manipulations. Conversation's "magic power" (Halliday 1976:574) of "reality-maintenance" (Berger and Luckmann 1967:152) is us talking so as to put our minds together by building a world to co-inhabit: a hostile world we jointly hold at bay, or a lovely world of lupins that we need one another to enjoy.

As he stands tiptoe to stare with shock or pleasure at the intriguing customs and strange beliefs of distant cultures, the anthropologist should be aware of the bizarre, exotic, more than slightly mad character of the ground under his own feet. The solidity of everyday reality stems from the shoring up and re-plastering we constantly give it as we talk about the world and inspect it for the materials which that talk requires. Beneath our busy scaffolding there may be nothing at all.

Those who have lived in alien cultures have thereby often distanced themselves from their own. This may chill the easy solace and security that home provides, but it also confers some freedom and awareness. The world of daily life, when its conversational texture is closely examined, reveals its managed quality. When we hold up our own world for inspection, our faces are less ground into it, and our lives so made more spacious.

Locations of Transcripts in Appendix A

Transcripts and Transcript Notation

Transcript Notation

Turn-taking

| | Bounds simultaneous speech (OVERLAP).

= Connects two utterances that were produced with noticeably less transition time between them than usual.

(number) Silences timed in tenths of seconds.

(·) Noticeable silence less than .2 second.

\# Bounds passages said very quickly.

Sound production

¢ Falsetto.

TEXT Upper case letters indicate noticeably loud volume.

° Indicates noticeably low volume. Usually placed before the soft word(s), but also used to indicate the end of a soft passage. Two °°s means very low volume.

<u>text</u>	Underlining indicates emphatic delivery.
–	Indicates that the sound that precedes it is CUTOFF, stopped suddenly and sharply.
:	Indicates that the sound that precedes it is prolonged (STRETCHED).
,	The comma is intonational, not a syntactic punctuation mark. It indicates a slight intonational rise of the sort that English speakers typically take to indicate that speaker plans to continue his utterance.
?	The question mark, like the comma, is intonational, not a syntactic punctuation mark. It indicates a sharp intonational rise, of the sort used by some English questions.

Breathiness

h, H	An audible outbreath. "H" is loud.
˙h, ˙H	An audible inbreath. "˙H" is loud.

Laughter

(h), ha, hə	Graded laughter particles described in Chapter Five, p. 73.

Comments

(text)	Transcript enclosed in single parentheses indicates uncertain hearings.
((comment))	Double parentheses enclose transcriber's comments. But note that double parentheses at the left margin of Thai transcripts indicate dialect.

Thai orthography

·	Long vowel. Sometimes indicated by doubling the vowel.

Thai tones are indicated by diacritics over the vowel. Aside from ⁻, added for the high level tone of Lue and Yuan, they follow Haas 1964.

Thai phonemes

h	following a consonant represents aspiration
c	palatal fricative, something like *J* in *John*
j	palatal continuant, something like *y* in *you*
k	unvoiced nonaspirate velar stop, something like *cc* in *hiccup*
ŋ	nasalized velar continuant, like *ng* in *sing*. Represented in text by *ng*.
p	unvoiced bilabial nonaspirate stop, like *p* in *sport*

t	unvoiced postdental nonaspirate stop, like *t* in *staff*
x	unvoiced velar fricative, like German *ach laut*
a	back unrounded low vowel, something like *o* in *mom*
e	mid front vowel, like *e* in *they*
ɛ	low front vowel, rather like *ai* in *hair*
ɘ	mid back unrounded vowel, rather like *i* in *third*
i	high front vowel, like *i* in *machine*
o	mid back rounded vowel, like *o* in *hope*
ɔ	low back vowel, like *au* in *caught*
u	high back rounded vowel, like *oo* in *soon*
y	high central unrounded vowel

For the rest, as the old guide books had it, vowels as in Italian, consonants as in English.

Thai dialects

Dialect is indicated in the left margin whenever a speaker first enters the conversation or changes the dialect he/she is using. The dialect indications are:

((L))	Lue
((S))	Siamese (= Central Thai)
((Y))	Yuan (= Northern Thai, Kham Myang)

Thai syntactic particles

ASPECT	Aspect of verb
AUX	Verbal auxiliary
CLSFR	Noun classifier
CNJ	Conjunction
CNTNT	Temporal continuer
D	Deictic, demonstrative
EPNYM	Eponym
FTR	Future particle
INDR	Indirect object marker
INTSFR	Intensifier
N	Proper name
Np	Personal name
Ns	Family name
NG	Negative
PRN	Pronoun
PRT	Unanalyzed sentential particle
!PRT	Hortatory particle
PRV	Pro-verb, like English "do," "make," etc.
PST	Past marker
Qprt	Question particle
QTVEprt	Quotative particle
RCP	Reciprocal
T	Title

Data Segment I: "The Leper"

1   S_{((L))}   xa·::w   lē·:w: án: (·)   mǔ·   fá·lǎŋ   an   tī·::   (·)
                occasion PST   um   group   foreign um   CNJ

                 O::nce um: (·) a bunch of foreigners um from:: (·)

2   xá·w jǔ·   kúŋthè·p ā·   jǔ· tī· náj   hū   nī
             they to be Bangkok Qprt to be CNJ where don't know PRT

             Maybe they were from Bangkok. I don't know where they were from.

3   ma·   āt   tī·   à·cá·n bá·j nï·
             come record CNJ T   N   PRT

             They came and recorded at Acan B's.

4   (.2)

5   MM_{((L))} ə·|:::|
             O|:::|h

6   S |á·w| á·w   bâ· nɔ̌· xá·w xāp
             PRV   PRV T   N   PRN   sing

           |Had| had Ba Nɔɔ sing,

7   (.4)

8   á·w   ná·n dá·   pá·j   pǎ·w pǐ·
             PRV T   N   PRV   blow pipe

             had Nan Daa play the pipe.

             (23 lines of transcript comprising about 30 seconds omitted)

32   DO_{((S))} khon   thî·   nǎj   kháp
              person   where sing

              Where was the singer from

33   (.7)

34   DO   khon   bâ·n   nî·   ly̌·
              person village this   Qprt

              Someone from this village?

35   S_{((L))} ān– (·) kun–   ān tí   jǔ·   hoŋja·   tī   pō   a·ca·n
             um   person um CNJ to be infirmary CNJ with T

             bá·j   hân   nɛ

N̩   DMNST   PRT

Um– (·) a guy– um who stays at the infirmary at Acan B's there.

36   (1)

37   B((L))   ĭsa·

What

38   (.3)

39   B   wā   kun   xàp   na·
            say   person   sing   PRT

You talking about the singer?

40   S   mɛ̃n lɛ̄.

That's right.

41   (.2)

42   bâ   nɔ̆ɔ   nân   nɛ·
            T   N   DMNST   PRT

That Ba Nɔɔ.

43   WS((L)) bâ   nɔ̆ɔ   xî·   t|ŭ·t   nɛ|
              T   N   leper   PRT

Ba Nɔɔ the   l|eper. |

44   S |man | pín   kun   phājā·:t
                        PRN   is   person   sick

                        nâŋkăw   lɛ:.   bâ   nân   kɔ·
                        somewhat PRT   T   DMNST   CNJ

                        |He| is sort of si:ck, that guy.

45   B?   hmm

46   S   man   há·   jŭ·   káp   a· |ca·n   bá·j|
            PRN   usually   be   with   T   N

He usually stays with   A|can B. |

47   WS |bâ   nɔ̆ɔ | lū·k   mɛ̄·thâ·w
                          T   N   child   T

                          mun   bâ·nce·ŋbá·n
                          N   N

47 (cont.)   ⌐Ba Nɔɔ⌐ the son of mɛthaw <u>Mun</u> of
                                                    Chiengban,

48   nɛ·   <u>tá·</u>
                        PRT   T

                        <u>uncle.</u>

49   B   ə·:::
                        O::h.

50   S   bâ   nɔ̌ɔ   nân
                        T   N   DMNST

                        That Ba Nɔɔ.

Data Segment II

19   George   Hey: (·) the place looks <u>different</u>

20   Gwen   Y::ea::h   ((falsetto rise-fall))

21   Helen   Ya see a⌐ll ou:r new⌐

22   Hal   ⌐It doe:s? ⌐

23   George   Oh yeah. ⌐(Since–) ⌐

24   Helen   ⌐all our new⌐ things

25   (·)

26   George   Since we were here you: rear<u>ran</u>ged things.

Data Segment III

530   MM$_{((L))}$ (kɔ)   mǔ·   la·w   nî·   pín   pín   phá·j
                     CNJ   group Lao   DMNST   be   be   who

                     (And) those Lao, who are they

531   (.7)

532   M   °əm

533 (KP) (pun)

(Over there)

534 KP$_{((Y))}$ |la·w| phā·k isǎ·n
Lao section Northeast

|Lao| from the Northeast

535 MK$_{((L))}$ |la·w| phā·k isǎ·n
Lao section Northeast

|Lao| from the Northeast

536 (.3)

537 KP$_{((L))}$ phā·k isá·n
section northeast

The Northeast

539 (.3)

540 KP pun. sa·lākhra·m kɔ mi·:,
DMNST N CNJ PRV

From far away. Some from Salakhram:,

541 MK i·sá·n
Northeast

The Northeast

542 KP lɔ·|j::: ē::t|
N

Ro|i:::e::t|

543 MK |khɔ́·nkhɛn|
N

|Khonkhaen|

544 (·)

545 KP cha·japhu·m
N

Chajaphum

546 (·)

547   caŋwāt   cha·jjaphu·m   (nân)
                   province   N   DMNST

                   Chajaphom Province.

548   MM   °ó   ma·   mǎ·j   ā
                   oh   come   new   Qprt

                   °Oh. Have they come recently

549   KP   khap⁼

                   Yes⁼

550   MK₍₍Y₎₎   ⁼ma·   mǎj
                   come   new

                   ⁼Came recently

551   KP₍₍L₎₎   ma·   mǎj
                   come   new

                   Came recently

552   DO   °ma·   dâ:ⁱⱼ::ⁱ
                   come   CMPL

                   °Came° aboⁱu::tⁱ

553   KP   ⁱma·ⁱ   jə̄·
                                   come   many

                                   ⁱCameⁱ in great numbers

554   DO   sɔ̌·ŋ   pi
                   two   year

                   two years ago

555   (.8)

556   sɔ̌·ŋ   sǎ·m   pi·
                   two   three   year

                   Two or three years ago

557   (1.3)

Data Segment IV

149   DO$_{((S))}$ na·:   sèt   mòt   lέ·w   lў·
                       fields   done   all   PST   Qprt   ((fast))

                       The fie:lds are they all done yet

150   (.7)

151   MK   °nέ·   a·   ((The Lue repair initiator 'nέ·(ā)' is like English "huh?"
                      °Whae?   in generality. DO hears/treats it like the Siamese '(thî·)nǎj'
                                    repair initiator = English "where?"))

152   (.5)

153   DO   na·   thuŋlɔ·   sèt   lá
                      fields   N   done   PRT

                      Are the Thunglaw fields finished

154   MK$_{((S'))}$ jaŋ   khāp.   ((S' = Siamese syntax, Lue accent))
                       not yet   PRT

                       Not yet.

155   (.7)

156   MK   kǎmlaŋ   tha·j: lɛ̃·w   kɔ·::,
                      CNTNT   plow   then   then

                      We're still plowing: and then::,

157   (1)

158   KP$_{((*))}$ kamlaŋ   phyŋ |sàj   kâ|·:   nī   ((in CT, *malsyntactic))
                       CNTNT   just   PRV   seedlings   PRT

                       still just   transp|lanting |

159   (MK) |(hmm)|

160   MK$_{((Y))}$ sàj   kā·.   tham:ᵊ
                       PRV   seedlings   PRV

                       transplanting. Making:,ᵊ

161   DO   ᵊɔ·   (tham)   na·   plù·k   lў·
                      oh   PRV   fields   plant   Qprt

                      ᵊOh. You're doing transplanted fields?

162	MK	⌈khap⌉	tham:					
		yes	PRV					

⌈yes ⌉ making:

163	KP((Y))	⌈khap⌉	tham	pen	na·	pǔ·k	mōt	bàdě·w
		yes	PRV	PRV	fields	plant	all	now

⌈Yes ⌉   making only transplanted fields now.

Data Segment V

248	B	We need <u>sum</u>pin that's for sure.
249	A	ts Yeah we need u:h sompin that the other countries are
250		afraid of us yo⌈u kno:w⌉ I mean uh w– whe:n Eisenhower
251	B	⌊° Yeah ⌋
252	A	was in there he didn't do a helluva lo:t ·hh but by God
253		those countries were afraid of us he kept us outta war anyway.
254		(.8)
255	B	We:ll, so did Kennedy (·) Ja:ck,
256		(1)
257	A	U– Yea::h, We:ll, yea:h, but he didn' have mu– you
258		kno:w ⌈he wasn' in– ⌉
259	B	⌊No: he wasn' in⌋ :long enough.
260	A	⌈No: ⌉
261	B	⌊We:ll,⌋ it's a sa:d thing when you think two,
262		(.7)
263	B	l⌈ovely⌉
264	A	⌊Go:d⌋

265   (.7)

266   A   did |yo:u |

267   B |me:n| :with their brains knocked out, °I mean it's just°

268   °°a horrible God.°° It's just like a nightmare.⁼

269   A   ⁼It seems like a <u>fair</u>y story.⁼ I |couldn'|t believe it.

270   B |I hh |

271   I thought it was just like <u>Or</u>sen <u>We</u>:lls.

272   (1)

273   A   Yeah.⁼

274   B   ⁼·HH Well honey I'll say goodby to Bud ⁼ he's leavin

275 |an' maybe later| on you cn–

276   A |Oh okay honey|

277   A   Aw:right,

278   B   Aw:right,

279   A   Bye hon|ie. |

280   B |Is–| is Sam there with y|a |

281   A |Ye|ah,

282   B   Uh huh.

283   A   Uh huh,

284   B   Okay dear.

            (*Call ends*)

Data Segment VI

215   (M) |THRT| ((Throat clearing))

216   MK$_{((Y))}$ |phom| tham   xán   wâj   mōt   lɛ·w.$^=$ $^=$lɛ̄ |dĕwnî·|
                     PRN   PRV   boundary[1]   PRV   all   PST   and   now/then

                     |I| made a boundary[1] all around. $^=$And |then|

217   M |(°) |

218   MK   mi·   nă·n   phĭan   haw   nī   ā   nă·n   phĭan::
                  PRV   T   N   PRN   PRT   PRT T   N

                  Our Nan Phian, Nan Phian::

219   (.8)

220   MK   phan   sɛ·n   nī
                  T   N   PRT

                  Police Major Saen's son

221   (.5)

222   DO   °hmm

223   (.3)

224   MK   aw   lōt,
                  PRV   vehicle

                  brought his tractor,

225   (.7)

226   MK   xâ·w,
                  enter

                  came in,

227   (.5)

228   MK   thăj   ləj   thăj   tī   xán   ləj
                  plow   just   plow   at   boundary[1] just

                  and just plowed plowed right at the boundary dike.

[1]In lines 216 and 228, 'xán' = "boundary" in L and Y, but is cognate with S 'kha·n'
= "dike."

229		(.7)
230	DO	°°khap
		°°Yes.
231		(1)

Data Segment VII

| 1 | A | Did Varda tell you what happened this weekend? |

Data Segment VIII

| 1 | A | If Percy goes with Nixon I'd sure like that. |

Data Segment IX

| 1 | B | ⁼Did they get ridda Kuhleznik yet hhh |
| 2 | A | No in fact I know somebody who ha:s her now. |

Data Segment X

1	A	Heloo?
2	B	'lo,
3	B	Is Shorty there,
4	A	O:h just– Who?
5	B	Eddy?
6	B	Wood₁ward?₁
7	A	₁Oh jus₁t a minute
8		(1.5)
9		It's for you dear.

Data Segment XI

710   B   Oh Sibbie's <u>sis</u>tuh had a <u>ba</u>:by <u>bo</u>: :y

711   A   Who?

712   B   <u>Sib</u>bie's <u>sis</u>ter

713   A   Oh <u>real</u>ly?

714   B   Myeah,

715   A   ₁(That's nice) ₁
              (Sibbie's sister)

716   B   ⌐She had it⌐ yesterday. Ten:: pou:nds.

717   A   Je:sus Christ.

Data Segment XII

1   A   . . . well I was the only one other than the uhm tch Fords?

2   Uh Mrs. Holmes Ford? You know uh ₁the₁ the cellist?

3   B   ⌐Oh yes⌐ She's the cellist.

4   A   Yes

5   B   Ye₁s

6   A   ⌐Well she and her husband were there . . .

Data Segment XIII

1   A   Ya still in the real estate business, Lawrence

2   B   Well uh uh no my dear heart uh ya know Max Rickler h

3   (.5)

4   hhh uh with whom I've been 'sociated since I've been out here

5   in Brentwood

6   A | Yeah

7   B | has had a series of um (·) bad experiences uhh hh I guess he

8   calls it a nervous breakdown. hhh

9   A   Yeah

Data Segment XIV

1   TM$_{((L))}$ pɔ̄·n   pɔ̄·n   xá·j   kǎ·t   ā·
                   PRN   PRN   sell   market   Qprt

                   Do they do they sell it in town?

2   (2.3)

3   W$_{((L))}$ hў·

                  Huh?

4   TM   já·:   pɔ̄·n   xá·j   kǎ·t   ka·
             medicine   PRN   sell   market   Qprt

             The <u>medicine</u>, do they sell it in town?

5   W   ə·:.

             Yeah.

Data Segment XV

1   DO$_{((S))}$ à·n   nǎŋsў·phim   ɔ̀·k   máj
                   read   newspaper   PRV   Qprt

                   Can [they] read the newspaper?

2   M | hǎ |

             | Huh? |

3   DO | nàklian |
             student

             | The students |

4   (1)

5   à·n   nǎŋsў·phim   ɔ·k   máj
           read   newspaper   PRV   Qprt

           can they read the newspaper?

6   (1.3)

7   KP   ɔ·k   khap
           PRV   PRT

           Yes they can.

Data Segment XVI

1   KP((L))   dēk   kɔ–   m̂·   bɔ·   dâj   ma·   DĒK   nǎ·
                kids   CNJ   NG   NG   PRV   come   kids   PRT

                The kids (·) haven't haven't come. THE KIDS.

2   TM   ((moans))

3   (1)

4   MK((L))   y·.   páj   lo·ŋlé·n   nân
                yeah   go   school   DMNST

                Yeah. They've gone to school.

Data Segment* XVII

1   L   khy·n   nán   raw   dâj   sâ·p   cà·k   khraj
           night   DMNST   PRN   PRV   know   from   who

           bâ·ŋ   rў·   plà·w
           example or   not

           That night did you find out from anyone or not

2   mỷa   we·la·   naaj   kràsɔ̂·n   ta·j   sâ·p   máj
           when   time   T   N   die   know   Qprt

           at the time that Naj Krasern died, did you know?

3   W   sâ·p   cà·k   phûak   thî·   paj   ra·jŋa·n
           know   from   group   that   go   report

           I found out from the group who were going to report it

           (15 lines of transcript omitted)

19   J   lɛ   raw   rú·   dâj   jaŋŋaj
              and   PRN   know   PRV   how

              And how did you find out?

20   W   hĕn   phûak   să·m   sì·   khon   kháp.
              see   group   three   four   person PRT

              I saw a group of three or four people.

21   cù·t   takiaŋ   mâŋ,   thỹ·   fajchâ·j   mâŋ
              light   lanterns   some   carry   flashlight   some

              Some were holding lanterns, some carrying flashlights

Data Segment XVIII

1   MM₍₍ₗ₎₎   lù:·k   (·)   lù·k   pháj
                child   child   who

                The chi:ld (·) child of who

2   (1.2)

3   S₍₍ₗ₎₎   lù·:k
                child

                The chi:ld of

4   MK₍₍ₗ₎₎ |kê·w|
                N

                |Kaew|

5   KP₍₍ₗ₎₎ |kê·w| na·
                |Kaew|'s   PRT

6   (1)

7   lù·k   (aj)   kê·w:
                child   T   N

                Kaew's child

8   (1)

9   kê·w   câ·w   tā   nī   na·:
                N   N   N   PRT   PRT

                Kaew Caw Ta!

10   MM   ə̰·:
           O̰:h.

Data Segment XIX

1   MM((L))   mi·   só·n   thī·   thī·   hà·ŋ   bâ·n
               PRV   garden   CNJ   CNJ   tail   village

               There's a garden at the tail end of the village.

2   KP   °hmm

3   MM   °khɔ́ŋ°   khɔ́ŋ   pháj
          of   of   who

          °It's° it's whose

4   (1)

5   MM   só·n   mi·:,
          garden   PRV

          A garden wi:th,

6   KP((L))   só·n   pûn   ā·
              garden   DMNST   Qprt

              The garden over there?

7   MM   ə·
          Yeah

8   (1)

9   KP   ā:n: |só·n|
          um   garden

          It's the |garden|

10 MM |( ) |

11 MK((L))   mὲ·   no·n   xáw   pûn=
              T   N   PRN   DMNST

              Mother Non from over there=

12   KP   ⁼mὲ·   <u>no·n</u>   xáw
           T   N   PRN

      ⁼Mother <u>Non</u>'s

13   (·)

14   mὲ·   thâw |no·n |
            T   T   N

            Old mother |Non |

15   MK |tī· | xáw   pɛ́·ŋ   tăkâ·   nân   nē̄
                                CNJ   PRN   make   seedbed   DMNST   PRT

                               |Where| they've made a seedbed.

(13 lines of transcript omitted)

29   (1.5)

30   KP   m̂·   cā·j   m̂·cā·j   mὲ·   no·n   nî·   nă·⁼
          NG   correct   NG   correct N   DMNST   PRT

          mὲ·   no·n   pûn   ná·
          T   N   DMNST   PRT

          We don't mean we don't mean Mother Non here.⁼ Mother Non from over there

31   mὲ·   thâw   <u>no·:n</u>   me·   thâw   bun   lâ·   nɛ·
          T   T   N   wife   T   N   N   PRT

          Old mother <u>No:n</u> the wife of old Bun-La,

32   (·)

33 |mὲ·   thâw   no·n   láŋ kɔ̌·ŋ   nɛ·: |
          T   T   N   EPNYM   PRT

          |Old mother Non the humpback |

34   MK |mὲ·   thâw   no·n   láŋ kɔ̌·ŋ |(   ) |
          T   T   N   EPNYM

          |Old mother Non the humpback |(   ) |

35   MM |ə· ə· |:: (·)
                                             yeah

          láŋ–   láŋ kɔ̌·ŋ
          back   EPNYM

|Yeah yea|:h (·)

the hum–the humpback

36   MK |ə· |
             |Yeah|

37   KP |ə· |
                     |::|
             |Yea:|
                     |::|

38   B((L)) |(nân lē)|
                     |(That's right)|

39   MK   hmn

40   (9)

Data Segment XX

259 MK((Y)) man   kɔ   pa·j   thɔ·n   l<u>āk</u>   an nân   <u>ɔ·k</u>
              PRN   CNJ   PRV   pull   post   CLSFR D   out

             He came and tore those <u>posts out</u>.

260   (1)

261 KP((S)) O·:   chɔ·b   j|uŋ | î·   nî·
                    like   t rouble   PRN   D

             OH he likes   t|rouble| that guy

262 (DO)((S)) |(khraj)|
                            (Who)

263 MK |chɔ·b   juŋ |
              like   trouble

              |Likes trouble |

264 KP |(chɔ·b   juŋ) | tè·
              like   trouble   true[1]

              |Likes trouble | really

[1] In line 264, 'tè·' is Y

265   DO   khraj

Who

266   (.8)

267   MK   nî·   ɔ·   nǎ·n   phǐan   xá·w   nân   ɔ
             D   PRT   T   N   PRN   D   PRT

Him! That Nan Phian.

268   DO   phǐan   nǎj
             T   N

Which Phian

269   MK   nǎ|·n   phǐ:an :,|
             T   N

Na|n   Phi:an:,|

270   KP |h HH   ·hh |

271   KP₍₍Y₎₎   tɛ̌·   phóm   jaŋ   bǎ·   paj   hǎ·   câwthâw   nǎ·⁼
                  but   PRN   still   NG   PR   look   T   PRT
                  ((smile voice))

I still hadn't gone to see you [i.e., DO] about it⁼

272   (DO)   ⁼ə·⁼

⁼uhuh⁼

273   KP   ⁼tɛ̌·   wâ·   phóm |û·   (kam)| taŋnɔ̂·k   aw
             but   CNJ   PRN   talk   (kan)   outside   PRV

⁼But we |talked about it| on our own

274   DO |phǐan   nǎj|
                                        N   which

|Which Phian |

275   MK   nǎ·n   phǐan   tǐ·:,   (·)   phû·   phan   sɛ·n   nî·   khàp
             T   N   CNJ   T   T   N   D   PRT

Nan Phian o:f:, (·) Major Saen, sir.

276   DO   wá·:   °phûak   nî·   juŋ   ma·k⁼
             EXCLM   group   D   trouble   much

WOW.   °That bunch is a lot of trouble°⁼

Data Segment XXI

435   (1)

436   KP((Y))   jaŋ   samu   wan–   (·)   nân   na· |kan | thâ·[1]
                 like   T   day   D   PRT   if   if
                 Like with the accounts officer that– (·) day |if| if

437   (DO) |ə |
                                                        |uhuh|

438   KP   dyat   kan   tè·   tɛ·:   na   phóm   páj   hǎ·   (·)   câwthâw
             angry RCP   true true   PRT   PRV   go   look for   T
             we had really quarreled I would have gone to (·) you

439   pun   °ɔ̄.
             D   PRT
             [to you]

440   (.4)

441   KP   thî   lɛ·k   phúm   jɛ·ŋ   hŷ–   (.5)   ta·n   na   (·)   ta·n
             CNJ   first PRN   divide INDR   PRN   PRT   PRN
             At first I gave– (.5) him,

442   khɔ̌·   kap   phóm   ɔ́
             request with   PRN   PRT
             (·) he asked me for

443   (.8)

444   KP   phóm   bɛ·ŋ   hŷ·   ta·n   lɔ·j   nỳŋ·
             PRN   divide INDR PRN   hundred one
             I gave him one hundred.

445   (.5)

446a   hŷ·::   (·)   ma·na
             INDR   N
             And wi::th (·) Mana

[1] In line 436, 'thâ·' is S.

446b   (.3)

446c   tī   pin: (·)   phû·cho·j   han–
                    CNJ   be   helper   D

                    who was: (·) my helper there–

447   DO   hmm =

448   KP   = hã·sīp   na·   ha
                    fifty   PRT   PRT

                    = fifty.

449a   DO   hmm

449b   (.5)

450a   KP   ((clears throat))   lɛwkɔ   lŷa   nân– (·)   pen   xɔŋ   phóm
                                         CNJ   over   D   be   of   PRN

                    And so the amount left over– (·) was mine,

450b   lɔ·j   hã·síp
                    hundred   fifty

                    a hundred fifty.

Data Segment XXII

1   L   la   dâ·n   ỳ·n   là
            and   side   other   Qprt

            And the other side?

2   W   dâ·n   ỳ·n   nà   bà   di·   kháp
            side   other   PRT   NG   good   PRT

            The other side was no good.

3   L   rút   lў·
            broke   Qprt

            Broken?

4   W   khàp

            Yes.

5   L   à·   na·j   thɔ·ŋ   mi·   kì·   dâ·n
            um   T   N   PRV   how   many side

Um:, how many sides to Nai Thorng's

6   W   sì·   dâ·n
        four   side

    Four sides.

7   L   sì·   dâ·n   ná
        four   side   PRTq

    Four sides?

8   W   khap

    Yes.

Data Segment XXIII

1   L   bâ·n   thî·   raw   jù·   nî·   khǎw   rîak   bâ·n   araj   na
        village CNJ   PRN   be   D   PRN   call   village what   PRT

    The village where you live, what is it called?

2   W   bâ·n   hajlǔaŋ
        village N

    Hailuang village.

3   L   bâ·n   hajlǔaŋ
        village N

    Hailuang village.

4   (10)

5   jù·   tâŋtè·   (.2)   kə̀·t   nâ   lə̌·
        be   since   born   PRT   Qprt

    Lived there since (.2) birth?

6   W   kháp

    Yes.

7   (8)

8   (J)   bâ·n   mù·   thî·   nỳ·ŋ
          village   group   CNJ   one

    Village number one

9   W   mù·   nỳ·ŋ   khap
                  group   one   PRT

                  Village one.

10   (3)

11   J   sŷŋ   rîak   wâ·   bâ·n   hajlŭaŋ
                  CNJ   call   CNJ   village N

                  The one that is called Hailuang Village

12   (.4)

13   L   khăw   rîak   bâ·n   araj   ná ⁼
                  RRN   call   village   what   PRT

                  What is it called?⁼   ((said fast))

14   W   ⁼bâ·n   hajlŭaŋ
                  village   N

                  ⁼Hailuang village

15   J   ⁼bâ·n   hajlŭaŋ
                  village   N

                  ⁼Hailuang village

16   W   kháp

                  Yes.

Data Segment XXIV

1   L   thî·   bâ·n   phuhɛ·n   mi·   phû·jàjbâ·n   máj
                  CNJ   village   N   PRV   headman   Qprt

                  At Phuhaen village was there a headman?

2   W   bɔ̀   mi·   kháp
                  NG   PRV   PRT

                  There was not.

3   L   mâj   mi·   phû·jàjbâ·n
                  NG   PRV   headman

                  There was not a headman

4   (17)

5   tɔ·n   nân   a·   tɔ·n   kɔ·n   nân   phû·jàjbâ·n   jù·   thî·nǎj
           while D   PRT while before D   headman   PRV   where

           At that time, um, before that where was there a headman

6   W   bâ·n   thǎj   kháp
           village N   PRT

           Thai village.

7   L   ɔ̌·   phû·jàjbâ·n   jù·   bâ·n   thǎj   rỷ·
           oh   headman   PRV   village N   Qprt

           O:h? The headman was at Thai village?

8   W   °kháp

           °Yes.

9   (1)

10   L   lɛ   thî·   bâ·n   phuhɛ·n   mi·:,
           and   CNJ   N   N   PRV

           And at Phuhaen village there was:,

11   (1)

12   khraj:

           who:

13   (1)

14   W   mi·   phû·chûaj   khráp
           PRV   assistant   PRT

           There was an assistant

15   L   mi·   tɛ̀·   phû·chûaj
           PRV   but   assistant

           There was only an assistant

16   W   khráp

           Yes.

17   (6)

18   L   khraj   pen   phû·chûaj
           who   be   assistant

           Who was the assistant

19   W   naaj   kam
             T   N

             Nai Kam

20   L   naaj   kam   camlə·j   thî· nỳŋ |pen| phû·chûaj
             T   N   defendant   first   be   assistant

             Nai Kam defendant number one |was| the assistant

21   W |Kháp|

                                                         |yes |

22   (12)

Data Segment* XXV

1   L   ə·:   thî·   bâ·n   nân   mi·   phû·chûaj phû·jàjbâ·n thî·
          um   CNJ   village   D   PRV   assistant headman   CNJ

2   naaj   kasɔ·n   tâŋ   kì· khon   ná
             T   N   appoint   how many   Qprt

           U::m, at that village how many assistant headmen were there who Nai
           Kasern had appointed

3   W   sɔ·ŋ   (khon)   khap
          two   person   PRT

           Two (people).

4   L   sɔ·ŋ   khon   chŷ·   araj   bâ·ŋ
          two   person   name   what   example

           What were the names of those two

5   W   naaj   sàŋŭan   kàp   naaj   banthom
             T   N   with   T   N

           Nai Sanguan and Nai Banthom

6   L   naaj   sàŋŭan   kàp   naaj   banthom
             T   N   with   T   N

           Nai Sanguan and Nai Banthom

7   W   khap

           Yes.

Data Segment* XXVI

1 L | lɛ́w kɔ̀· pá phǎj
and then meet who

And then who did you meet

2 W | bɔ̀· pá phǎj
NG meet who

Didn't meet anybody

3 L | mâj pá phǎj lə·j ná
NG meet who at all PRT

Didn't meet anybody at all?

4 | raw troŋ paj bâ·n naaj kasə̌·n lə·j
PRN straight go house T N at all

You went straight to Nai Kasern's house

5 W | khap

Yes.

6 L | phà·n bâ·n khraj máŋ
pass house who instance

Whose houses did you pass

7 W | phà·n lǎ·j bâ·n kháp
pass many houses PRT

I passed a lot of houses

8 L | NÂNSI phà·n bâ·n khraj
exactly pass house who

FOR SURE! Whose houses did you pass

9 W | bâ·n naaj sàŋǔan bâ·n naaj phan
house T N house T N

Nai Sanguan's house, Nai Phan's house

10 L | ə̀·. bâ·n khraj ì·k
oh house who more

Oh. And who else's house

11 W | naaj lat
Nai Lat's

12   L   bâ·n   naaj   lat   phà·n   lǎ·j   bâ·n   ná
            house   T   N   pass   many   house   Qprt

            Nai Lat's house. You passed many houses?

13   W   kháp

            Yes

14   L   khŷn   tha·ŋ   nÿa   páp   kɔ̂·   khŷn   paj   bâ·n   naaj
            PRV   along   north   instant   PRV   go   house   T

            kasɔ̂·n   lə·j
            N   directly

            Went toward the north and went up to Nai Kasern's house straight away

15   W   kháp

            Yes

16   L   mâj   pá   phǎj   thî·   nâ·   pàtùu
            NG   meet   who   at   front   gate

            Didn't meet anyone in front of the gate

17   W   bɔ̀   pá   phǎj   à
            NG   meet   who   PRT

            Didn't meet anyone at all

18   L   phà·n   bâ·n   naaj   sàŋǔan   bâ·n   naaj   lat
            pass   house   N   N   house   T   N

            bâ·n   naaj   phan
            house   T   N

            Passed by Nai Sanguan's house, Nai Lat's house, Nai Phan's house

19   W   khap

            Yes

Data Segment* XXVII

1   L   naaj   kyn   khŷn   paj   bon   bâ·n   phóp   raw   lɛ́·w
            T   N   PRV   go   no   house   meet   PRN   PST

            phû·t   kan   na·n   sák   thâwràj
            speak   RCP   long   how   long

            Nai Kyn came up to the house and talked with you for how long?

2   W   mâj   khỹn   paj   kháp
          NG   PRV   go   PRT

He didn't come up.

3   L   jù·   toŋŋǎj   lâ
          PRV   where   PRT

Then where was he?

4   W   jù·   khâŋlâ·ŋ   kháp
          PRV   below   PRT

He was downstairs.

5   L   ɔ·:.   jù·   khâŋlâ·ŋ.   jù·   tha·ŋnǎj   là
          oh   PRV   below   PRV   where   PRT

Oh:. He was downstairs. Where was he?

6   W   jù·   tǐ·n   kha–   bandaj   khap
          PRV   foot   stai–   stairs   PRT

He was at the foot of the stai– stairs.

Data Segment XXVIII

1   L   prachum   rŷaŋ   araj   kan   là
          meeting   subject   what   RCP   PRT

What was the subject of the meeting

2   W   pasum   rŷaŋ cà   lŷaktâŋ   phû·jàjbâ·n   nîa   khap
          meeting   subject   elect   headman   PRT   PRT

A meeting for electing a headman

3   L   ɔ·:? kháw   bɔ·k   wâ·   jaŋaj   bɔ·k   kà
          oh   PRN   say   CNJ   how   say   PRT

         cha·wbâ·n   wâ·   jaŋaj
         villagers   CNJ   how

O:h? What did they say? How did they talk to the villagers.

4   W   bɔ·k   wâ·   wanphûk   ní·   câwnaj   cà   ma·   lŷaktâŋ
          said   CNJ   tomorrow   D   officials   FTR   come   elect

5   phû·jàjbâ·n   hŷ·   pha·kànma·   mót   nə̂·   wâ·   î·
          headman   INDR   gather   all   !PRT   say   QTVEprt

They said tomorrow the officials would come for election of a headman so you'd better all be there. That's what they said.

6   L

ɔ̂·.	hâj	ma·
oh	INDR	come

Oh. They ordered you to come.

7   (2)

8

kháw	hâj	ma·	thî·nǎj
PRN	INDR	come	where

Where did they order you to come?

9   W

ma·	thî·	bâ·n	naaj	kam	hǐakɔ̀·n
come	CNJ	house	T	N	first

To go to Nai Kam's house first

10   L

lɛ́·w	kɔ̀·	cà	paj	thî·nǎj	paj	lŷak	kan	thî·nǎj
then	CNJ	FTR	go	where	go	elect	RCP	where

And then where were you to go for the election

11   W

thî·	wát
at	temple

To the temple

12   L

ɔ̂·.	cà	paj	tham	ka·nlŷakkan	thî·	wát.	wát	araj
oh	FTR	go	PRV	election	at	temple	temple	what

Oh. You were to go to the temple for the election. What temple?

13   W

wát	phu·hɛ̌·n
temple	N

Phuhaen Temple

14   L

wát	phu·hɛ̌·n
temple	N

Phuhaen Temple

15   (6)

16

kháw	bɔ̀·k	rŷ·	plàw	(wâ·)	kháw	cà	lŷakkan
PRN	say	or	no	CNJ	PRN	FTR	elect

kì·	mo·ŋ
what	time

Did they say or not what time the election would be

17   W   bɔ·k.   (·)   lîak   kâw   mo·ŋ
              said   elect   nine   hour

They did say. (·) They said the election would be nine o'clock.

18   L   kâ·w   mo·ŋ
              nine   hour

Nine o'clock.

19   (3)

Data Segment* XXIX

1   L   lɛ́·w   we·la·   lŷak   paj   lŷakkan   jaŋŋaj
              and   time   elect   PRV   election   how

And at the time of electing, what kind of voting

2   W   tî·   naj   wìhǎ·n   khàp
              at   in   temple   PRT

In the temple.

3   L   ɔ́·.   mǎ·jkhwa·m   wâ·   lŷak   bè·p
              oh   meaning   CNJ   elect   type

Oh. I meant what kind of election

4   W   kháp

Yes

5   L   pɔ̀tphɔ̌·j   rýwâ·   láp
              open   or   secret

Open or secret

6   W   láp

Secret

7   L   ɔ́·.   loŋ   khanɛ·n   láp
              oh   drop   ballot   secret

Oh. Using secret ballots.

Data Segment XXX

1   L   âj::
            U:mm::,

2   (2)

3   ((sniffs))   bɔ·riwe·n
                       neighborhood

        In the area

4   (1.5)

5

khɔ̌ŋ	n·aj	krasɔ̌·n	phû·	ta·j	(.4)	nîa
of	T	N	person	die		PRT

tha·ŋ	dâ·n	nǎ̆ya
along	side	north

of Nai Krasern the deceased (.4), along the north side

6

man	pen	( )	( )	rý	man	pen	araj
PRN	be			or	PRN	be	what

is it ( ) or what is there

7   W

pen	pà·
be	forest

It's forest

8   L

pen	pà·
be	forest

It's forest

9   W   khráp

        Yes.

10   (3.5)

11 L

khon	də·n	paj	dâj	mǎj	paj	dâj	mǎj
person	walk	go	can	Qprt	go	can	Qprt

Could someone walk that way? Could someone go that way?

12 W

dâj	khrà·p
can	PRT

He could.

1ɔ	L	dâj

He could.

14		(6)

15		lέ·w	tha·ŋ	dâ·n	tawantòk
		and	along	side	west

And along the west side?

16	W	tit	bâ·n	na·j	kham
		join	house	T	N

It joins with Naj Kham's house

17	L	tìt	ka?	ryan	rý	wâ·	bɔ·riwe·n	bâ·n
		join	with	house	or	CNJ	neighborhood	house

Joins with the house or with the house compound

18	W	bɔ·riwe·n

The compound

19	L	bɔ·riwe·n.	MÂJ	thỹŋ	tǔa	hyan	kâ·
		neighborhood	NG	reach	body	house	PRT

The compound. It DOESN'T connect with the house itself.

20		pen	bɔ·riwe·n	⌐rỹ· ⌐	pen	sǔan	ka·
		be	neighborhood	or	be	garden	PRT

Is it a compound   ⌐or ⌐   is it a garden

21	W			⌐khap⌐	pen	sǔan,	SǓAN	MÁJ
				yes	be	garden	garden	wood

⌐Yes. ⌐   A garden, AN ORCHARD.

22		(1.5)

23	L	la	thâ·ŋán	ɔ·k	paj	thî·nǎj	dâj
		and	in that case	out	go	where	PRV

And from there, where does one get to

24	W	ɔ·k	paj–	(.7)	ta·ŋ	pà·	pûn
		out	go		direction	forest	D

From there– (.7) to the woods beyond

25   L   ɔ·k   paj   <u>pà·</u>
               out   go   forest

          One gets to the <u>forest</u>

26   W   kháp

          Yes

27   L   ɔ·k   paj   pà·   hǎ·   araj
               out   go   forest   seek   what

          And from the forest where does one get

28   W   hǎ·   thûŋ na·   pûn
               seek   fields   D

          Toward the ricefields over there

29   L   hǎ·   thûŋna·   dâj.   naj   thǎ·ná   khǒn   thî·nǎj
               seek   fields   PRV   in   position   proceed   where

          One can get to the ricefields. And from there, where?

30   W   bòkphan   khap
               N   PRT

          Bokphan.

31   L   ɔ·

          Oh.

32   (3)

33   J   ɔ·k   bâ·n   na·j   kham   kɔ   pen   thûŋna·   ná
               from   house   T   N   CNJ   be   fields   Qpre

          Beyond Nai Kham's house are the ricefields?

34   W   khâp

          Yes.

35   (3.5)

Data Segment XXXI: "Father"

1   L   la   raw   kɔ   lə·j   tɔ·nca   khá·   klàp   law
        and   PRN   CNJ   while   way   back   PRN

        kɔ   wɛ́   bɔ̀·k
        CNJ   stop   tell

        And on the way back you stopped off and told

2   phɔ̂·   mɛ̂·   raw   paj dûaj
            father   mother   PRN   also

            your father and mother as well

3   W   kháp

        Yes

4   (10)

5   L   phɔ̂·   raw   chŷ·   araj
        father   PRN   name   what

        What is your father's name

6   W   na·j   inta·   sɛ·ŋjaj   khap
        T   Np   Ns   PRT

        Nai Intaa Saengjai.

7   L   na·j   inta·   sɛ·ŋjaj   kháw   pen   araj
        T   Np   Ns   PRN   be   what

        What is Nai Intaa Saengjaj

8   W   pen   khru·   kháp
        be   teacher   PRT

        He is a teacher

9   L   pen   khru·   araj
        be   teacher   what

        What kind of teacher

10 W   khru·:

        A teacher:

11   (.3)

12   khru·   châ·wbâ·n   kháp =

> teacher   villager   PRT
>
> A village teacher＝

13 L   ＝khru·   jàj   khru·   nɔ́·j
         teacher   big   teacher small

         ＝A headmaster or a regular teacher

14 W   khru·   jàj   °kháp
         teacher big   PRT

         A headmaster.

15 L   khru·   jàj   roŋrian   nǎj
         teacher big   school   which

         Headmaster of what school

16 W   roŋrian   bâ·n   ɔ́·   khap
         school   village   N   PRT

         Ban Or school.

17 L   ɔ̂·   roŋrian   bâ·n   ɔ̂·
         oh   school   village   N

         Oh, Ban Or school

18   (.8)

19   pen   tambon   chiaŋkha·n   nâ lɔ̌
         be   borough   N   Qprt

         In Chiengkhan borough?

20 W   kháp

         Yes

21 L   lɛ́   wɛ́   bɔ̀·k   bìda·   khru·:   inta·   sɛ·ŋjaj   sŷŋ
         and   stop   tell   father   teacher   Np   Ns   CNJ
                                formal   formal

         And stopped off to tell your father teacher: Intaa Saengjaj who

22   pen: (·)   thamŋa·n   pen   khru·   jàj:
         be   work   be   teacher   big

         is: (·) works as a hea:dmaster

23 W   kháp

         Yes

24   L   mŷa   də·n   phà·n
               while   walk   past

               while walking by.

Data Segment XXXII: "The Cell"

1   L   tɔn   khăw   aw   raw   paj   wàj   naj   hɔ̂ŋkhăŋ   nâ,
          while   PRN   PRV   PRN   PRV   PRV   in   cell   PRT

          When they put you in the cell,

2   mi·   phû·tɔ̂ŋhă·   ỳ·n   jù·   dûaj   rý   plà·:w:
          PRV   suspects   other   PRV   also   or   not

          were there other suspects there too or no::t

3   (.4)

4   thî·rê·k

          At first.

5   W   mâj   mi·   °khap
          NG   PRV   PRT

          There were not

6   L   mâj   mi·:   (·)   raw   khon   dĭaw   nâ lɔ̌·
          NG   PRV   PRN   person single PRT

          There weren:'t (·). Just you, right?

7   W   kháp

          Yes

8   (4)

9   L   ⁄   lɛ́·w   tɔ̀·   ma·   lâ
               and   later   PRV   PRT

               And then?

10   W   tɔ·njen   kɔ̂   aw   phúak   mêw   khâw   paj:
          evening   CNJ   PRV   type of   Miaw   enter   PRV

          In the evening they brought in some Miaw:

11   (.4)

12   nɔ·n   dûaj   kháp
              sleep also   PRT

              to spend the night with me.

13   (1)

14   L   phû·tɔ̂ŋhǎ·   phûak   nǎj
              suspects   kind of which

              What kind of suspects?

15   W   phûak–   (.2)   nákka·nmyaŋ   nákthô·t   ka·nmyaŋ   (khap)
              kind of   political   culprit   political PRT

              Some– (.2) politicals, political prisoners.

16   L   thô·t   araj   ná
              crime   what   PRT

              What crimes?

17   W   thô·t   ka·nmyaŋ   kháp.   phû·   kɔ̂   ka·nrá·j
              crime   political PRT   person   PRV   violence

              Political crimes. Insurgents

18   L   ɔ̂·:.   hɔ̂ŋ   dǐaw   kàp   phû·kɔ̀ka·nrá·j
              oh   room   single   with   insurgents

              O:h. In the same cell with insurgents

19   (.5)

20   pen   phûak   (.2)   araj   nà
              be   kind of   what   PRT

              They were (.2) what kind?

21   W   nákthô·t   ka·nmyaŋ
              culprits   political

              Political prisoners

22   (.2)

23 |mɛ́w |
              |Miaw|

24   L |rú· | lɛ́·w   mâj   tɔ̂ŋ   athíba·j   hâj   thana·j   faŋ
              know   PST   NG   must explain   INDR   lawyer   listen

ǀI knowǀ that. You don't have to explain it to me.

25 na·j na·j rú· di· kwà· raw. ka·nmyaŋ
    T T know better more PRN political

    pen ka·nmyaŋ.
    be political

    I I¹ understand better than you do. Political is political.

26 mŷa bɔ̀·k rŷaŋ phû·kɔ̀ka·nrá·j kɔ̂ phɔ· <u>lɛ́·w</u>.
    when say subject insurgents CNJ enough PST

    When you've said insurgents that's already <u>enough</u>.

27 mâj tɔ̂·ŋ athíba·:j:
    NG have explain

    You don't have to explai:n:.

28 W <u>mɛ́:w</u> kháp

    Mia:w.

29 tè· jà·k cà sâ·p wâ· pen (·) khraj bâ·:ŋ
    but want FTR know CNJ be who instance

    And I would like to know (·) who they were <u>specifically</u>

30 W mɛ́w lɛ ja·w
    Miaw and Yao

31 L ə̂·:. lɛ́ khraj ì·k
    oh and who more

    O:h. And who else

32 W thìn

    Thin.

33 L phûak <u>thìn</u> mɛ́w <u>jà·w</u>

    There were <u>Thin</u> Miaw and <u>Yaw</u>.

34 W °khap

    °Yes

¹In line 25, because Ts are used as labels for co-present persons including speaker (see Chapter Three), na·j might refer to the judge rather than to the lawyer.

Data Segment XXXIII

574　　　　　　　(14)

575　MK$_{((L))}$　　o·:　　　bȳt　　　nỳŋ　　(nī/mi·)　　kun nī　　ma·　　lá·::j
　　　　　　　　　exclm　　moment　　one　　　　　　　　people　　come　　many

　　　　　　　　　lɛ̃·　　kan　　　((smile voice))
　　　　　　　　　PRT　　if

　　　　　　　　　Oh! in a short time, lo:ts and lo:ts of people will be here, once
　　　　　　　　　　　　　　　　　　　　　　　　　　　　　　　　　((smile voice))

576　　　　　　　xá·w　　hû·　　nǎ
　　　　　　　　　PRN　　know　　PRT　　　((smile voice))

　　　　　　　　　they find out.　　　　　　((smile voice))

577　MM　　　　hm

578　　　　　　　(1)

579　KP　　　　°ha ha ha°

580　MK　　　　ha ha ha　　|ha ha ha　　　　　　　|

581　KP$_{((S^1))}$　　　　　　　　　|xáw　　chɔ·p　　na|　　ha ha ha ha ha$^=$
　　　　　　　　　　　　　　　　　　　PRN　　like　　　　　((high pitch))

　　　　　　　　　　　　　　　　　|They really like him|　　ha ha ha ha ha$^=$

582　MK　　　　$^=$xáw　　pa·j　　tuŋ　　　|paj　　na·|　　bȳt　　　nýŋ
　　　　　　　　　PRN　　go　　fields　　　go　　fields　　moment　　one

　　　　　　　　　They've gone to the fields, |to the farms|. But real soon

583　KP　　　　　　　　　　　　　　　　　　|(　　　　　)|

584　MK　　　　kan　　h|û·　　pɔ·　　cá·n　　ma·　　nī|　　ho·:
　　　　　　　　　if　　know　　T=N　　　　　come　　　　　exclm

　　　　　　　　　once they know that Por-can's come, wow!

585　KP　　　　　　　　|(　　　　　)　　　　　ha ha ha$^{o|}$

586　　　　　　　(.5)

587　MK　　　　ma·　　thȳt　　thȳt　　lɛ̃
　　　　　　　　　come　　pell　　mell

---

[1] In line 581, S is spoken with an L accent.

They'll come pell mell

588	DO$_{((S))}$	nî·	lê·w	lɔ·:.			
		D	AUX	PRT			

And so::,

589		(.2)

590	(MK)	hə

591		(.2)

592	DO	(ma·)	khûj	kap	kè·	mi·	lŷaŋ	mi·
		PRV	chat	with	PRN	PRV	topic	PRV

|la·w| °àla·j kɔ
 story what CNJ

(Come) and talk with him about whatever subject or |stories|

593	M	|( )|

594	DO	°àlaj	lâ·w	hâj	faŋ°
		whatever	tell	INDR	listen

°there are just tell him about them°

595	KP	khap.

Yes.

596	DO	thùk	súk	dŷadlɔ́·n	àlaj	kɔ	lâ·w
		pain	pleasure	quarrel	whatever	CNJ	tell

Good things and bad, any quarrels, just tell him about them

597	MK	khap=

Yes=

598	KP	=khap

=Yes

599		(1.5)

600	KP$_{((Y))}$	an	pàwǎt,	pàwǎ·t	dâŋdə·m	nī (·)	pɔ̌	phǒm	ɛ̌·
		um	history	history	ancient	D	father	PRN	PRT

The histories, the old stories, (·) my father,

601 DO ˚mm

602 (KP)   hɛ hɛ hɛ   ˭pə̄·n   là·w   ha ha ha ha   tā·n   kɔ
          ((smile voice)) PRN   tell   PRN   CNJ

          |cōt| ta·m   nân   (ɛ/a)
          write   follow D

          hɛ hɛ hɛ ˭He told them hahahaha and he |wrote| them down

603 DO |˚hm|

604a DO   ˚mm˚   #lɛ́·w   kɔ·:::#
                  AUX   CNJ

          ˚mm˚ # And so:::#   ((# = squeaky voice))

604b (.3)

604c   a·hă·n   kankin   kɔ   jà·   hâj   (man) khà·t
          food   food(Y) CNJ don't INDR PRN   lack

          Don't let there be insufficient food.

605 KP ˚˚khà:p

          ˚˚Ye:s

606a DO ((clears throat))   mi·   ala·j   kɔ·:
                              PRV   what   CNJ

          ((clears throat)) Whatever it i:s:

606b (.3)

607   paj   hă·   phóm.   ˭tɔ̂ŋkan alaj   thî·   tàlàt   lɔk
          PRV   seek   PRN   want   what   CNJ   market !PRT

          come and look for me. ˭Whatever is needed from the market.

608 KP ˚khap

          ˚Yes

609 (1.5)

610 DO   khiăn   nâŋsў· kɔ   dâj.   ˚mâj   tɔ̂ŋ   paj   è·ŋ˚
          write   letter   CNJ PRV   NG   must PRV   self

          Writing a note is all right. ˚You don't have to go yourself.˚

611   (KP)   °khap
             °Yes

612   (.8)

613   DO   tɔ̂ŋkan   àlaj   cà   paj   sý.
             want   what   FTR   PRV   buy

             Whatever has to be bought

614   (.8)

615   hâj   lɔ̌ɔ·n   paj   °kɔ   dâj°
             INDR   ((Y))   PRV   CNJ   PRV
                      child

             °You can just° send a kid

616   (KP)   °(khap)
             °(Yes)

617   MK   hy   ((chuckle))

618   DO   phɔ́   baŋ   sǐŋ,   âj   ta·m   bâ·n   nî   man   mâj   mi·
             for   some   thing   um   follow village D   PRN   NG   PRV

             For some things, um aren't available in villages

619a MK   khap.
             Yes.

619b   (.2)

619c   mâj   mi·   ā
             NG(S)   PRV   PRT

             Are not available.

620   KP((S/Y))   tɛ̌·   pén: (·)   kǎ·j   pen   ñáŋ   mi·
                   but   PRV   chicken   PRV   what   PRV

             But as for: (·) chicken and things like that we have them

621   DO   ə·::.   jàŋ   nân   mi·   (à)   phya   kin   mǔ·   kin   nŷa
             yeah   like   D   PRV   in order eat   pig   eat   meat

             Yeah:. There's that kind of stuff. But to eat pork or meat

622   àla·j   kɔ
               what   CNJ

               of any kind

623   MK   hm

624   DO   bɔ̀·k   paj
               tell   PRV

               Send a message

625   (MK)   °hm

626   (1.8)

627   DO   khɔ·ŋ   khɛ·n   námsôm   námwǎ·n   àla·j   kɔ   dâj
               things   can   juice   sugar water   what   CNJ   PRV

               Canned goods, bottled drinks, anything like that

628   M   khap

               Yes

629   (4)

630   MK₍₍L₎₎   hy hy ·h   lùk   ká·j   haj   nī   no   ma·   no =
                         from   far   INTSFR   PRT   Qprt   PRV   Qprt
                                 ((smile voice))

               hy hy ·h ((chuckle))   You've really come from far away, Haven't you =
                         ((smile voice   ))

631   MM   = hə ⌐hə hə hə =

632   MK   ⌐hə hə

633   MK   = kamkín   kɔ   bǎ   xá·j   mɔ́·n   pə·n
               food   CNJ   NG   nearly   like   others   ((smile voice))

               Your food is hardly like other people's   ((smile voice))

634   KP   əm   hɔ́   hɔ́   ((high-pitched laughter))

635   MK   hm   mm

636   MM₍₍L₎₎   °û·   kɔ   ⌐bǎ   mɔ́·n⌐   pə̄·n°=
                       talk   CNJ   NG   like   others

               °My speech   ⌐isn't like other⌐ people's°

637   W |xâ·wtûm   xâ·wnúm   kɔ| |bá   dâj   kín|
                                  boiled rice   sweets   CNJ   NG   PRV   eat

                                  |Boiled rice and goodies | you|won't| get to eat

638   MK   = |hm :: |

639   kɔ   bá·   dâj   kín   lɛ̄   (no)   ((smile voice))
                    CNJ   NG   PRV   eat   PRT   Qprt

                    You won't get to eat, (right)?   ((smile voice))

640   MK   ((cough cough))

641   MK   mècá·n   m̀|m̀   ma·   ba   dâj   het   lɛ̄ |
                    T   NG   PRV   NG   PRV   PRV   PRT

                    Maecan hasn|'t come to make them for you |

642   WI((L)) |mè·cá·n   m̀m̀   ma·   nī. |m̀m̀   mi· |
                                 T   NG   PRV   PRT   NG   PRV

                                 |Maecan hasn't come. |There won't be any|

643 | ((noise)) |

644   WI   phá·j |hēt   lè | ::   ha ha ha
                    who   PRV   PRT

                    There's no::body to |make them| ha ha ha

645   MM |hm hm hm | ((chuckles))

646   WP((L))   kín   xâ·w   nŷŋ   lɔ̄
                    eat   rice   sticky PRT

                    Eat sticky rice!

647   W(I)   mè·cá·n   ma·   nī   hú· |:|
                    T   PRV   PRT know

                              Had Maecan com|e

648   KP((S)) |mŷ|a   ma·   khá·ŋ   lè|·k
                                          when   PRV   time   first

                                         |Wh|en he came the first ti|me

649a WI |xâ·|w tûm
                                                              |Boi|led rice

649b xâ·wnum hó·ŋ dâj kín nī
     goodie ASPCT PRV eat PRT

|Boi|led rice and goodies you could have eaten

650 KP khâ·w nĭaw kɔ– (.4) tā·n kɔ pòn mÿankan
       rice sticky CNJ PRN(Y) CNJ mix also
                        ((smile voice))

Sticky rice–, (.4) he mixed right in
         ((smile voice))

651 ha-ha-ha-ha ha-ha-|ha-ha ·hh| ((high pitched))

652 (DO) |hm hm | ((chuckle))

653 KP ·hh pon kan |khâ·w nĭaw| | (__)
          mix AUX rice sticky

·hh He mixed in |sticky rice|

654 W ((Off mike)) |KÍN XÂ·W NÉ·W| ba dâj hâ·n
                     eat rice sticky NG PRV CMPLTV

|Can't eat sticky rice |!

655 lè ka·= ha ha ha:, ha ha

                                 (1)

at all= ha ha ha:, ha ha

656 KP kɔ::, (.2) thî·lè·k phóm kɔ câ·:w na. wâ· (__)
       CNJ   at first PRN CNJ boil PRT QTVE

So::, (.2) at first I boiled rice, but he said

657 KP((Y)) o:: bɔ– (·) tôŋ câ·w. (.3) mi· anda·j
              NG   must boil   PRN anything

       kɔ a·w annân kă·
       CNJ PRV that PRT

O::h don– (·) don't have to boil rice. (.3) Whatever there is, I'll just have that.

658 ((S)) lên xâ·w nĭaw (w(h)aj) ha-ha-ha h|a:: ((smile voice))
                      (lə:(h)j)
        PRV rice sticky AUX

So I just made st(h)icky rice ha-ha-ha h |a::

659 MK |hhm ((chuckle))

660 DO
kɔ· kin jù· tâŋ pi· sɔ̌·ŋ pi· nī
CNJ eat PRV entire (Y) year two year PRT

tɛ̌·kɔ̌·n nā
formerly PRT

Because he had already been eating it for a year or two, see?

661 KP
khāb

Yes

662 DO
tɛ̀· |khon tha·j| la·w è·:ŋ khon phâ·k
but people Thai PRN self people region

kla·ŋ nā,
central PRT

But we | Thai people | ourselves the Central Thai,

663 TM | belch/moan |

664 DO
jaŋ kin xâ·w nɛ̌·w mâ·j pen lə·j
AUX eat rice sticky(Y) NG PRV AUX

Just can't eat sticky rice at all.

665 M
khap

Yes

666 DO
kin mâj dâj ɔ̄
eat NG PRV PRT(Y)

Just can't eat it.

667 (1)

668 DO
kin lɛ́·w mâj sàba|a·j ca(j)|=
eat PST NG comfortable

If we eat it we're uncom|fortable |=

669 TM |((moan)) |

670 KP =hɛ hɛ hɛ ((chuckle))

671 DO
pen jà·ŋ nán khàw ì·k
be like D reason more

It's like that for another reason too

672   (.4)

673   khon   mâj   khə·j   à
             people NG   accustomed

             We're people who aren't used to it

674 (MK) |hə| ((chuckle))

675 DO |khon| tha·j   tê·   tê·   na
             people   Thai   true   (Y)   PRT

             The real Thai |people.|

676 M   hmm

677 DO   (hȳ)   kin   khâ·w |nǐaw   mâj   pen | °mâj   khə·j
                    eat   rice   sticky   NG   PRV   NG   accustomed

             |Can't eat sticky| rice. °We're not used to it°

678a TM |((groan   ))|

678b   (1.5)

679 DO   JÀ·ŋ KHRU·   ŶA
             like T   N

             LIKE TEACHER YA

680   (.3)

681   khlu·   ŷa   sàj   wɛnta·   mȳa   khynnî·   a,
             T   N   PRV   glasses   when   last night PRT

             Teacher Ya who wore eyeglasses last night,

682   (·)

683   kin   khâ·w   nǐaw   mâj   dâj   lɔ·k
             eat   rice   sticky   NG   PRV   PRT

             Can't eat sticky rice at all.

684   (.8)

685 MM   ɔ·:

             O:h?

686 DO   ə́·:.   kin   dâj   kɔ·:   (.2)   sàk   <u>mý·</u>   sɔ̌·ŋ   <u>mý·</u>
            yeah   eat   PRV   CNJ   only   meal   two   meal

            <u>Yea:h</u>. He can eat jus:t (.2) a <u>meal</u> ((alternatively: a <u>handful</u>)) or two

687   thâwnân   lɛ̄ =
            only   PRT

            at most =

688 M(M)   = ə́·

            = Oh

689 DO   kin   pàcam   mâj   dâj
            eat   regular   NG   PRV

            He can't eat it regularly

690   (2)

691 DO   SȲKSǍ·   kɔ   °mŷankan
            T   CNJ   same

            THE EDUCATION OFFICER is °the same

692 M   hmm

693   (.8)

694 MM_((S))   kɔ·:   khlu·   ŷa   mâj–   mâj   chaj   khon
               CNJ   T   N   NG   NG   right   person

               phâ·k   nŷa   lў·
               section   north   Qprt

               But: isn– isn't Teacher Ya a northerner?

695 DO   khon   phâ·k   nŷa   tɛ̀·:   w– (·)   khon   phà:ja·:w
            person   section   north   but   person   N ((clearly
                                                                 enunciated))

            A northerner bu:t (·) from Pha:ja:w ((town name clearly enunciated))

696   (.7)

697   khon   phâ·k   nŷa   mŷankan   tɛ̀·:   m–
            person   section   same   but   NG

            A northerner all the same bu:t n–

698   (1)

699   kin::   jàŋ   châ·w bâ·n   nî·   °mâj   kin°
             eat   like   villagers   D   NG   eat

             but to ea::t like these village people °he can't°

700   MK_((Y))   khu·   ŷa   tī·   sɔ̌n: (.2)   lo·ŋlian   wìtthàja·khōm?
                 T   N   CNJ   teach   school   N

                 Teacher Ya who teaches: (.2) at the Technical school?

701   DO   mm

702   (2.3)

703   MK_((L))   pɔ̄   mǎ·j   kɔ   paj   sɔ̌·n
                 T   CNJ   PRV   teach

                 I teach there

704   KP_((L))   xá·j   lab   ka· |(pɔ̄   cán)|
                 want   sleep   Qprt   T

                 Are you sleepy | Paw Can | ((to MM))

705   MK |paj   sɔ̌·n| sǎ·n
                                         |teach | basketry
                                         |I teach | basketry

706   KP_((L))   tɛ̀·   á·
                 true   Qprt

                 Really?

707   MM_((L)) |sɔ̌·n   sá·n |
                 |teach   basketry|
                 |Teach basketry |

708   DO |SȲKSĂA | thî·   ma·   khuj   mŷa   khynnî·   kɔ
                 T   CNJ   PRV   chat   time   last   night

                 khon   myaŋ   phrɛ̀·
                 person   town   N

                 |THE EDUCATION OFFICER| who came and chatted last night is
                 from Myang Phrae

709   (.7)

710	°khon	phâ·k	nỹa	mỹankan°	khon	myaŋ phrɛ̀·
	person	region	north	same	person	N

°Also a northerner° from Myang Phrae

711   (3.5)

Data Segment XXXIV

1	Ada	What's ₎ne– ₎
2	Bea	⎸Well⎸I had compny Saturdee night 'n Sundee, so:,
3		₎Bud's₎ gonna play golf now at Riverside he's just leavin.
4	Ada	⎸Yeah ⎸
5		Oh::.
6		(.8)
7	Bea	So Katherin 'n Harry were spoze to come down las' night but
8		there was a death 'n the family so they couldn' come so
9		Bud's asked Bill to play with the company deal so I guess
10		he can play with 'em so, ((delivered without intonation
11		change. Sounds bored.))
12	Ada	°Oh goo:d.
13	Bea	WHAT A MISERABLE WEEKEND.
14	Ada	Yeah an' gee it's been beautiful down here.⁼I know yoyu've
15		had it– lousy in town⁼have'n₎cha ₎
16	Bea	⎸Yeah⎸ it <u>rained</u> yesterday.
17	Ada	But the sun was out here it was beautiful y₎ester₎day
18	Bea	⎸Yeah⎸
19	Ada	₎But it's–₎

20	Bea	|(What–)|
21	Ada	been <u>co:ld</u>,
22	Bea	I know it. ⁼I hadtu turn the furnace u:p, I tol' Bud my
23		<u>Go:d</u>, .hh <u>Oh</u> it's cold up tow:n too. It rained yesterday
24		morning till about ele:ven
25		(1.2)
26	Ada	I:t rained about uh:: le's see, Thursdee morning real |hard	
27	Bea	|(Yeah)|
28		(Yeah)
29	Ada	about five o'clock down here.⁼
30	Bea	⁼Did i:t?
31	Ada	Yeah

Data Segment XXXV

1	GW	ha ha ha |ha
2	HH	|You can tell it again if you li:ke
3	GH	No:
4	HW	ha ha ha
5	GH	It's not that good. heh heh
6		(.2)
7	( )	U::m
8		(1.2)
9	GW	But (·) u:m:,⁼
10	HW	⁼Ye|ah the–|

11	GW	⌈(as a) ⌉ #matter of fact ya know:,# the– thee– thee
12		uh My <u>gir</u>lfriend (.2) who u:m
13		(.5)
14		I <u>off</u>ered the house to in the count(h)r(h)y,
15	HH	°mmm?
16	GW	She has a– an invalid <u>moth</u>uh
17	HH	mmhm
18	GW	who's bed–<u>rid</u>den
19	HH	mhm
20	GW	An' they still haven't figured ou:t, <u>how</u> they gonna get
21		to the country⁼ who's gonna take care of her MOTHuh while
22		they'⌈re ⌉ y'know up in the c<u>ou</u>ntry on the weekends
23	HW	⌈mm⌉
24		(.2)
25	GW	So:: you know,
26		(.5)
27		An bes<u>i</u>des <u>tha</u>:t,
28	GH	You c'n go <u>any</u>way
29	( )	Don' don' you
30	GW	They won't be:
31	HH	No, there's ther–'s no no long explanation is necessary
32	GW	Oh ᶜnonono: I'm not– I jus–ᶜ I wanted you to k<u>now</u> that
33		you can go up <u>any</u>ways⁼
34	GH	⁼Yeah

35	GW	You kn<u>o</u>w,
36		(.2)
37		Because uh,
38		(3.5)
39	GH	They don't mind honey they're just not gonna talk to us
40		ever again
41	HH	huh huh
42		(.5)
43	HW	We don't mind ⌈we just⌉ never gonna talk to you ever
44	HH	⌈(No)⌉
45	HW	agai(h)huh
46	GH	heh heh heh heh heh heh
47	HW	So:: °that's awright
48	GW	Ya kn⌈ow that⌉ we're gonna # In fact– I'm gonna– (She/See)
49	GH	⌈( )⌉
50	GW	I haven't seen her# since I spoke to you but I'm going
51		to talk to = What a' you making?
52	HW	It's a blanket.
53	GW	Did you weave that your⌈s<u>e</u>lf ⌉
54	HW	⌈I wo:ve⌉ I wove this myself.
55	HH	She wove ⌈all of this ⌉ herself
56	GW	⌈¢Ya kidding⌉
57	(HW)	(No)
58	GH	No j<u>o</u>ki⌈ng ⌉

59	HH	|ʳThat| was a Ca– that was a <u>Camp</u>bell <u>tar</u>tan.
60		(.2)
61	GW	You're ᶜk|i:dding	
62	GH	|Ya kno:w,|
63		(1.2)
64		I looked at that an' I said to meeself, to meeself I
65		said,	that's Abysinnian if I ever s|aw it.
66	(HH)	¹(ha) ·
67	HW	|HA haha ha

Data Segment XXXVI

1	B	SA:Y gosh has– This is really been a week ⁼ha:sn' it,
2	A	O:h, it really has.
3	B	|It's real–|
4	A	|It's real |ly it really has.
5	B	I won't even turn the <u>tee</u>vee on.
6	A	Well I had it <u>tur</u>ned o:n when I first got <u>up</u> just to see how
7		things were progressing, but the thing was so sad an' all
8		that horrible sad music they kep– keep |playing| all the |time ya|
9	B	|O::h| |Go::d	
10	A	know.
11	B	They go on an' on an' on |with thi|s ⁼Like yesterday, showin'
12	A	|Yea:uh	
13	B	'em goin' in the ch– ·hh I mean so much I know it's sa:d, but

14		my <u>God</u> let's don't throw it at the public constantly.
15	A	Well, I think it's sad that they don't– uh, allow:, ya know,
16		the families at least the decency ˎof ⌐ having some <u>pri</u>vacy.
17	B	˥Yeah˥
18	B	Yeah in the church yesterday they– ·hh flashin' the <u>cam</u>eras
19		on 'em when they were there yaknow went into pra:y, an–
20		an' (·) Go<u>:</u>d, ˎJa–
21	A	˥I think it's˥ <u>terr</u>ible.
22	B	Jackie looked u::p, ·hh ⁼<u>He</u>y that was the <u>same</u> sp<u>o</u>t we took
23		off for Honolulu
24		(.2)
25		where they put him on,
26		(.5)
27		at that chartered place,
28	A	Oh really?
29	B	Yea::h.
30	A	Oh:/ for heaven saˎkes. ˎ
31	B	˥Exa_ˌctly. It says on West Imperial Boulevard
32		an' uh, they– I could see the building, an' then the World Airways
33		was uh, .HH on the side there, where it comes in⁼ an' that's
34		just where ((smile voice)) <u>we</u> took off.
35	A	Well I'll be darnˎed.
36	B	˥Yea:h. ·hhˎhhˎ
37	A	˥Oh:˥:, well I'm glad it didn't

38		happen while <u>you</u> were tryin' to get off,
39	B	O::h my Go:⌐d.
40	A	⌐God⌐ <u>that</u> would of been a mess you'ld a never
41	A	gotten ta Hawaii.
42	B	No, <u>woul</u>dn' that been some⌐th–⌐
43	A	⌐J<u>h</u> ⌐immeny Christmas. (·) No kidding.

Appendix B

On "Understanding" in the Analysis of Natural Conversation

MICHAEL MOERMAN and HARVEY SACKS

1987 Introduction

This paper was first read at a Symposium on the Relations between Anthropology and Linguistics in Honor of Charles Friederich Vogelin at the 70th Annual Meeting of the American Anthropological Association in New York City on 20 November 1971. Never published, I present it here because it is a good statement of our position at that time, and because it has proved to be a helpful introduction to the subsequent, and current, conversation analysis literature.

Conversation analysis was little known in 1971. It seemed necessary then to emphasize that there exists an empirically discoverable social organization of speech exchange that must not be confused with what linguistics, anthropology, and sociology had heretofore studied or assumed. I think that position has been established, indeed over-built, by now. The paper, like much early work in sequential analysis, tends to depict conversation as a natural phenomenon whose properties are entailed by how the requisites of a communications system intersect with human sensory capacities. For reasons I hope this book makes clear, I now think it is a mistake to study conversation independently of the languages, cultures, and settings in which it occurs.

We cannot know how Harvey Sacks would view this paper now. That is the least his tragic and untimely death deprives us of. Were *I* to revise it, I would give much greater prominence to its statement that "We are not proposing that what is called 'understanding' consists entirely of what it takes to accomplish proper speaker transition." Rather than "what is called 'understanding'," I would make the subject "the events that pass or fail to pass as understandings." As Chapter Three (especially p. 45) argues, "understanding" is variegated in form and content, situated, and negotiated. So are "speaker transition" and "speaker selection." "Selection" is too general, "transition" too non-local and impersonal. At various points in the course of an utterance, various others may be required, proposed, invited, or allowed to speak next, or discouraged or enjoined from doing so. And "next" can be "right now." Moreover, type of speaker, content of on-going utterance, degree of transition relevance, and placement of transition all interact. By laughing before I finish, you can try to make my utterance into a joke. If you wait until I am finished, you may be required to speak immediately next, and to do so in a way that will be heard as responding to my insult.

M.M.

■

It would clearly be impossible and unproductive to try in a single paper to report exhaustively on the theory, findings, assumptions, etc., of our work on the analysis of natural conversation. Nor would it be very helpful to allude to our few published results. Rather, we hope to allow you to position our work in relation to the disciplines with which this symposium is concerned: linguistics and anthropology. Our device for doing this will be to pose a problem obviously central to our common interest in language, culture, and society. Neither this paper nor our entire work to date provides a full and satisfying solution to that problem. But we do entertain these hopes for our work, and for this paper. First, since the problem is obviously central, merely posing it requires us all both to deal with it and to wonder why we have not heretofore. Second, that the problem suggests itself to us may encourage you to share our conviction that the field from which it comes is lively and interesting. Third, by proposing some key observations and sketch arguments, we hope to convince you that a good part of any reasonable solution to the problem, and to a host of problems affiliated with it, both requires and can be accomplished through the systematic analysis of the sequential organization of natural conversation.

The problem, in its first version, is simply this: Why do people understand one another? We pick the phenomenon "understanding" as the problematic object for a paper which aims to permit the positioning of our work because both disciplines have hung their fundamental issues on it: whether by anthropology's loose formulation of a culture as a system of understandings, or by linguistics' goal of accounting for the fact that speakers understand novel sentences.

By hanging assertedly fundamental questions on the notion "understanding," both disciplines make understanding matter a great deal. It becomes, at least to their theories, a formally central but unmotivated concern. If understanding also matters a great deal to the natural phenomenon which our disciplines study, the human capacity for society and for language, then all that we know about life in society would lead us to expect that elaborate aspects of social organization would be devoted to assuring its recurrent achievement. Note, for example, that food gathering and distribution, the preservation of public order, the acquisition and training of new personnel all matter in ways that can be seen as fundamental; and all are elaborately achieved by social organizational means. If understanding matters in anything like the ways that these do, then social organization is likely to be decisively involved in its accomplishment. Or, to take that expectation rather more seriously, were there not such forms of organization, the fundamental status of understanding as a natural phenomenon would be suspect. So our initial question: Why do people understand one another? can be reformulated: What forms of social organization secure the recurrence of understanding among parties to conversation, the central institution of language use? What forms of social organization get participants to occasions of talk to do the work of understanding the talk of others in the very ways and at the very times at which they demonstrably do that work? And what are the understandings which those forms secure?

A characterization of those forms of social organization, *for they do indeed exist,* will secure the status of understanding as a natural phenomenon, specify the work members do to accomplish it, and determine some of the interests and capacities which members must have as part of the social and conversational competence which permits their work, their accomplishment, and their commitment to them.

■

Let us consider a feature which we assert to be always potential, widely achieved, and theoretically fundamental to the organization of conversation, and some of its implications for "understanding." The occasions of transition between speakers in a conversation are manageable so as to have it happen without gap or overlap between the talk of different speakers that on both sides of the transition exactly one person is speaking. That is, even when more than two parties are involved, even when their talk consists of utterances of widely ranging length and composition, only one party talks on both sides of a transition, and there is neither gap nor overlap across that transition.

In asserting this as a fundamental feature of conversation, we are not ignoring the fact that gaps, overlaps and silence often do occur. But since we shall show that no-gap/no-overlap transitions require work for their accomplishment, that participants typically do bring this off shows participants to have the competence for doing that work. Further, it can be shown that gaps, overlaps and more than one at a time are violations in two serious senses. First, members notice, interpret and correct them as violations of those features. Second, many occasions of violation can be shown to be consequences of the very system that accomplishes proper speaker transitions.

We thus recognize that the notion of error or violation is often a weak one in the social sciences, for the mistake may be the analyst's, not the actor's. For example, we now all realize that the speaker who says "It's me" is not violating a rule of English by which he should say, "It's I." Rather, the mistake belongs to the grammarian who calls it an error. We claim for our work, but cannot show within the limits of this paper, that our description of violations can be established in the same ways as our description of rules.

Speaker transition without gap or overlap is a feature of the social organization of conversation, achieved always then and there. For example, participants do not retrospectively attain it by editing their memory of a conversation. They do not, in the first instance, go outside the conversation in order to report violations to referees, policemen, oracles, etc., in the hope that external agencies will punish the violators. There is, then, a social organization to turn-taking which has as one of its proper products that one person talks at a time. Achieving this product requires participants to encounter and solve at least two tasks: the collaborative location of transition points, and the collaborative use of means for arriving at who speaks after any current speaker. These are tasks which, on the situated occasions of their solution, are tasks of understanding. And participants so interpret them. They take failing to talk when one has been selected to and another stops as evidence of failing to understand what has been said.

The specific kinds of understanding required for achieving proper turn-taking are determined by how turn-taking is socially organized. For example, if conversation were structured so that the order of speakers and the lengths of their utterances were pre-assigned for whole conversations, turn-taking would impose rather minimal tasks of understanding upon participants. But the empirically found turn-taking systems of American and Thai conversation work differently. They work in such a way as to require that parties to a conversation do extensive work of understanding if their system of turn-taking is to operate as it does. Both employ utterance units which need to be constantly monitored for their completion. Both operate to select future speakers in an one utterance at a time fashion. And both, thereby, impose upon conversation participants demanding and identical tasks of understanding and of demonstrating understanding.

If speaker transition is to occur with neither gap nor overlap, any intended next speaker must work on understanding the current utterance so as to know what it will take for that utterance to be completed. Utterances must be built so that attention to them permits projecting their future. Participants must be trained in an ability to understand that permits them to use such information in a timely fashion. It is possible to design a system in which the work of such understanding would be minimal. A linguistic particle or other sign might be required to be emitted at some specific point before the ending of an utterance. Or utterances might have to be of some pre-specified size. But, in fact, utterance completion does not operate in these simple ways in Thai or American conversation. Roughly, both systems use an utterance unit that is sequentially analyzable for its possible completions, but in which the possible completions projectable at one point are modifiable in a rather large range of ways, such that each state of an utterance is *relevant* to determining what it will take to complete the utterance, but no state definitely forecasts completion with a fineness sufficient for proper speaker transition. Participants therefore are never relieved from current and future listening and analysis for the utterance completeness they must locate for that transition. In other words, the syntactic, intonational and—we presume—kinesic knowledge which members use over the course of an utterance to predict when it will be over yields them only a *possible* prospective completion. Such syntactic examples as possible sentences becoming embedded phrases or, in Thai, possible declaratives being given question particles or the option between using continuent and final particles at the end of phrases should make it clear that co-participants must attend to utterances over their entire course to do the work which yields understanding of their completion. Understanding completion requires, to maintain our syntactic examples, gleaning and using grammatical parsing with all the other kinds of understanding which such parsing implies.

In addition to the collaborative locating of utterance endings, any conversational system in which turns are taken one at a time, must have ways of allocating future speakership. Some formula which pre-assigned the order of all speakerships for a conversation might both reduce the chances of more than one speakership happening at once and assure that someone would be responsible to talk upon each completion. But the turn-taking systems of Thai and American conversation do not operate this way. Instead, they work one utterance at a time, employing an ordered mix of alternative ways by which next speaker is arrived at. Roughly, either current speaker selects a next, or—current speaker not selecting a next—first starter on completion gains rights to make an utterance. Even within these empirically found rules, participant work of understanding for who should or might speak next could be minimized by requiring, for example, that utterances which select a next speaker begin or end with some signal of unique designation, such as a name or social security number. Obviously, neither Thai nor American next-speaker selection operates in this way. Rather, information relevant to whether a next speaker is being selected, and as to who he is, is tucked into the current utterance in such forms and at such places that the current utterance must be attended to and analyzed over its course to yield an understanding of whether anyone, and if so, who, should speak immediately next and, sometimes, of what he should do with his speech. So, for example, questions make answers appropriate as a next utterance. Not answering, if one has been selected to, is a noticeable failure, as also is talking then when some other participant has been selected to answer. So all must listen and analyze in order to know whether a question has been asked and who has been selected to answer it. And in that, for example, both conversational systems have forms—like the American "why?" or the Thai-Lue "*wāāsáng kɔ*"— which select last speaker as next speaker, the requirement of such analysis both devolves immediately upon a speaker when he has done talking and requires attention to the sequencing of utterances.

Since it may not be intuitively obvious that sequencing rules are used to determine who should speak next, let us examine a further example—this one from a real conversation among more than two Americans. Roger says: "Ken face it, you're a poor little rich kid." Ken then says: "Yes, Mommy. Thank you." Roger then says: "Face the music." We are sure that you, like those present, heard Ken's "Mommy" as a deliberate and consequential misidentification of Roger, and not as an error, or as a correct identification of someone not present—Ken's mother. The hearing rests on our knowing the sequential relationship: an insult can get an insult-return by the insulted. Ken's "Yes, Mommy" is examined for whether it is hearable as an insult return. Since it is so hearable, it is heard as addressed to Roger, the original insultor, who is thereby known to have been deliberately misidentified as "Mommy." Hence his similarly analyzable "Thank you."

■

There are further formal properties of conversational sequencing, like topical continuity, that provide social organizational means and requirements for doing the activity of understanding. For these, as for the properties of one at a time and utterance-by-utterance selection of next speaker which we have examined in this paper, two points should be stressed again. First, the kinds of understanding required for conversational sequencing implicate and provide social organizational sanction for other, more conventionally recognized, kinds of understanding. Second, the elaborated understandings which conversational sequencing requires are done locally, immediately, publicly, accessibly, sanctionedly, and continually. We are not saying just that understanding is as central to a theory of conversational sequencing as it is to other theories in anthropology and linguistics. Rather, we are asserting that understanding matters as a natural phenomenon in that conversational sequencing is built in such a way as to require that participants must continually, there and then—without recourse to follow up tests, mutual examination of memoirs, surprise quizzes and other ways of checking on understanding—demonstrate to one another that they understood or failed to understand the talk they are party to. That a person is silent while another speaks and when another has been selected to speak, that and how a person speaks when selected, and at the end of another's utterance, are continually used to show whether and how he understood the utterance that selected or permitted him to speak. Typically, understanding *that* utterance requires, and so publicly demonstrates, that he has understood the preceding utterances upon the analysis of which, in turn, its form and placement was based.

We are not proposing that what is called "understanding" consists entirely of what it takes to accomplish proper speaker transition, although the inescapable difficulty of following a lecture or of knowing that one has been understood in giving one makes that proposition appealing right now. We can demand, however, that any forms of understanding which are said to be important be shown to matter as natural phenomena in conversation.

The instant availability of elaborate rules of grammar shows that our naive notion of how little the human brain can do quickly is wrong. But that such analysis must be done on an utterance just to take care of speaker transition, and must be done under severe time limits, may constrain the other understandings that can be pulled out of an utterance, the procedures used to extract such understandings, and what a speaker can put into an utterance for others to pull out. We suggest that the forms of understanding that demonstrably matter as natural phenomena might profitably be used to constrain the forms of understanding that matter as problematic objects of research in anthropology and linguistics.

Notes

CHAPTER ONE

1. This chapter was stimulated by comments made at seminar presentations at the University of Sydney and the Australian National University, has benefited from conversations with Matthew Ciolek, Lawrence Cromwell, and Anthony Diller, and from criticism by Bruce Kapferer, Roger Keesing, Paul Kroskrity, Peter Wilson, and Michael Young.

2. The sufis say that when a sage walks by a pickpocket, the pickpocket doesn't know who walked by, since he sees only pockets.

3. The exemplary research of Adam Kendon (1977) and of the Goodwins (1979, 1980) demonstrates the interpenetration of the verbal with the non-verbal, the heard with the seen.

4. Little conversation analysis has been done, and still less published, on "exotic" materials. Gail Jefferson has examined British conversation, Atkinson and Drew (1979) British courtroom talk. For the Mayan languages, Irene Daden (1982) has described Quiché bargaining, Penelope Brown is working on Tzeltzal litigation, and John Haviland on Tzoltzil. Stephen Levinson is investigating Tamil. I (1972, 1977) have written about Thai.

5. This proposal is not exclusively mine. Schegloff (in press) shows an interesting correspondence between pecularities of the organization of repair on the island of Tuvalua and what Niko Besnier reports about Tuvaluan values and expectations.

6. In "Finding Life in Dry Dust" 's analysis of overlaps.

7. In "Motives in Action" 's analysis of person-reference repairs.

8. In Chapter Five.

9. See Appendix B.

10. Ervin-Tripp's (1974:268–9) definition of "microsociolinguistics."

11. Bauman and Sherzer's (1975:96) characterization of "the ethnography of speaking."

12. To quote from *Discourse Structures* (Gumperz 1982):

> [I]nterpretation at the level of conversation is a function of an inferential process that has as its input syntactic, lexical, and prosodic knowledge (p. 117).

> Prosodic cues . . . carry some of the weight of selecting among a variety of possible interpretations by directing the listener among shades of meaning inherent in the semantic range of the words used (p. 104).

> Where an utterance is syntactically ambiguous, tone groupings can function to provide information that is not otherwise available through lexical content (p. 110).

The paralinguistic phenomena that make the third of our basic categories of prosodic signs tend to be regarded as basically emotive or expressive in nature (p. 113).

13. Appendix A lists transcript conventions and describes the phenomena they record.

14. Some of the ways in which my presence undeliberately and unconsciously influenced the talk at a scene at which I was present are discussed in Chapter Five.

15. Much of Schegloff's work on overlap is still unpublished. "Finding Life in Dry Dust" makes use of his lectures to undergraduate courses at UCLA.

16. Chapter Three presents findings based on re-transcribing to standards required by new discoveries.

17. It would be intriguing to have actors play a scene for which a conversation transcript was the script, record their performance on videotape or film, and compare it to the record of the original interaction. This could tell us about relations among words, voice, and bodies that hold (or fail to) among the members of a society, across societies, and between the conventions of drama and of real life.

18. Fieldwork and equipment were supported by a grant from the Committee on Research of the Academic Senate of UCLA; transcription and preliminary analysis by the Air Force Office of Scientific Research (Research Grants #66-1167 & 68-1428).

19. Fieldwork was supported by the National Science Foundation.

20. For a fuller description of local history and ethnicity see Moerman 1965, 1967, 1968:12–14. Chapter Five, pp. 70–71, provides more information on dialect use.

CHAPTER TWO

1. This chapter began as talks presented at the Naropa Institute Summer Science Program that were later polished by alert attention and criticism from colleagues at Tsukuba, Kyoto, and Mindanao State Universities, and at the University of the Ryukyus. I am grateful to the Committee on Research of the Academic Senate of UCLA for its support of my 1979 trip to Asia. It is a pleasure to thank Professors Masori Higa of Tsukuba, Yoneo Ishii and Yukata Tani of Kyoto, Yabiku Hiroshi of the University of the Ryukus, and Fred Tiamson of Mindanao for their hospitality and intellectual stimulation.

The chapter's next appearance was at the Santa Barbara Arts Council's 1981 Conference on Creativity. A much modified version was read to the joint Annual Meetings of the Australian Anthropological, Linguistics, and Applied Linguistics Associations at Canberra in 1981. This was revised for seminar presentations at the University of Adelaide, the University of Western Australia, and UCLA. I am grateful for the hospitality of those universities, and especially to Professors Basil Sansom and Adrian Peace. Participants' comments on those occasions moved this chapter toward its present form. It is largely the vagaries of memory which select N. Anderson, K. Anderson-Levitt, J. Dwyer, P. Fitzhenry, J. Irvine, B. Kapferer, D. Kerman, R. Kirsner, B. LeMaster, L. Miller, A. Peace, J. R. Ross, B. Sansom, E. Schegloff, M. Silverstein, and G. Wijeyewardene for individual thanks. For the kindness and acuity for their detailed written comments, I am pleased to be able to thank Jack Bilmes, Penelope Brown, Kathryn Cleland, Lawrence Cromwell, Joseph Goguen, John Haviland, Roger Keesing, Ken Liberman, Charlotte Linde, Francesca Merlin, Emanual Schegloff and Michael Young.

2. Overlap is recorded on a transcript by vertical bars marking its onset and its end. See Appendix A.

3. My phrasing stumbles with overuse of the word "possibly." It is a reminder that a turn, no less than any other conversational event, is an interactive accomplishment and therefore negotiated, contingent, etc. My ticket and excuse for climbing aboard your ongoing

utterance is my claim to have heard that you were ending. But you might keep on going, therein claiming that I heard you wrong.

4. I report this as an ethnographer familiar with this community and its people. But a conversation analyst could see from the (translated) transcript that the speaker assumed his recipients would know and recognize the persons he referred to. Chapter Three demonstrates that the sequential organization of references to non-present persons is the same in Thai and American conversation. In terms of that organization, reference is done here by means of non-try-marked recognitional labels. These make recognition relevant and assume that it will be accomplished. The issue of using conversation analysis as an ethnographic discovery procedure will be returned to in Chapters Four and Five.

5. The translation is lexically and syntactically correct, but the Thai question is somewhat more an attempt to recognize and identify its referent than, "Where was the singer from?" would be in American talk.

6. Sealing wax, crocodiles, cabbages, and kings—in principle an infinite number of things are absent at this, and every, moment. One of the strengths of conversation analysis is its capacity to recognize what is *significantly* absent.

The best published description of "adjacency pairs" can be found in Schegloff and Sacks 1973. The direction in which the concept must be reformulated is indicated in Pomerantz 1978, note 6.

7. Dr. Gehan Wijeyewardene, whose command of Myang dialect is better than mine, found this an unusual translation for /nângkǎw lɛ/, although not inadmissible. A standard justification for a divergent translation would be to point out that Myang and Lue are different dialects, and that I "own" Lue, as does S, who is speaking it. But such a claim is based on the very views of culture, language, meaning, and ethnography than this book challenges: that a culture is a coherent single system of meanings encoded in a language. It is better to point to the particular occurrence and to procedures. The particular occurrence is the one I have described: these very people at this very scene. My procedure was to transcribe and translate along with a native Lue speaker (Mr. Dheerawattana Wongyai) from the district where the recordings were made. While we were listening to line #44, I asked him, "nângkǎw lɛ?" He answered (in Thai), "It means the same as *myǎnkan* in Siamese."

Making public use of conversational data requires and enables ethnographers to justify the translations upon which all their reports are based. This is of priceless, although admittedly costly, benefit to ethnography. Ethnographers must accord native talk no less respect than literary translators, classicists, and biblical scholars give their materials.

8. "Obliterative" is a social, not a mechanical or acoustic matter. Conversants sometime show themselves (and so may always be able) to understand overlapped speech.

9. Chapter Six develops some ways in which noticing is a social, not a perceptual, event.

10. Hence the title of the major paper on this subject (Schegloff, et al. 1977), "The preference for self-correction . . .".

11. In conversation transcripts (see Appendix A), single parentheses enclose words not heard clearly. These might sometimes be noises other than words, as well as words other than the ones the transcriber hears.

12. One difficulty with the notion of "adjacency *pairs*" is that the conversationally coordinated unit is sometimes a triplet rather than a pair (see Jefferson and Schenkein 1977). In some environments, the standard, perhaps normative, sequence is:

1 A: First part of paired action
2 B: Second part of paired action
3 A: Token of acknowledgement, agreement, understanding, etc. (e.g., "Uh huh, "thanks," etc.).

An environment especially rich in such third turns is after a second pair-part that follows an inserted repair sequence. Participants in Segment IV might have expected, and so found missing, some token of understanding from DO at line #155. MK's #156 is ambiguous as evidence for his understanding of #155. As an expansion (i.e., repair) of his answer at #154, #156 is a typical object after an insufficient show of understanding. But it is also a standard way of moving into talk on the topic that the asker of a question proposed.

13. The reader of V:279–80 can note both how the turn gained by (re-cycled) overlap can be used for new business, and that ending talk even after such leave-takings as #276–9, like all conversational events, is negotiated, contingent, and without guarantees (see Schegloff and Sacks 1973).

14. Chapter Three returns to the tension between the natural and cultural modes of conversation, Chapter Four to the actor's place in embodying and resolving it.

15. Coming to agree, and therein replicating a pattern that other transcripts show to characterize their relationship.

16. Chapter Five returns to this issue.

CHAPTER THREE

1. Correspondence of sequential organization between Thai and American references to persons was first reported at the Annual Meetings of the American Anthropological Association in 1975. An incoherent version of this chapter was then presented at the Social Science Research Council/British Sociological Association International Conference on Practical Reasoning and Discourse Processes held at St. Hugh's College, Oxford in 1979. For their kindness on that occasion, I am pleased to be able to thank the SSRC and the BSA, St. Hugh's, and Dr. J. Maxwell Atkinson.

The subsequent presentations were seminars at The University of Adelaide (where Prof. Bruce Kapferer and Dr. Roy Fitzhenry, especially, helped me to discover what I was trying to say), at the Australian National University, at Sydney University, at the International Workshop at the Australian National University with which our Working Group on Language in Social and Cultural Context ended its program in July of 1982, and at UCLA in November 1982. I am sure that I omit many when I note my appreciation of the comments of Alton Becker, Lawrence Cromwell, John Gumperz, John Haviland, and Roger Keesing. For their written comments and suggestions, I am grateful to Nancy Anderson, Anthony Diller, John Haviland, Roger Keesing, Katie Anderson-Levitt, Daniel Kerman, Laura Miller and Jean Wong. This chapter and I have both benefited from the challenging yet sympathetic comments of Emanuel Schegloff.

2. Sacks and Schegloff 1979's domain of data is *initial* references to *non-present* persons. I, too, will concentrate on these but, like them, make use of the phrase "reference to persons" for ease of exposition. In English conversation, non-initial references usually make use of pronouns.

3. Universality was first claimed in Sacks, et al.'s canonical paper on turn-taking (1974, note 10) and given substance by Daden 1982 for Quiché, a Mayan language, and by Moerman 1977 for Thai.

4. The quotations and the formulation come from Stephen Toulmin's insightful review (1978) of Vygotsky.

5. As this chapter develops, so will the ways in which my sense of "preference," "form," "reference occasion," and of conversational rules and principles differs from theirs. Where they speak of forms, I see ways of making specific interactional tasks relevant or irrelevant, ways of proposing that an interactional task—here, identifying an individual—be done. But I will use their words and gradually stuff my meanings into them.

6. A host of issues concerning types of talk, speakers, populations, occasions, etc.

hides under the convenient label of "American (sic!) conversation (sic!)" for a corpus of transcripts.

7. The term "one-bit" is not from Sacks and Schegloff 1979. I use it to emphasize, as further evidence of minimization, that although a very long series of descriptors *could*, in principle, be used, only one item for referent indentification is preferred.

8. So, for example, a student of "criticisms" (e.g., "You forgot to buy coffee.") should also collect "suggestions" (e.g., "A shopping list can be helpful.") and conjoint "complaints" (e.g., "The shops are really confusing this time of year.").

9. In the course of examining these materials, whether as ethnographers or as conversation analysts, we will have to consider both how equivalent and how representative they are. Thai lawyer-client conversation is presumably at least as special-purpose and as power-biased as such talk is in America. Chapter Four, pp. 50–53 describes how turn-taking in Thai courtroom testimony differs from conversation.

10. Lines 39 and 37 of "The Leper" (Data Segment I) were a prior instance of this. Chapter Two also presented descriptions of overlap and of repair insertions. The claim, or offer, or dare made in Chapter One is always on the table. Every line of every transcript may be examined to see whether it contains an instance of a described conversational phenomenon, like "overlap," "adjacency pair," "repair." If it does, that newly encountered instance should behave as the description says it does.

11. Not only did people come and go during the recording, but those physically present drifted in and out of the conversation. Women were occasional participants, but often engaged in business of their own.

12. If try-making is done in Thai talk with any device other than just leaving a pause after a recognitional label, some of the devices that may be used are:

1) stretching the last continuant (e.g., the /:/s of /phǐan:/ [VI:218] and /kɛ·w/ [XVIII:7]);

2) pairing the particle /nǐ/, usually phrase-final, with the particle /ā/ which usually marks a question (Segment VI:218). /nǐ ā/ seems generally to promise more talk by its speaker.

13. Chapter Four develops what I mean by "motivated." Here it is enough to stipulate that I do not mean conscious, planned, or deliberate in the usual senses of those words.

14. Sacks and Schegloff's 1979 use of "preference" relies upon such formulations as "*massively* accomplished," "*maximum* exploitation," "*overwhelmingly* used," and "*heavy* use" (pp. 17, f., emphases added). This assumes that recognitional forms vs. non-recognitional forms are exhaustive alternatives, and that the incidence of the two has been compared and measured. But there are many ways to talk, other than using a specifically non-recognitional form, that do not make identification relevant. The set of "non-recognitional forms" whose frequency can be compared with that of recognitional forms is thus not very meaningful. A speaker can use the passive voice, for example. In Data Segment V, had B asked "Are you alone?" rather than "Is Sam there with you?" (line #280), identification would have been made irrelevant by the verbal phrase without the use of a non-recognitional form. At Data Segment XXXIV, line #3, Bea's "Bud's gonna play golf now at Riverside" makes the identification of his golf partners irrelevant without using such a non-recognitional form as "with some guys."

15. My Thai corpus is smaller than the American one. I presume that this may be why I have not encountered in it such major evidence of a "preference" for recognitional "forms" as:

> A nonrecognitional having been done, recipient may find from other resources in the talk that he might know the referred-to, while seeing that the speaker need not have supposed that he would. He may then seek to confirm his suspicion by offering the name or by asking for it, characteristically offering some basis for independently knowing the referred-to (p. 17).

If I encounter instances of a recipient proposing that the work of recognition be done for a referent person whom he had previously let pass unrecognized, I will look, as we should in American instances, to what was being said to see why it would matter to the recipient that he might know who was being talked about. In some instances of initially non-identificatory talk, I would guess that slyness or concealment, rather than ignorance, might be recipient's "suspicion."

16. Sacks and Schegloff 1979 claims that:

   1) Recognitionals are used "if they are possible," and by "if they are possible" we mean: *If recipient may be supposed by speaker to know* the one being referred to, and if *recipient may suppose speaker to have so supposed* (p. 17, emphases added).

   2) Try-markers are used if a speaker *anticipates* that the recognitional form being used will on this occasion, for this recipient, possibly be *inadequate for securing recognition* (p. 18, emphasis added).

By reading backward to cognitive concerns from finished states of affairs, the paper invites us to impute a single over-riding motive to all participants in every conversation in which persons are mentioned.

17. By "story" I mean a multi-turn description of personal experience, the turns largely made out to parallel the temporal sequence claimed for the events they purport to describe.

18. Still other interpretations of DO's action are possible.

   1) Alton Becker suggested that the district officer's requiring repetitions of the plaint may certify rather than deny its importance.

   2) It can also be noted that the district officer's "Who" (XX:262) follows a peasant's use of a very deprecating pronoun (the /ii/ of line #261) for Nan Phian, an official's son. Were the district officer's repair initiations to be in reaction to this, he would, of course, have had to have already identified who the referent was.

These interpretations are not inconsistent with the analysis I have offered. The point is that any acceptable interpretation requires us to respect the cultural context of the particular occasion and to recognize motives born of the immediate situation rather than importing such ready-made ones as cognitive recognitional adequacy.

19. Footnotes are sanctuaries for speculation. Here is a classical one, borrowed from C. Perelman (1963:161, ff). Plato (*Gorgias* 487) recommends dialogue by having Socrates tell Callicles:

   . . . if you agree with me in an argument about any point, that point will have been sufficiently tested by us and will not require to be submitted to any further test.

Pareto (1935, Sect. 612) rejects this by observing that:

   The good Plato has a simple, easy and effective way of obtaining universal consent. . . . He has it granted to him in his dialogues by an interlocutor whom he makes say anything he himself desires.

In this, I think, Pareto underestimates the potency of real dialogue. Were Socrates' interlocutors real men engaged in real talk, they might well have gone along with him in many of the ways the Dialogues present. And only later—upon realizing that their situated confirmatives and permissions for Socrates to get on with it might stand (as indeed they do) for all time as total, abstract, and substantive agreement—would they want to take back their nods, mutterings, and demotic "yeah's."

CHAPTER FOUR

1. This chapter began as a seminar presented to the Department of Anthropology of the University of Adelaide. It was given direction through discussions with Professor Bruce Kapferer, has benefited from a critical reading by Professor Emanuel Schegloff, and been pruned in response to the written comments of Bruce Kapferer and Jean Wong.

2. I gratefully acknowledge the National Science Foundation's support of fieldwork in 1968–69 on the administration of justice in Thailand. I am also pleased to have this opportunity to thank the Ministry of Justice of the Kingdom of Thailand for its facilitation of this research, and especially for granting permission to tape record trial proceedings. The research reported in this chapter could not have been done without the knowledgeable advice and active cooperation of Sansern Kraichitti, Som Intrapayung, Duang Kiwajin, Winit Winitnaipak, Boonsong Klaikaew, Thavee Chemnasiri, and Prawin Nivaswat.

3. Each of the items I have capitalized from Blount's conclusions (1975b: 134) is made recognizable to Blount and (insofar as the ethnography is sound) to the elders solely by the operation of rules for the organization and interpretation of speech. It is those rules which permit us to describe the capitalized items and to show their force and their vulnerability.

"The FINAL VERSION of the genealogy for any speech event is the product of what the elders AGREE TO AGREE upon. Any elder can make AN ASSERTION ABOUT a given feature of genealogical history, but he has to consider that he may be CALLED UPON for CLARIFICATION. If so, he must be able to REFER to some specific objects or events that VERIFY his POINT. If the object or event is the THEME of a *sigana,* his position is strengthened. Other elders may COUNTER with their own STORIES, and SIDES may be chosen on THE ISSUE. . . . The more successful an elder, the more he can DIRECT the DISCUSSION. . . . However, he must EXERCISE CAUTION not to be TOO SUCCESSFUL. If the group OBJECTS to his DOMINATION, they may THREATEN to rework the genealogy so as to MALIGN his lineage."

4. In civil cases, documents are prominent, and compromises and decisions often made in chambers.

5. Officially, two or three judges hear and decide the case, but rarely is more than one present on the bench.

6. A large proportion of Northern criminal verdicts are appealed. In the case from which Data Segments "Father" (XXXI) and "Cell" (XXXII) come, defence counsel had warned his clients that he thought an appeal would be necessary.

7. A program to introduce tape recorders and stenographers was initiated in 1978.

8. Data Segments marked "*" are transcripts that have not been re-checked against tape, and thus lack timed pauses.

9. The best overview is Chapter 6 of Levinson 1983. Interesting and interactionally sensitive descriptions of parts of the organization of repair can be found in Jefferson 1972, 1974, Jefferson and Schenkein 1977, and C. Goodwin 1980. But one must not too long postpone the most general and systematic report, Schegloff, et al. 1977, which uses English language data from conversations in a wide range of American social classes and situations, as well as a few British instances. Moerman 1977 shows that the features of repair described by Schegloff, et al. 1977 for British and American conversation, and specifically the "preferences" for self-correction and for repair-as-soon-as-possible, also characterize a smaller corpus of conversations in various Thai dialects in a range of social settings. This finding is based on the procedures described in Chapter Three, and thus subject to criticisms parallel to those made in that chapter.

10. "Discovery markers" are collectable and partially studied (Jefferson 1973) conversational objects, not gratuitous characterizations of these data. Initial inspection indicates that they are organized similarly in Thai and American conversation.

11. It is rare for witnesses to reject a question. XXVII: 2 shows one way in which this is done.

12. The earlier theories turned variation into uniformity by the gloss of "subculture," made it a-social by the concept of "deviance," ascribed it to the differential operation of unexamined uniform forces like "socialization," or—with notions like "acculturation" and "culture change"—blamed it on time's corruption.

13. See Acciaioli 1981 for an excellent critique of *Outline for a Theory of Practice.*

14. See Schegloff, et al. 1977 and Moerman 1977 on the "three-turn repair space"

for the analytic finding, and Data Segment XIX:30 for one format used to target non-contiguous repairables.

15. When these materials were presented at the University of Adelaide, Dr. Roy Fitzhenry independently made this observation. This illustrates both the benefits of public data and his perspicacity.

16. In addition to portraying the prosperity and good character of the defendant, and the coercedness of his confession, counsel planned to find an alibi, allude to unapprehended persons who had more motive and better connections to the police, and cite the loyalty, affection, and gratitude defendant felt toward the deceased.

17. Chapter Five, pp. 85–86, provides instances of less clearly motivated, but no less instrumental, person-reference repairs.

18. Schutz cites *Human Nature and Conduct III,* Modern Library Edition, p. 190.

19. According to Jones' (1962:33) interpretation of the *Poetics,* Aristotle "assault[ed] the now settled habit by which we see action issuing from a solitary focus of consciousness—secret, inward, interesting." For Aristotle, and for Aeschylus, the person is the " 'enactor'— *prattontes* or *drōntes,* the doer of what is done" (Jones 1962:59). The "personalizing of the dramatic individual" (Jones 1962:153) came with Sophocles.

CHAPTER FIVE

1. This chapter's segment contains utterances that are simultaneously orders, means of being ingratiating, and ways of aligning participants.

2. My recognition of dialect use, choice, and switch as components of speaker selection/exclusion does not deny the undoubted, but unavailable, import of who the speaker is looking at or away from.

3. The Scollons (1981) report this about Athabaskans *vis-à-vis* American missionaries, as do I about villagers *vis-à-vis* officials in Thailand and about friendly Americans in La Junta, Colorado, *vis-à-vis* the Bronx.

4. This does not imply that Thai laugh at the same places, in the same situations, and for the same purposes as Americans.

5. Transcripts record this as /(h)/ within words.

6. Its absence from #578 is less noticeable than it would be after a higher graded form of laughter.

7. The latch (/=/) records that MK started #582 with less transition time than standard in this segment. This could make it difficult for other speakers to *talk* at this point. But laughter thrives during other talk. So MK's latch does not challenge the observation that DO refrains from laughing.

8. The female's equivalent is *kha.*

9. It actually began at the start of this occasion and persisted throughout it.

10. In the orders, requests, and invitations (the list is not exhaustive) that I have encountered in transcripts, they typically are.

11. On pages 78–80 we will attend to those that were not.

12. Statements about "awe" and "will" (Rubin 1973) for example.

13. To these, claimedly universal distinctions, an ethnographer of this village should add "red meat" (*cín mii lɔ̌ɔt*) vs. food less violative of the Buddhist precepts.

14. And "the truth" and agreement will thus always "lie between" them.

15. Douglas happens to be referring specifically to the meanings of food.

16. Anthropologists and folklorists who do not take account of this may be getting them wrong.

17. By withholding his #650 during her talk, KP may be trying to get her attention, and the attention of those who have been talking Lue with her (through #s 630–47).

18. *na* and *tὲ·* are both discourse ties: *na* points forward; *tὲ·*, back.

19. By /a/ + /,/.

20. By invoking repair outside of the normal three-turn repair space, MM may be enacting surprise.

21. In his admiring, and admirable, essay, "The life of a farmer," Caw Khun Phya Anuman Rajadhon (1961:8) eschews *khon bâan nɔ́·k* as the term for the people he writes about because it connotes "backwardness."

22. In this segment, DO pronominalizes MM or uses 0-form. Earlier in this conversation, before our segment begins, he referred to MM as /majkə·n mɔmɛ·n/ ("Michael Moerman"), a term unknown to villagers.

23. This is not to imply that DO would have difficulty figuring out who either term referred to.

24. The more refined scholarly terminology developed since 1973 (e.g., Jakobson and Pomorska 1983:154; Singer 1984:42–50) would call Geertz' Saussurian approach "semiologic," reserving "semiotic," for approaches informed by the theories of Charles Sanders Peirce.

25. I note these rather obvious facts because Geertz writes (n. 16): "This use of a descendant's personal name as part of a teknonym in no way contradicts my earlier statements about the lack of public currency of such names" and that (n. 17) teknonymy "underscores another theme which runs through all the orders of person-definition discussed here: the minimization of the difference between the sexes which are represented as being virtually interchangeable. . . ."

26. It may be that Geertz is unaware of the inconsistency between his claims and his activities. Although "Thick Description" was written well after *Person, Time, and Conduct in Bali,* it introduces the volume in which that study is reprinted, and is the only new essay in that volume.

27. Including "From the Native Point of View," published in 1974 and reprinted (in Basso and Selby) in 1976.

28. Geertz may well be right about the Balinese. He has much more to go on than the data he proffers: the experience of living with the Balinese, of observing and talking to them, and of thinking, quite profoundly, about all of it. When Geertz turns to *Javanese* notions of the person (1974:59–61), he makes explicit use of what Javanese say about the person, and often reports the circumstances in which they said it. His description of Java is thereby far more convincing.

29. In these transcripts: I:47, XIX:31, XXXIII:600.

30. In these transcripts: I:8, VI:218, XX:267, 269, 275.

31. In these transcripts: VI:220, XX:271, 275, XXI:436, 438.

32. In these transcripts, XIX:11.

33. In these transcripts: I:32, 47, III:540–7.

CHAPTER SIX

1. Some of the ideas in this chapter were first presented at the EST Foundation's Conference on the Construction of Realities in 1978, and developed at the Summer Science Program of the Naropa Institute, 1978–80. A fuller version was then presented to the Department of Anthropology of the University of Adelaide and to the Anthropological Society of Western Australia in 1981. That version was published in *Anthropology News,* Proceedings of the Anthropological Society of Western Australia 19.1: 3–8, February 1982. For their thoughtful and detailed comments, I am grateful to Jack Bilmes, Larry Cromwell, Joseph Goguen, John Haviland, Ken Leberman, Charlotte Linde, Patricia Miller, Herbert Phillips, and Michael Young, as well as to participants in the UCLA EPOS Seminar which discussed this chapter in 1985.

2. I have no evidence of a case being thrown in this way, but Thai legal practitioners agreed that it is a lively possibility.

3. In "Levy-Bruhl's Theory of Primitive Mentality," 1934, p. 29, as quoted in Douglas 1980:29.

4. These are the same two sisters, and the same phone conversation, as in Data Segment V.

5. This report is based on Emanuel Schegloff's lectures on noticings and Pomerantz' (1975, 1978) study of assessments.

6. I first heard this distinction from Heinz von Foerster at the 1978 Conference on the Construction of Realities.

7. This observation makes use of Jefferson's analysis of laughter.

8. Chapter Two pointed out that saying the same thing, making the same noises, at the same time is a device that enacts unity. Notice, here, the partial overlap of B's "Go:d" with A's "God" (lines #39/40). The transcript does not capture the acoustics of the striking similarity between B's "th-" and the harsh aspiration of A's "J*h*" (lines #42/3).

9. These observations come from American conversations.

Bibliography

Acciaioli, Gregory L.
   1981   "Knowing what you're doing: a review of Pierre Bourdieu's *Outline of a Theory of Practice.*" *Canberra Anthropology* 4.1:23–51.

Agar, Michael
   1973   *Ripping and Running.* Orlando, Fla.: Academic Press.

Anderson, William E.
   n.d.   "Religion and mystical experience." Unpublished paper.

Atkinson, J. Maxwell and Drew, Paul
   1979   *Order in Court.* London: Macmillan Press Ltd.

Auerbach, Erich
   1953   *Mimesis.* Princeton, N.J.: Princeton University Press.

Barwise, Jon and Perry, John
   1983   *Situations and Attitudes.* A Bradford Book. Cambridge, Mass.: MIT Press.

Basso, Keith H. and Selby, Henry A., eds.
   1976   *Meaning in Anthropology.* Albuquerque: University of New Mexico Press.

Bateson, Gregory
   1972   "The cybernetics of 'self': a theory of alcoholism." *Psychiatry* 34.1:1–18
           [1971], as reprinted in *Steps to an Ecology of Mind.* New York: Ballantine
           Books.

Bauman, Richard and Sherzer, Joel, eds.
   1974   *Explorations in the Ethnography of Speaking.* Cambridge and New York:
           Cambridge University Press.

Becker, Alton L.
   1979   "Communication across diversity." In *The Imagination of Reality,* A. L.
           Becker and A. Yenogyan, eds., pp. 1–5. Norwood, N.J.: Ablex Publishing
           Corp.

Beers, Sir Stafford
  1980   Introduction to *Autopoiesis and Cognition: The Realization of the Living* by
           Humberto R. Maturana and Francisco J. Varela. Boston Studies in the Philoso-
           phy of Science, 42. Dordrecht: D. Reidel.

Berger, Peter and Kellner, Hansfried
  1964   "Marriage and the construction of reality." *Diogenes* 46:1–24.

Berger, Peter L. and Luckmann, Thomas
  1966   *The Social Construction of Reality.* [1967] New York: Anchor Books Edition.

Berlin, Brent and Kay, Paul
  1969   *Basic Color Terms.* Berkeley and Los Angeles: University of California
           Press.

Bloch, Maurice, ed.
  1975   *Political Language of Oratory in Traditional Society.* Lakewood, Calif: Aca-
           demic Press.

Blount, Ben G.
  1975a   Introduction to Sanches and Blount 1975, pp. 1–10.
  1975b   "Agreeing to agree on genealogy: A Luo sociology of knowledge." In Sanches
           and Blount 1975, pp. 117–36.

Blum, Alan F. and McHugh, Peter
  1971   "The social ascription of motives." *American Sociological Review* 36:
           98–109.

Bourdieu, Pierre
  1977   *Outline of a Theory of Practice.* Richard Nice, trans. Studies in Social An-
           thropology, #16. Cambridge and New York: Cambridge University Press.

Bronowski, Jacob
  1978   *The Origins of Knowledge and Imagination.* Silliman Lectures. New Haven,
           Conn.: Yale University Press.

Brown, James Marvin
  1962   *From Ancient Thai to Modern Dialects.* Ph.D. dissertation in linguistics,
           Cornell University, Ithaca, N.Y.

Brown, Penelope and Levinson, Stephen
  1978   "Universals in language use." In *Questions and Politeness,* Esther N. Goody,
           ed., pp. 56–310. Cambridge and New York: Cambridge University Press.

Cage, John
  1968   *Silence.* New York: Calder & Boyars.

Campbell, Russell
  1969   *Noun Substitutes in Modern Thai.* The Hague: Mouton.

Cicourel, Aaron
  1980   "Language and social interaction." *Sociological Inquiry* 50.3-4:1-30.

Cole, Michael and Scribner, Sylvia
  1974   *Culture and Thought: a Psychological Introduction.* New York: Wiley.

Collins, Steven
1982   *Selfless Persons: Imagery and Thought in Theravada Buddhism.* Cambridge and New York: Cambridge University Press.

Cromwell, L. G.
1982   *Toward an Anthropology of Idiom.* Unpublished dissertation in anthropology, The Australian National University, Canberra.

Daden, Irene.
1982   *Bargaining in a Guatemalan Highland Quiche-Mayan Market.* Unpublished Ph.D. dissertation in anthropology, University of California at Los Angeles.

Douglas, Mary
1973   *Rules and Meaning.* New York: Penguin.
1980   *Evans-Pritchard.* Sussex: The Harvester Press.
1984   *Food in the Social Order.* New York: Russell Sage Foundation.

Dufrenne, Mikel
1963   *Language and Philosophy.* Bloomington: Indiana University Press.

Engel, David M.
1978   *Code and Custom in a Thai Provincial Court.* Association for Asian Studies Monograph.

Ervin-Tripp, Susan M.
1974   "Sociolinguistics." In *Language, Culture, and Society,* Ben G. Blount, ed., pp. 268–334. Cambridge, Mass: Winthrop.

Frake, Charles D.
1980   *Language and Cultural Description.* Stanford, Calif: Stanford University Press.

Frank, Lawrence K.
1966   "The world as a communication network." In Kepes 1966, pp. 1–14.

Freeman, Derek
1981   "The anthropology of choice." *Canberra Anthropology* 4.1:82–100.

Garfinkel, Harold
1967   *Studies in Ethnomethodology.* Englewood Cliffs, N.J.: Prentice-Hall.

Garfinkel, Harold, Lynch, Michael and Livingston, Eric
1981   "The work of discovering science construed with materials from the optically discovered pulsar." *Philosophy of Social Science* 11:131–58.

Geertz, Clifford
1966   *Person, Time, and Conduct in Bali.* New Haven, Conn.: Yale University Southeast Asia Series, Cultural Report #14, as reprinted in *The Interpretation of Cultures.* New York: Basic Books, 1973.
1973   "Thick description: toward an interpretive theory of culture." In *The Interpretation of Cultures,* pp. 3–30. New York: Basic Books.
1974   " 'From the native's point of view': on the nature of anthropological understanding." *Bulletin of the American Academy of Arts and Sciences* 28.1, as reprinted in Basso and Selby 1976.
1975   "Common sense as a cultural system." *Antioch Review* 33:5–26.

Goldberg, Jo Ann
    1975   "A system for the transfer of instructions in natural settings." *Semiotica* 14.3:269–96.
    1978   "Amplitude shift." In Schenkein 1978, pp. 199–218.

Goodenough, Ward H.
    1956   "Residence rules." *Southwestern Journal of Anthropology* 12:22–37.

Goodwin, Charles
    1979   "The interactive construction of a sentence in natural conversation." In Psathas 1979, pp. 97–122.
    1980   "Restarts, pauses, and the achievement of a state of mutual gaze at turn-beginning." *Sociological Inquiry* 50.3–4:277–302.

Goodwin, Marjorie Harkness
    1980   "Processes of mutual monitoring implicated in the production of description sequences." *Sociological Inquiry* 50.3–4:303–17.

Grima, J. A. and Strecker, D.
    1976   "Zero anaphora in Thai texts." Paper presented to The IXth International Conference on Sino-Tibetan Languages and Literatures, Copenhagen.

Gumperz, John J.
    1982   *Discourse Strategies.* Cambridge and New York: Cambridge University Press.

Gumperz, John, ed.
    1983   *Language and Social Identity.* Cambridge and New York: Cambridge University Press.

Haas, Mary R.
    1964   *Thai-English Student's Dictionary.* Stanford, Calif.: Stanford University Press.

Halliday, M. A. K.
    1976   "Anti-languages." *American Anthropologist* 78:570–84.

Haviland, John
    1977   *Gossip, Reputation, and Knowledge in Zinacantan.* Chicago: University of Chicago Press.

Heidegger, Martin
    1967   *What is a Thing?* W. B. Barton, Jr. and Vera Deutsch, trans., with an analysis by Eugene T. Gendlin. Chicago: Henry Regenry Co.

Hoijer, Harry
    1954   "The Sapir-Whorf hypothesis." In *Language in Culture,* Harry Hoijer, ed. American Anthropological Association, Memoir #79, Vol. 56.2:92–105.

Jakobson, Roman and Pomorska, Krystyna
    1983   *Dialogues.* Cambridge, Mass.: MIT Press.

Jefferson, Gail
    1972   "Side-sequences." In Sudnow 1972, pp. 294–338.
    1973   "A case of precision timing in ordinary conversation." *Semiotica* 9.1:47–96.

1974   "Error correction as an interactional resource." *Language in Society* 3:
            181–206.
1978a   "Sequential aspects of storytelling in conversation." In Schenkein, 1978.
1978b   "What's in a 'n'yem'?" *Sociology* 12.1:135–39.
1979   "A technique for inviting laughter and its subsequent acceptance/declina-
            tion." In Psathas 1979, pp. 97–122.

Jefferson, Gail and Schenkein, Jim
1977   "Some sequential negotiations in conversation." *Sociology* 11.1, as reprinted
            in Schenkein 1978.

Jones, John
1962   *On Aristotle and Greek Tragedy.* New York and Oxford: Oxford University
            Press. (1968 paperback edition).

Kapferer, Bruce
1976   *Transaction and Meaning.* Philadelphia: ISHI
1983   *A Celebration of Demons.* Bloomington: Indiana University Press.

Keesing, Roger
1981   "Kwaio women speak: the micropolitics of autobiography in a Solomon Is-
            land society." Paper presented at the Meetings of the Australian Anthropologi-
            cal Association.

Kellner, Hansfried
1973   "On the cognitive significance of the system of language in communication."
            As published in *Phenomenology and Sociology,* Thomas Luckmann, ed. New
            York: Penguin Books, 1978, pp. 324–42.

Kendon, Adam
1972   Review of *Kinesics and Context* by R. L. Birdwhistell. *American Journal of
            Psychology* 81:441–55.
1975   Introduction, pp. 1–16 of *The Organization of Behavior in Face-to-Face In-
            teraction,* A. Kendon, R. M. Harris and M. R. Key, eds. The Hague: Mouton.
1977   *Studies in the Behavior of Face-to-Face Interaction.* Lisse, The Netherlands:
            Peter De Ridder.

Kepes, Gyorgy, ed.
1966   *Sign, Image, Symbol.* New York: Braziller.

Labov, William
1973   *Sociolinguistic Patterns.* Philadelphia: University of Pennsylvania Press.

Labov, William and David Fanshel
1977   *Therapeutic Discourse: Psychotherapy as Conversation.* New York: Aca-
            demic Press.

Leach, Sir Edmund
1960   "Animal categories and verbal abuse." In *New Directions in the Study of Lan-
            guage,* Eric H. Lenneberg, ed. Cambridge, Mass: MIT Press.

Levi-Strauss, Claude
1970   *The Raw and the Cooked.* J. and N. Weightman, trans. and eds. Chicago:
            University of Chicago Press.

Levinson, Stephen C.
1983   *Pragmatics.* Cambridge and New York: Cambridge University Press.

Lienhardt, G.
1961   *Divinity and Experience: the Religion of the Dinka.* New York and Oxford: Oxford University Press.

Leiter, Ken
1980   *A Primer on Ethnomethodology.* New York and Oxford: Oxford University Press.

Lorenz, Konrad
1978   *Behind the Mirror.* [Translation of *Die Rueckseite des Spiegels.* 1973.] San Diego: Harcourt, Brace, Jovanovich.

Maturana, Humberto R. and Varela, Francisco J.
1980   *Autopoiesis and Cognition: The Realization of the Living.* Boston Studies in the Philosophy of Science, 42. Dordrecht: D. Reidel.

Moerman, Michael
1965   "Ethnic identification in a complex civilization: Who are the Lue?" *American Anthropologist* 67:1215–30.
1966   "Ban Ping's temple: the center of a 'loosely structured' society." In *Anthropological Studies in Theravada Buddhism,* Manning Nash, ed., pp. 137–74. Yale University Southeast Asia Studies Cultural Report Number 13, New Haven, Conn.
1967   "Being Lue: uses and abuses of ethnicity." *American Ethnological Society, Proceedings of 1967 Spring Meeting,* as reprinted in Turner 1974.
1968   *Agricultural Change and Peasant Choice in a Thai Village.* Berkeley: University of California Press.
1969a   "A little knowledge." In *Cognitive Anthropology,* Stephen A. Tyler, ed., pp. 449–69. New York: Holt, Rinehart & Winston.
1969b   "A Thai village headmen as a synaptic leader." *Journal of Asian Studies* 28.3:535–49.
1972   "Analysis of Tai conversation: making accounts, finding breaches and taking sides." In Sudnow 1972, pp. 170–228.
1973   "The use of precedent in natural conversation." *Semiotica* 9.3:193–218; *Rechtstheorie* 4.2:207–29.
1977   "The preference for self-correction in a Tai conversational corpus." *Language* 53.4:872–82.

Moore, Sally Falk
1977   "Individual interests and organizational structures." In *Social Anthropology and Law,* Ian Hamnett, ed, pp. 159–87. A.S.A. Monograph #14. Lakewood, Calif.: Academic Press.
1978   *Law as Process.* New York: Routledge & Kegan Paul.

Nida, Eugene A.
1959   "Principles of translation as exemplified by Bible translating." In *Language Structure and Translation: Essays by Eugene A. Nida,* Anwar S. Dil, ed., pp. 24–46. Stanford, Calif.: Stanford University Press, 1975. Originally

published in *On Translation*, Reuben A. Browser, ed. Cambridge, Mass.: Harvard University Press, 1959.

Ong, Walter J.
1982   *Orality and Literacy*. New York: Methuen & Co.

Panupong, Vichin
1970   *Intersentence Relations in Modern Conversational Thai*. Bangkok: Siam Society.

Pareto, V.
1935   *The Mind and Society*. Cambridge and New York: Cambridge University Press.

Parkin, David
1976   "Exchanging words." In Kapferer 1976, pp. 163–90.

Perelman, Ch.
1963   *The Idea of Justice and the Problem of Argument*. New York: Routledge & Kegan Paul.

Piaget, Jean
1954   *The Construction of Reality in the Child*. Margaret Cook, trans. New York: Basic Books.

Pomerantz, Anita
1975   *Second Assessments*. Unpublished Ph.D. dissertation, School of Social Sciences, University of California at Irvine.
1978   "Compliment responses." In Schenkein 1978, pp. 79–112.

Powdermaker, Hortense
1962   *Coppertown*. New York: Harper & Row.
1966   *Stranger and Friend*. New York: Norton & Co.

Psathas, G., ed.
1979   *Everyday Language*. New York: Irvington.

Rajadhon, Caw Khun Phya Anuman
1961   "The life of a farmer." In *Life and Ritual in Old Siam*, William J. Gedney, trans. and ed. New Haven, Conn.: HRAF Press.

Richards, I. A.
1932   *Mencius on the Mind*. New York: Routledge & Kegan Paul.

Ricoeur, Paul
1976   *Interpretation Theory: Discourse and the Surplus of Meaning*. Fort Worth: Texas Christian University Press.

Rosaldo, Michell Z.
1980   *Knowledge and Passion: Ilongot Notions of Self and Social Life*. Cambridge and New York: Cambridge University Press.

Rubin, Herbert J.
1973   "Will and awe: illustrations of Thai villager dependency upon officials." *Journal of Asian Studies* 32.3:425–45.

Sacks, Harvey
  1972a   "An initial investigation of the usability of conversational data for doing sociology." In Sudnow 1972, pp. 31–74.
  1972b   "On the analyzability of stories by children." In *The Ethnography of Communication,* John J. Gumperz and Dell Hymes, eds., pp. 327–45. New York: Holt, Rinehart & Winston.
  1972c   "Notes on police assessment of moral character." In Sudnow 1972, pp. 280–93.
  1974   "An analysis of the course of a joke's telling in the course of conversation." In Bauman and Sherzer 1974, pp. 337–53.
  1975   "Everyone has to lie." In Sanches and Blount 1979, pp. 57–79.

Sacks, Harvey and Schegloff, Emanuel
  1979   "Two preferences in the organization of reference to persons in conversations and their interaction." In Psathas 1979, pp. 15–21.

Sacks, H., Schegloff, E. and Jefferson, G.
  1974   "A simplest systematics for the organization of turn-taking for conversation." *Language* 50.4:696–735. Reprinted in Schenkein 1978.

Sanches, Mary and Blount, Ben G., eds.
  1975   *Sociocultural Dimensions of Language Use.* Orlando, Fla.: Academic Press.

Sapir, Edward
  1929   "The status of linguistics as a science." *Language* 5:207–14, as reprinted in *The Selected Writings of Edward Sapir,* David Mandelbaum, ed. Berkeley: University of California Press.

Schegloff, Emanuel
  1968   "Sequencing in conversational openings." *American Anthropologist* 70.4: 1075–95.
  1979   "Identification and recognition in telephone conversation openings." In Psathas 1979, pp. 23–78.
  1981   "Discourse as an interactional achievement." In *Analyzing Discourse: Text and Talk,* D. Tannen, ed. Georgetown University Roundtable on Language and Linguistics. Washington, D.C.: Georgetown University Press.
  in press   "Between macro and micro: contexts and other connections." In *The Micro-Macro Link,* J. Alexander, B. Gissen, R. Munch, and N. Smelser, eds. Berkeley: University of California Press.

Schegloff, E. and Sacks, H.
  1973   "Opening up closings." *Semiotica* 8.4:289–327. Reprinted in Turner 1974.

Schegloff, E., Jefferson, G. and Sacks, H.
  1977   "The preference for self-correction in the organization of repair in conversation." *Language* 53.2:361–82.

Schenkein, Jim
  1978a   "Sketch of an analytic mentality for the study of conversational interaction." In Schenkein 1978, pp. 1–6.
  1978b   (ed.) *Studies in the Organization of Conversational Interaction.* New York: Academic Press.

Schutz, Alfred
    1962   "Choosing among projects of action." In *Collected Papers, Vol. I: The Prob-
                lem of Social Reality*, Maurice Natanson, ed., pp. 67–96. The Hague: Mar-
                tinus Nijhoff.
    1964   "The Homecomer." In *Collected Papers, Vol. II: Studies in Social Theory*,
                Arvid Brodersen, ed., pp. 106–19. The Hague: Martinus Nijhoff.

Scollon, Ron and Scollon, Suzanne B. K.
    1981   *Narrative, Literacy and Face in Interethnic Communication*. Norwood, N.J.:
                Ablex.

Seyfarth, Robert M. and Cheney, Dorothy L.
    1980   "The ontogeny of vervet monkey alarm calling behavior." *Zeitschrift für
                Tierpsychologie* 54:37–56.

Sharp, Lauriston and Hanks, Lucien M.
    1978   *Bang Chan*. Ithaca, N.Y.: Cornell University Press.

Sherzer, Joel
    1983   *Kuna Ways of Speaking*. Austin: University of Texas Press.

Singer, Milton
    1984   *Man's Glassy Essence: Explorations in Semiotic Anthropology*. Bloomington:
                Indiana University Press.

Sturrock, John
    1979   *Structuralism and Since*. New York and Oxford: Oxford University Press.

Sudnow, David, ed.
    1972   *Studies in Social Interaction*. New York: The Free Press.

Tannen, Deborah
    1981   "New York Jewish conversational style." *International Journal of the Sociol-
                ogy of Language* 30:133–49.

Tedlock, Dennis
    1983   *The Spoken Word and the Work of Interpretation*. Philadelphia: University of
                Pennsylvania Press.

Terasaki, Alene Kiku
    1976   *Pre-Announcement Sequences in Conversation*. University of California, Ir-
                vine. School of Social Sciences. Social Sciences Working Paper #99.

Toulmin, Stephen
    1978   "The Mozart of psychology." *New York Review of Books*, Sept. 28:51–7.

Turner, Roy
    1974   *Ethnomethodology*. Harmondsworth, Md.: Penguin Education Series.

van Velsen, J.
    1967   "The extended case method and situational analysis." In *The Craft of Social
                Anthropology*, A. L. Epstein, ed. London: Tavistock.

Volosinov, V. N.
    1973   *Marxism and the Philosophy of Language*. Cambridge, Mass.: Seminar Press.

von Foerster, Heinz
    1966   "From stimulus to symbol: the economy of biological computation." In
                Kepes 1966, pp. 42–61.
    1970   "Thoughts and notes on cognition." In *Cognition: a Multiple View,* Paul
                Garvin, ed., pp. 25–48. East Lansing, Mich.: Spartan.

von Frisch, Karl
    1967   *The Dance Language and Orientation of Bees.* Leigh E. Chadwick, trans.
                Cambridge, Mass.: Belknap Press of Harvard University.

Wales, H. Q. Quaritch
    1934   *Ancient Siamese Government and Administration.* New York: Paragon Book
                Reprint, 1965.

Weber, Max
    1947   *The Theory of Economic and Social Organization.* T. Parsons, ed. New York:
                Free Press [1964].

Whorf, Benjamin Lee
    1940   "Linguistics as an exact science." *The Technology Review* 43:61–3, 80–3,
                as reprinted in *Language, Thought, and Reality: Selected Writings of Ben-
                jamin Lee Whorf.* John B. Carrol, ed. Cambridge, Mass.: Technology Press
                of MIT & John Wiley, 1956.

Wieder, D. Lawrence
    1980   "Behavioristic operationalism and the life-world." *Sociological Inquiry*
                5.3–4:75–103.

Witherspoon, Gary
    1977   *Language and Art in the Navajo Universe.* Ann Arbor, Mich.: University of
                Michigan Press.

Subject Index

Transcript Index

University of Pennsylvania Press
Conduct and Communications Series

Erving Goffman and Dell Hymes, *Founding Editors*
Dell Hymes, Gillian Sankoff, and Henry Glassie, *General Editors*

Erving Goffman. *Strategic Interaction.* 1970
William Labov. *Language in the Inner City: Studies in the Black English Vernacular.* 1973
William Labov. *Sociolinguistic Patterns.* 1973
Dell Hymes. *Foundations in Sociolinguistics: An Ethnographic Approach.* 1974
Barbara Kirshenblatt-Gimblett, ed. *Speech Play: Research and Resources for the Study of Linguistic Creativity.* 1976
Gillian Sankoff. *The Social Life of Language.* 1980
Erving Goffman. *Forms of Talk.* 1981
Dell Hymes. *"In Vain I Tried to Tell You."* 1981
Dennis Tedlock. *The Spoken Word and the Work of Interpretation.* 1983
Ellen B. Basso. *A Musical View of the Universe: Kalapalo Myth and Ritual Performances.* 1985
Michael Moerman. *Talking Culture: Ethnography and Conversation Analysis.* 1988
Dan Rose. *Black American Street Life: South Philadelphia, 1969–1971.* 1988
Charles Briggs. *Competence in Performance: The Creativity of Tradition in Mexicano Verbal Art.* 1988
J. Joseph Errington, *Structure and Style in Javanese: A Semiotic View of Linguistic Etiquette.* 1988